CHILDREN AND YOUTH IN PREMODERN SCOTLAND

St Andrews Studies in Scottish History

Sponsored by the Institute of Scottish Historical Research at the University of St Andrews, St Andrews Studies in Scottish History provides an important forum for the publication of research on any aspect of Scottish history, from the early Middle Ages to the present day, focusing on the historical experience of Scots at home and abroad, and Scotland's place in wider British, European and global contexts. Both monographs and essay collections are welcomed.

Proposal forms can be obtained from the Institute of Scottish Historical Research website: http://www.st-andrews.ac.uk/ishr/studies.htm. They should be sent in the first instance to the chair of the editorial board at the address below.

Professor Roger Mason
Institute of Scottish Historical Research
St Andrews University
St Andrews
Fife KY16 9AL
UK

Previous volumes in the series are listed at the back of this book

CHILDREN AND YOUTH IN PREMODERN SCOTLAND

Edited by
Janay Nugent and Elizabeth Ewan

THE BOYDELL PRESS

First published 2015
The Boydell Press, Woodbridge

ISBN 978 1 78327 043 9

The Boydell Press is an imprint of Boydell & Brewer Ltd
PO Box 9, Woodbridge, Suffolk IP12 3DF, UK
and of Boydell & Brewer Inc.
668 Mount Hope Ave, Rochester, NY 14620–2731, USA
website: www.boydellandbrewer.com

A catalogue record for this book is available
from the British Library

This publication is printed on acid-free paper

Printed and bound in Great Britain by
TJ International Ltd, Padstow, Cornwall

FSC www.fsc.org MIX Paper from responsible sources FSC® C013056

For
Jasper and Jonas Moulton
and
Maureen and George Ewan

Contents

Illustrations

Plates

Maps

Notes on Contributors

Katie Barclay is an ARC Discovery Early Career Research Fellow in the ARC Centre for the History of Emotions and School of History & Politics, University of Adelaide, Australia. She is the author of *Love, Intimacy and Power: marriage and patriarchy in Scotland, 1650–1850* (2011) which won the Women's History Network Book Prize and the Hume Brown Prize in Scottish History, and of numerous articles on emotion and family life in Scotland and Ireland. She has recently edited, with Deborah Simonton, *Women in Eighteenth-Century Scotland: Intimate, Intellectual and Public Lives* (2013).

Jamie Reid Baxter is Honorary Research Fellow in Scottish History at Glasgow University. He has published widely on sixteenth- and early-seventeenth-century Scottish history, music, literature, and religious life, including *Elizabeth Melville, Lady Culross: Poems from Manuscript, with Ane Godlie Dreame* (2010) and *Jhone Angus, Monk of Dunfermline, and Scottish Reformation Music* (2011). He was responsible for 'Elizabeth Melville Day' in Edinburgh on 21st June 2014, which included the unveiling by Germaine Greer of an inscribed flagstone commemorating the poet.

Stuart Campbell is Head of the Treasure Trove Unit, National Museums of Scotland, responsible for assessing newly discovered archaeological objects in Scotland. He specialises in the material culture of the medieval and early modern period and has a particular interest in the material culture and consumer economy of the post-medieval period, particularly in how material can be used to express personal and community identities.

Mairi Cowan is Associate Professor in the Department of Historical Studies, University of Toronto, Canada. Her teaching and research interests include the social and religious history of late medieval and early modern Scotland, and intercultural contact in the early Atlantic world. She is author of *Death, Life, and Religious Change in Scottish Towns c.1350–1560* (2012), several articles on medieval and early modern Scottish history, and pedagogical resources for the teaching of world history and Canadian history at the elementary, secondary, and post-secondary levels.

Sarah Dunnigan is Senior Lecturer in English Literature at Edinburgh University. She is author of *Eros and Poetry at the Courts of Mary Queen of Scots and James VI* (2002) and editor of numerous collections, including *Scottish*

Traditional Literatures (2013), co-edited with Suzanne Gilbert. She has published in the areas of medieval and early modern Scottish literature; Scottish women's writing; ballads; and children's literature.

Elizabeth Ewan is University Research Chair in History and Scottish Studies at the University of Guelph, Canada. Her research focuses on gender, towns, and crime in late medieval and early modern Scotland. She is author and editor of several books and articles on Scottish women, including *Women in Scotland c. 1100–c. 1750* (1999) and *The Biographical Dictionary of Scottish Women* (2007), and co-editor with Janay Nugent of *Finding the Family in Medieval and Early Modern Scotland* (2008).

Anne Frater is Senior Lecturer in the Gaelic section at Lews Castle College, University of the Highlands and Islands in Stornoway, and is programme leader for the University of the Highlands and Islands Gaelic Scotland degree course. She is also a poet who writes in Scottish Gaelic. Her work has appeared in many magazines and anthologies, as well as in her own collection *Fo'n t-Slige (Under the Shell)* (1995). Her historical research focuses on the poetry of Scottish Gaelic women up to 1750.

Dolly MacKinnon is Senior Lecturer in Early Modern History at the University of Queensland, Australia. She is currently the chief investigator (with Megan Cassidy-Welch) on the ARC discovery project, 'War and Remembrance in England and Scotland 1200–1700. Author of *Earls Colne's Early Modern Landscapes* (2014), she has co-edited a number of collections and published numerous journal articles and book chapters that explore the intersection of cultural history with mental illness, family, gender, and religion.

Cynthia J. Neville is George Munro Professor of History and Political Economy at Dalhousie University, Halifax, Canada. She is author of numerous articles and book chapters that examine the legal, social, and cultural history of Scotland 1150–1400, including *Native Lordship in Medieval Scotland: the Earldoms of Strathearn and Lennox, c. 1140–1365* (2005) and *Land, Law and People in Medieval Scotland* (2010). She is editor, with Grant G. Simpson, of *Regesta Regum Scottorum, Vol. IV, Pt 1: the Acts of Alexander III King of Scots 1249–1286* (2013). Her current research explores the history of royal mercy and royal pardon in medieval Scotland.

Janay Nugent is an Associate Professor of History and a founding member of the Institute for Child and Youth Studies at the University of Lethbridge, Canada. She is co-editor with Elizabeth Ewan of *Finding the Family in Medieval and Early Modern Scotland* (2008), and author of several journal articles and book chapters on family, gender, social history, and the Reformation in Scotland. Her current research is on children, youth, and parenting in early modern Scotland.

Heather Parker is a Postdoctoral Fellow and the assistant director of the Centre for Scottish Studies at the University of Guelph, Canada. She co-edited *The Shaping of Scottish Identities: family, nation, and the world beyond* (2011) and is the editor of the *International Review of Scottish Studies*. Her recent research has focused on medieval and early modern marriage contracts.

Cathryn R. Spence is an Assistant Professor of History at the University of New Brunswick, Saint John, Canada. She has published on the intersecting topics of Scottish women, credit and debt, and work. She is author of *Women, Credit, and Debt in Early Modern Scottish Towns* (2015) and co-editor of the *Edinburgh Housemails Taxation Book, 1634–6* (2014). Her research interests include urban and economic history, and the impact of gender and socioeconomic status when navigating economic relationships in Western Europe.

Laura E. Walkling is a graduate of the Honours BA program at University of Toronto Mississauga, Canada, and the Master of Teaching program at the Ontario Institute for Studies in Education. Her research has included an examination of the status of foreigners at the court of James IV, the development of world history resources for secondary school teachers, and a phenomenological investigation entitled 'Taking the "Dis" out of "Disability": how a school's community of teachers works to empower students with disabilities in an ableist education system'. She currently teaches English and History at the secondary level in London.

Nel Whiting is undertaking an AHRC funded inter-disciplinary PhD at the University of Dundee. She is using Scottish family group portraits from the second half of the eighteenth century as primary sources to investigate constructions of gender, national, and familial identity. She was awarded the Leah Leneman Essay Prize 2010 by Women's History Scotland for new writing in Scottish gender history.

Acknowledgements

Like children who receive a great deal of help from others as they grow up, this book represents the culmination of many people's efforts. First of all we would like to thank our authors who have contributed their research, enthusiasm and time, responded gracefully to suggestions from the editors and external readers, and produced such excellent studies. We are especially grateful to those contributors who came to our rescue at a late date when some of the original authors were forced to pull out by unforeseen circumstances. The external readers of both the individual articles and the entire collection have made valuable suggestions that have contributed greatly to improving the book.

Roger Mason, as editor of the series St Andrews Studies in Scottish History, has been very supportive from the time when we first proposed the idea of a collection on children and youth. We are very pleased to have this book included as one of the series, and thank Caroline Palmer, Rohais Haughton, Rob Kinsey, and Rosie Pearce of Boydell and Brewer for help and support. Elizabeth also appreciates the wonderful opportunity to spend the winter of 2014 in St Andrews as a Visiting Fellow of the Institute for Scottish Historical Research, and to do 'fieldwork' among the university youth of St Andrews in the many coffee shops around town recommended by Alex Woolf. Alex, Roger, Norman Reid, Ann Kettle, Chris and Anne-Marie Smout, Michael Brown, Barbara Crawford, Margaret Connolly, Katie Stevenson, and their postgraduate students provided great hospitality and many stimulating discussions about medieval and early modern Scottish history. Katie's loan of her office with its view of the University Library reminded its temporary occupant of why she was there. Elizabeth would also like to thank the staff and visiting scholars of Strathmartine House for the friendly and intellectually lively home away from home. Janay would like to thank all of her colleagues and postgraduate students at the Institute for Child and Youth Studies [I-CYS] who have been instrumental in shaping the concepts and questions running through the collection. I-CYS was birthed and has grown up during the writing of this collection, and it has become a family where the members constantly test and push one another while offering undying support and good humour. There are many Institute affiliates at the University of Lethbridge and across Canada, the United States, and Britain who have contributed to the stimulating atmosphere of I-CYS, but particular thanks go to the core group of Jan Newberry, Kristine Alexander, Louise Barrett, Elizabeth Galway, Sergio Pellis and Amy von Heyking, as well as to Jenny O'Seen whose administrative support is greatly appreciated. Janay would also like to thank Heidi MacDonald and Carol Williams for their support, sage advice, and their diligence and commitment to the writing group where much of her work for this collection was completed.

Both of us would like to thank colleagues and friends at the Universities of Lethbridge, Guelph, St Andrews, Edinburgh, Strathclyde, and Glasgow, the National Museums of Scotland and the National Records of Scotland – too many to name individually – for their support and interest in the collection. Our husbands and families once again have patiently borne our absences and our long Skype conversations on 'the book' with good grace, even when these have intruded on family time as academic projects are wont to do. We could not have done this work without the help and support of Kris Inwood and Jason Moulton. They will be especially delighted, and not entirely for academic reasons, to see publication of the collection at last. Elizabeth would also like to thank Janay for her unfailing good humour and incredible work ethic, as well as for enlivening research trips to Edinburgh. Janay would like to thank Elizabeth for her hospitality in her lovely flat over the last two research trips to Edinburgh, her insight and unwavering dedication to the collection, as well as her incredible generosity over twenty years of mentorship. Elizabeth's skills with New Town boilers are also appreciated, without which there would have been many summers of cold showers as this collection has come together.

Financial aid has been provided by the Social Sciences and Humanities Research Council of Canada, the College of Arts at the University of Guelph through its University Research Chairs programme, and the University of Lethbridge through the Internal SSHRC and Community of Research Excellence Development Opportunities grants. We would also like to thank the Treasure Trove Unit of the National Museums of Scotland, the National Galleries of Scotland, the Blair Castle Estate, and Alan and Carol Murray for their kind permissions to reproduce the images in this collection.

The child–parent relationship is lifelong and one of the most important in people's lives. In recognition of the affection and support we have personally received, we have dedicated the collection to Janay's children and Elizabeth's parents, as a small token of our love and thanks.

Abbreviations and Conventions

APS	T. Thomson and C. Innes (eds), *Acts of the Parliaments of Scotland*, 11 vols (Edinburgh, 1814–44)
CL	Jane E.A. Dawson (ed.), *Campbell Letters, 1559–1587* (Edinburgh, 1997)
DSL	*Dictionary of the Scots Language*, online at www.dsl.ac.uk
EUL	Edinburgh University Library
JHCY	*Journal of the History of Childhood and Youth*
JSHS	*Journal of Scottish Historical Studies*
NGS	National Galleries of Scotland
NLS	National Library of Scotland
NMS	National Museums of Scotland
NRS	National Records of Scotland
ODNB	*Oxford Dictionary of National Biography* (Oxford, 2004)
PSAS	*Proceedings of the Society of Antiquaries of Scotland*
RMS	T. Thomson et al. (eds), *Registrum Magni Sigilli Regum Scottorum. The Register of the Great Seal of Scotland*, 11 vols (Edinburgh, 1882–1914)
ROSC	*Review of Scottish Culture*
SHR	*Scottish Historical Review*

Until 1600, the calendar year began on 25 March. All dates have been given in modern form. Money is given as pounds (£), shillings (s) and pence (d). A merk was worth 6s 8d.

Unless otherwise noted, in quotations 'y' has been modernized as 'th'.

Introduction
Adding Age and Generation as a Category of Historical Analysis

Elizabeth Ewan and Janay Nugent

Historical interests often develop from personal experiences. When we were editing a previous collection, *Finding the Family in Medieval and Early Modern Scotland* (2008),[1] we experienced a minor baby boom as many of our contributors and one of us welcomed children into our lives during the process. It served as a salutary reminder that in that collection, we were not able to devote as much space to children's experiences and identities as we would have liked. This volume begins to redress this gap and to demonstrate the value that child and youth studies can bring to our understanding of medieval and early modern Scotland. The essays range from the thirteenth to the turn of the nineteenth century, from the Highlands to the Lowlands, and from the country to the city to the royal court.

The history of children and youth has developed rapidly as a field since the 1980s. Partly spurred on by the controversial work of Philippe Ariès and Lawrence Stone, who argued that childhood did not exist in the West as a distinct stage of life until the eighteenth century and that parents felt little affection for their offspring before this period, historians such as Linda Pollock began examining more personal sources to uncover parents' real attitudes towards their children.[2] The conclusions of Ariès and Stone are now largely rejected by historians, but still play a role in popular impressions of the past;[3] as a result, several of our contributors address these ideas in their chapters. Historians also began to engage in general studies of childhood and youth to determine what could be found out about young people in the past. A number of studies emerged in the late 1980s and 1990s that mainly grappled with questions of what it was to be a

1 Elizabeth Ewan and Janay Nugent (eds), *Finding the Family in Medieval and Early Modern Scotland* (Aldershot, 2008).

2 Philippe Ariès, *Centuries of Childhood* (New York, 1962); Lawrence Stone, *The Family, Sex and Marriage in England 1500–1800* (New York, 1977); Linda Pollock, *Forgotten Children* (Cambridge, 1983). For further discussion and examples of both European and Scottish sources, see 'Guide to Further Reading' in this volume.

3 For a summary of the last four decades of research, see Margaret L. King, 'Concepts of Childhood: What We Know and Where We Might Go', *Renaissance Quarterly* 60 (2007), 341–407. No works on Scotland are mentioned.

child, if youth was a distinct stage of life, and what can be known about topics such as child-rearing practices, education, child and youth culture, work, illness, death, and child–parent relations. The types of sources available and how the experiences and perceptions of children and youth have changed over time have also been significant historical questions.[4]

In Scotland, the study of children and childhood is a relatively new development. In the 1980s, some attention was paid to attitudes towards children during the Scottish Enlightenment.[5] Rosalind Marshall considered the upbringing of female children in her study of Scottish women between 1080 and 1980.[6] Young people have figured in the population data used by demographers to examine the country's population history; infant mortality and age at marriage were two factors which needed to be considered.[7] There have also been studies of wet-nursing, illegitimacy and infanticide, all of which by their nature include children.[8] But few of these sources considered children as subjects in their own right, with the exception of an exhibition on seventeenth-century children at the National Portrait Gallery, for which Rosalind Marshall wrote the accompanying text.[9] In the last two decades, more works on Scottish history have included material on children and youth, although these topics are rarely the main concerns of these studies. These recent developments are discussed at more length in the 'Guide to Further Reading'.

Over the last fifteen years, the monograph-length studies of children and youth in medieval and early modern Europe have largely moved away from simply finding children and youth in the past, to engaging in larger questions of historiographical significance. Politics, religion, poverty, gender, the history of emotions, and many other themes have been the focus of recent historical studies. The premise of these discussions is that unlike modern western societies with their rapidly aging populations, premodern societies had a very high proportion of young people. Therefore in order to understand what it was to be a medieval or early modern person necessarily requires an understanding of what it was to be a boy or girl in that society. 'Traditional assumptions about

4 For specific references see 'Guide to Further Reading'.

5 Craig Beveridge, 'Childhood and Society in Eighteenth-Century Scotland', in R.A. Mason et al. (eds), *New Perspectives on the Politics and Culture of Early Modern Scotland* (Edinburgh, 1982), 265–90.

6 Rosalind Marshall, *Virgins and Viragos: A History of Women in Scotland 1080–1980* (London, 1983).

7 R.A. Houston, *The Population History of Britain and Ireland, 1500–1750* (Cambridge, 1992); Michael Flinn (ed.), *Scottish Population History: From the Seventeenth Century to the 1930s* (Cambridge, 1977); Karen Cullen, 'The Famine of the 1690s and Its Aftermath: Survival and Recovery of the Family', in Ewan and Nugent (eds), *Finding the Family*, 151–62. See also King, 'Concepts of Childhood', 385–6.

8 Gordon DesBrisay, 'Wet-Nurses and Unwed Mothers in Seventeenth-Century Aberdeen', in E. Ewan and M.M. Meikle (eds), *Women in Scotland c. 1100–c. 1750* (East Linton, 1999), 210–20; Leah Leneman and Rosalind Mitchison, *Sin in the City* (Edinburgh, 1994); Deborah Symonds, *Weep Not for Me* (University Park, 1997).

9 Rosalind Marshall, *Childhood in Seventeenth Century Scotland* (Edinburgh, 1976).

what counts as history and who gets counted in making that history'[10] have not generally included young people, yet young people were everywhere, and their experiences and lives have much to reveal about medieval and early modern society. The essays in this collection seek to explore how the lens of age can help us to further our understanding of broader historical issues such as urban economic development, consumption patterns, clan politics, personal piety, medieval kingship, court life, slavery, constructions of gender, the history of emotions, and the dynastic concerns of noble houses.

Children and Youth in Premodern Scotland demonstrates the feasibility of studying young people by identifying and analysing the breadth of sources available to scholars of medieval and early modern Scotland. Our contributors have made use of such sources as government financial and land records, as well as court proceedings, asking new questions of these well-known documents. More individual records such as marriage contracts and personal correspondence throw light on the role and experience of children and their relationship with their parents in individual families.[11] Poems and treatises of advice for children and their parents illustrate perceptions of how children develop into responsible adults. Songs written by Gaelic women tell of the powerful emotional bond between a mother or foster-mother and her child. Legal treatises and judgements in inheritance cases are interrogated to uncover developing ideas about natural affection between parent and child, while archaeological finds of toys provide a glimpse into the world of play and work of early modern children. Portraits reveal how the patron wanted the children in the family to be perceived, while family manuscripts attempt to fashion a particular identity for a family and its children. The sources explored by our contributors just begin to scratch the surface of how we can find young people in the historical record. Additional sources for the study of children and youth have been identified by Lauren Martin, Lizanne Henderson and Ted Cowan, Scott Moir, and Diane Purkiss, who have found children in witch trials and fairy beliefs; Melissa Hollander has located children and fathers in the kirk session records; and still ripe for examination are the archaeological record, and the cheap and widely distributed chapbooks of the period.[12]

[10] Martha Saxton, 'Introduction', *JHCY* 1:1 (2008), 2.

[11] *CL*, Jane Dawson's publication of Campbell family correspondence, has been particularly helpful in making such sources more widely accessible. For an online version of the letters, see http://www.ed.ac.uk/schools-departments/divinity/research/resources/breadalbane/letters (accessed February 2015).

[12] Lauren Martin, 'Witchcraft and Family: What Can Witchcraft Documents Tell Us About Early Modern Scottish Family Life?' *Scottish Tradition* 27 (2002), 7–22; Lizanne Henderson and Edward J. Cowan, *Scottish Fairy Belief: A History* (East Linton, 2001); Scott Moir, 'The Crucible: Witchcraft and the Experience of Family in Early Modern Scotland', in Ewan and Nugent (eds), *Finding the Family*, 49–59; Diane Purkiss, 'Losing Babies, Losing Stories: Attending to Women's Confessions in Scottish Witch-Trials', in M. Mikesell and A. Seeff (eds), *Cultural Change: Attending to Early Modern Women* (Newark, 2003), 143–58; Melissa Hollander, 'The Name of the Father: Baptism and the Social Construction of Fatherhood in Early Modern Edinburgh', in Ewan and Nugent (eds), *Finding the Family*, 63–72.

In addition to exploring how studies of young people can contribute to broader questions of historiographical significance, and to identifying sources, this collection seeks to push forward the types of questions that historians ask when exploring children and youth. 'The study of children, often seen as peripheral to the important work of understanding social, political, national, and ethnic structures, allows us to rethink the very foundations underlying these structures.'[13] It is this premise that has inspired the section breakdown of the collection, with each section signalling key issues in child and youth studies that we want to address in the collection. Each theme provides insights into what the study of young people can contribute to broader historical questions. Although each section is organized to highlight a particular aspect of childhood in the premodern period, these are not exclusive or competing themes but instead are overlapping and entwined throughout the collection. The experience of being a young person in medieval and early modern Scotland was necessarily connected with how the young were represented and how adults shaped childhoods to construct the next generation of Scots. The stages of childhood and youth were critical for shaping the future direction of families, communities, the church, and the state.

Part I, 'Experiences of Childhood and Youth', seeks to question our understanding of the young in history. Most sources that survive in the past are produced by adults or filtered through the voice of adults. Literature on how to raise children and how to categorize and understand the ages and stages of childhood, legal records which present children only as property of their parents, adult correspondence describing and discussing child-rearing practices, and religious and prescriptive texts are all written by adults describing children and their perceptions of what childhood should be. It is these records that inform the basis of what historians believe to be 'true' about childhood. In this model, the voices, perspectives, and actual experiences of children and youth are lost. The voices of children in the past are elusive, yet it is worthwhile to try to seek them out where possible and to find children experiencing their lives. By doing this, we can begin to bring a more balanced, humanistic understanding to this segment of the population.[14] Although this is a difficult goal to achieve for the premodern period, the essays in this section do shed light on how children lived and experienced their lives. The lives of children in and around the court of James IV are discussed by Mairi Cowan and Laura Walkling, while Cathryn Spence studies the young women who contracted themselves into apprenticeship arrangements in the perling (silk-weaving) trade in early modern Edinburgh. Janay Nugent examines the fosterage experience of Archibald Campbell, future 9th earl of Argyll, while further down the social scale, Stuart Campbell interrogates the uses and meanings of children's toys. Collectively these essays shed light on the material possessions of children and youth such as clothing and toys, their educational experiences, and how they spent their time. Play and work are two sides of the same coin,

13 Anna Mae Duane (ed.), *The Children's Table: Childhood Studies and the Humanities* (Athens, GA, 2013), 1.
14 Duane, *The Children's Table*, 2–4.

preparing children for the social and cultural adult world that their social status, gender and race would have them inherit. The identification and exploration of children's voices and experiences, where they are discernible in the records, continues as a theme throughout the collection.

In Part II, 'Representations of the Young', the authors seek to explore how children and youth were represented in medieval and early modern society. Contemporaries clearly understood childhood and youth to be separate and distinct stages of life, characterized by vulnerability and dependence. 'Age inevitably intersects with other categories of social organization and social difference',[15] so exploring how the young were represented helps to bring about a nuanced understanding of childhood and youth, as well as expanding our understanding of the power constructions of gender, class and race. Elite parents were able to use children to advance their own claims to family dynasty, clan politics, and the distribution of family wealth. Although there was clear affection for these young people, as demonstrated in Anne Frater's examination of Gaelic women's songs to children, and an expectation – indeed, as Katie Barclay shows, a legal obligation – that the adult members of their families were to care for them, children were vulnerable to the demands of adults. Dolly MacKinnon's chapter adds another complexity to the power relationship, with race and age working to cultivate the prestige of slave owners. Nel Whiting's examination of David Allan's group family portraiture is a clear expression of how children represented a family's status in the community, which is reflected in all of the essays in this section. It is clear that age signifies 'a historically contingent system of power relations and cultural expectations'.[16] This theme expands beyond this section, as representations of the young and the consideration of age as a category of historical analysis are woven throughout the collection.

The final section, 'Constructing the Next Generation', explores how children were raised and shaped to fulfil specific adult roles. The essays in this section shed light on how the grooming of the young can reveal much about the values of society, what they feared, and how these ideals shifted with gender and social status. Cynthia Neville's paper considers the socializing of Prince Alexander, heir to Alexander III, and the symbolic significance of the heir in the dynastic politics and lineage of his family. Heather Parker examines the marriage contracts which were made by parents for their children, reflecting concerns about the continuation of the lineage but also shaping those children's future lives. Adults at all periods are full of advice to children about how to behave and concerns about misbehaviour, providing practical guidance on how they should become constructive members of society. Sarah Dunnigan examines literary sources, several of which are part of a broader European literary tradition of tutelary advice for boys and girls.

15 Steven Mintz, 'Reflections on Age as a Category of Historical Analysis', *JHCY* 1:1 (2008), 92.

16 Leslie Paris, 'Through the Looking Glass: Age, Stages, and Historical Analysis', *JHCY* 1:1 (2008), 107.

The actual words of counsel from one mother to her son form the final chapter of the collection. Drawing together the various goals of this volume, Jamie Reid Baxter's transcription consists of an edition of two letters of the celebrated poet Elizabeth Melville to her son James, as he embarked on a life of his own. Through presenting a never-before-published source, he demonstrates how much can be ascertained about how children experienced their relationship with their parents, how they represented family interests, and how parenting was used to construct the next generation.

The division of the collection into these three themes is intended to signal some of the questions that are important in child and youth studies. The remainder of this introduction explores a myriad of additional themes that emerge within the collection. One particularly challenging discussion is about how long childhood lasts. Concrete definitions of childhood are notoriously difficult to pin down.[17] Medieval thinkers recognized various schemes of the ages of man (and occasionally of women), which might consist of anything from three up to seven life stages. A common one, articulated in the fifteenth-century Scottish poem *Ratis Raving*, described seven stages, with full development as a rational adult not coming until age thirty.[18] On the other hand, boys could marry at fourteen, and girls at twelve, and other ages marked full legal capacity in various areas of life. Moreover, perceptions of youth might not necessarily reflect calendar age – hence servants or slaves might be called boys or girls no matter how old they were. The great diversity of terms used to refer to children and youths is discussed in more detail by Cowan and Walkling.

For this collection, we have adopted a flexible definition of youth, from the very young to those who were just starting to enter upon household responsibilities, such as the 'young wives' of Dunnigan's essay. This was especially important for girls, as marriage marked a different turning point in their lives than it did for boys. Marriage changed women's legal position from one of independence to one of dependence on their husbands, while for men it marked a new level of legal responsibility and authority over a wife and household.[19] For women who married, then, achieving adulthood resulted in a loss of legal independence. One intriguing example of such a 'young wife' was Margaret Tudor, who became queen when she married James IV at the age of thirteen. Parker discusses elite young people in the fifteenth and sixteenth centuries who were betrothed or married at a young age, primarily to fulfil the plans of their parents. We lack the demographic data to ascertain how common such young ages of marriage were. It seems likely that such practices were mainly typical of the elite rather than

17 Naomi Miller and Naomi Yavneh, 'Introduction: Early Modern Children as Subjects: Gender Matters', in Naomi Miller and Naomi Yavneh (eds), *Gender and Early Modern Constructions of Childhood* (Farnham, 2011), 12.

18 Ritchie Girvan (ed.), *Ratis Raving and Other Early Scots Poems on Morals* (Edinburgh, 1939).

19 For a summary of the legal position for women and men, see Angelo Forte, 'Some Aspects of the Law of Marriage in Scotland: 1500–1700', in Elizabeth Craik (ed.), *Marriage and Property* (Aberdeen, 1984), 104–18.

the majority of the population, although there is some evidence suggesting that marriage ages for girls in the Highlands were lower than those in the Lowlands.[20]

One lively debate in the literature on childhood and youth is whether a distinct stage of adolescence was recognized in the past.[21] For elite women, the passage from childhood to married life could be immediate. On the whole, however, our contributors accept the idea of adolescence while recognizing that its form could vary according to gender, social status and time period. For urban youth, this was often a period of transition from the domestic world of the natal family to a world of work outside the household, often living in another family's home. Boys often entered apprenticeships to learn the craft which would sustain them as adults, living in their master's home, while girls commonly went into domestic service,[22] although some did enter apprenticeships or apprenticeship-like arrangements. Boys of the middling and upper classes might begin the transition away from the domestic family (a world often gendered feminine as the domain of the mother) earlier, around the age of seven, if they were sent to school, or in the case of the elite, began instruction with a tutor. Any formal education of elite girls was usually focussed on preparing them for their role as wife and mother. Sons and some daughters of elite Gaelic families were often fostered in other families as part of a complex web of family alliances and obligations, while for young Lowland gentlemen (and some Highland ones as well), the place to seek one's fortune was at the royal court.

As several of our contributors point out, adults might try to shape the lives of their children, but young people also exercised agency in determining their own experiences.[23] Campbell argues that while the early modern toys found in various parts of Scotland may have been fashioned by adults, their use also reflects choice on the part of the children who played with them. Parker provides examples of young people who resisted parental plans for their marriage, while the letters of Elizabeth Melville strongly suggest that her son James did not always take her advice to heart. The concept of agency is one fraught with controversy, and this is particularly so for studies of children and youth. To what extent can children assert agency? What do we mean by the concept of agency? To what extent

[20] Michael Anderson, 'The Demographic Factor', in T.M. Devine and J. Wormald (eds), *The Oxford Handbook of Modern Scottish History* (Oxford, 2012), 41–2.

[21] For a Scottish perspective, see John Dwyer, 'The Construction of Adolescence in Late Eighteenth-Century Scotland', Chapter 3 of his *Virtuous Discourse: Sensibility and Community in Late Eighteenth-Century Scotland* (Edinburgh, 1987). European works accepting the concept of 'adolescence' include Ilana Krausman Ben-Amos, *Adolescence and Youth in Early Modern England* (New Haven, 1994) and Konrad Eisenbichler (ed.), *The Pre-Modern Teenager* (Toronto, 2002).

[22] See for example, A.M. Allen, *The Locksmith Craft in Early Modern Edinburgh* (Edinburgh, 2007); Elizabeth Ewan, 'Mistresses of Themselves? Female Domestic Servants and By-Employments in Sixteenth-Century Scottish Towns', in A. Fauve-Chamoux (ed.), *Domestic Service and the Formation of European Identity* (Bern, 2004), 411–33.

[23] This was common throughout Europe, Colin Heywood, *A History of Childhood* (Cambridge, 2011), 2–5.

are actions the strategies of an individual or, alternatively, embedded in social relations, institutions and history?[24]

Despite evidence of children as historical actors, parents had their own ideas about how children should act, what they should be, and what they represented to the family. Of especial importance to royalty and the elite was the role of children in continuing their lineage. The marriage of Prince Alexander, arranged at the highest political levels, was of crucial importance in securing Alexander III's dynasty for the next generation – his early death in 1284 and lack of an heir was eventually to plunge the country into the Wars of Independence. In Gaelic Scotland, the young foster-sons and -daughters and their foster families constructed bonds of loyalty and friendship that would bring cohesion to clan society. The importance of the child as representative of the family rather than an individual can be seen in the practice, strange to modern sensibilities, of providing for the 'substitution' of another sibling if something befell the first-named one before a fosterage or marriage contract was completed. Here, the child was to a certain extent a pawn in the dynastic plans of parents, although as Parker points out, many parents did consider their children's happiness as well, and some children refused to go along with their parents' plans. The marriage laws of Scotland, which allowed marriage to be made through the simple consent of the couple, enabled some young people to make their own marriage choice. At the levels of society below the aristocracy, there seems to have been a fair degree of freedom of choice for both men and women.[25]

Gender was an important determinant in the lives of medieval and early modern children, playing a role in both their experiences and in the perceptions that others had of them.[26] The practical implications of gender difference are demonstrated by the restrictions placed on female workers by guilds in the early modern period at the same time as boys were being apprenticed into these trades. Town councils and kirk sessions were concerned about young women living alone, for both moral and economic reasons.[27] Advice literature also ascribed different characteristics to boys and girls, with boys seen as more capable of developing the powers of reason and self-governance than girls. A seventeenth-century

[24] Mary Jo Maynes, 'Age as a Category of Historical Analysis; History, Agency, and Narratives of Childhood', *JHCY* 1:1 (2008), 114–124, especially 119.

[25] Ballads often show the unfortunate consequences of young people's exercise of independence in courtship, Katie Barclay, '"And Four Years Space, being Man and Wife, they Loveingly Agreed": Balladry and Early Modern Understandings of Marriage', in Ewan and Nugent (eds), *Finding the Family*, 23–34. Freedom of marriage choice further down the social scale was also found in other countries such as England. See John Gillis, *For Better, For Worse: British marriages, 1600 to the Present* (New York, 1985) and Diana O'Hara, *Courtship and Constraint: Rethinking the Making of Marriage in Tudor England* (Manchester, 2000).

[26] For European societies, see the essays in Miller and Yavneh (eds), *Gender and the Construction of Childhood*. Some of the papers delivered at a recent conference on Scottish masculinities, held in St Andrews in March 2014, will be published in a forthcoming collection edited by Lynn Abrams and Elizabeth Ewan.

[27] Michael Graham, 'Women and the Church Courts in Reformation-Era Scotland', in Ewan and Meikle (eds), *Women in Scotland*, 187–98.

Gaelic song sets out the qualities expected of the ideal noble girl in Highland society, while portraits present boys and girls very differently once they are past infancy. Advice literature also spelled out the dangers of female sexuality, if it was not strictly regulated. Honour for girls was linked more closely to acceptable sexual behaviour than it was for boys, although sexual propriety and economic honesty played a role for both sexes.[28] Although its nature shifted and changed over time, premodern Scottish society was still patriarchal.[29]

Many concerns over female sexuality revolved around the problems of illegitimacy. Although this topic has been studied in some depth since the 1980s, the focus has tended to be on the women bearing the children, rather than the children themselves.[30] Acceptance and legal treatment of illegitimate children varied over time and place. In the Gaidhealtachd, illegitimate children, at least those fathered by elite men, were largely accepted and acknowledged by their fathers, although their inheritance rights were commonly less than those of their legitimate brothers. Ethnicity and gender also played a role, as demonstrated by the ambivalent views of white fathers to their mixed-race offspring with slave women. In Lowland Scotland, the illegitimate sons of kings were treated well and elite families often made provision for illegitimate children, although not on the same terms as their legitimate siblings.

Legitimate children were critical for elite families to ensure family lineage. The way in which parents saw their children in the context of the family is represented in the family portraits which became particularly popular in the eighteenth century, although earlier pictorial evidence such as the thirteenth-century seal of young Prince Alexander also reveals something about perceptions of identity. As Whiting points out in her examination of two family portraits by David Allan, it was the commissioner of the portrait who decided how the children would be represented. The son and heir is portrayed as the hope for the future of the lineage, but his siblings are also depicted in gendered roles. Play has a role in these portraits as well, suggesting a consciousness of childhood as a distinct stage. A more sombre side of childhood is shown in the portraits which depict, or at one time did depict, African slave children with their Scottish masters. If white children were to a certain extent marginalized in Scottish society, black children were almost invisible, not only to contemporary society, but also to twenty-first-century conceptions of the Scottish past.

[28] Recent work has argued that the distinction between female and male honour was not as clear-cut as once assumed. See Garthine Walker, 'Expanding the Boundaries of Female Honour in Early Modern England', *Transactions of the Royal Historical Society*, 6th ser. 6 (1996), 233–45.

[29] Katie Barclay, *Love, Intimacy and Power: Marriage and Patriarchy in Scotland, 1650–1850* (Manchester, 2011). For expectations for the behaviour of wives, see Chapters 10 and 11 in this collection.

[30] Among the most influential studies in this area, although now somewhat dated, is Leah Leneman and Rosalind Mitchison, *Sexuality and Social Control: Scotland 1660–1780* (Oxford, 1989). For a critique, see Andrew Blaikie, 'Scottish Illegitimacy: Social Punishment or Moral Economy', *Journal of Interdisciplinary History* 29:2 (1998), 211–42.

Children were not merely pawns to be used in furthering family fortunes, however; their relationships with their parents were much more complex. Evidence exploring the emotions of children and those in their families can be found in letters to offspring, letters to friends showing pride in children's achievements, in the grief expressed when a child died, and in the concern shown through works of advice. Elizabeth Melville's letters to her son continue a tradition of parental guidance shown by her own father Sir James Melville of Halhill, who wrote two treatises of advice for his sons and daughters (now unfortunately lost). Indeed, such instruction was found also at the very top of society, as instanced by the *Basilikon Doron*, written by James VI for his young son.[31] The songs and poems of Gaelic mothers, foster-mothers and nurses show the depth of feeling of these women toward the children under their care, while maternal love motivated Margaret Douglas, Lady Lorne's acts of influence (and interference) in her son's fosterage experience. Recent work in the history of emotions has revealed a multitude of sources to explore children and emotion.[32] Even law was not immune. In legal disputes over family inheritance in the eighteenth century, ideas of 'natural affection' between a parent and child not only affected the pleading of cases, but even influenced the law itself. Another area of affection, and one which the essays in this collection have only been able to treat fleetingly, was that between siblings.[33]

David Mullan has shown how the religious autobiographies of seventeenth- and early eighteenth-century Scottish women and men provide a glimpse into their emotions, both about their own children, and in their memories of their own parents. Advice literature on how to teach children piety was written throughout the early modern period, including work by James Kirkwood and the anonymously authored *The Familie Exercise*.[34] Indeed, occasionally we can hear children's own voices, either in the reports of their parents, or in the biographies of godly children which were popular with seventeenth-century readers. The godly child Emilia Geddie scolded fellow children for playing on the Sabbath day; such actions probably appealed to parents more than to her playmates.[35] The letters home from a sixteenth-century schoolboy asking for more money echo down the ages, including to those of our contributors and readers who have university-age children.[36]

31 James Craig (ed.), *The Basilikon Doron of King James VI* (Edinburgh, 1950).

32 Claudia Jarzebowski and Thomas Max Safley (eds), *Childhood and Emotion: Across Cultures 1450–1800* (London, 2014).

33 Naomi Miller and Naomi Yavneh (eds), *Sibling Relations and Gender in the Early Modern World* (Aldershot, 2006).

34 James Kirkwood, *The True Interest of Families: or, directions how parents may be happy in their children, and children in their parents* (London, 1692); *Familie Exercise, or, The Service of God in Families* (Edinburgh, 1641).

35 David G. Mullan, *Narratives of the Religious Self* (Aldershot, 2010), 172. See also the mothers' narratives in David G. Mullan (ed.), *Women's Life-Writing in Early Modern Scotland* (Aldershot, 2003).

36 Robert Vans Agnew (ed.), *The Correspondence of Patrick Vaus of Barnbarroch, Knight* (Edinburgh, 1887).

Due to high mortality rates, children were often challenged with the loss of one or both parents. When one parent died, it was not uncommon for the surviving spouse to remarry, and many children grew up in blended families with a step-parent and half siblings. Many young people took on adult responsibilities early in order to help support a widowed parent, especially a mother who did not remarry.[37] Other children lost both parents and often faced an uncertain future. If they were wealthy heirs or heiresses, their wardship was often assigned to other members of the elite, not necessarily their kin. At the other end of the social scale, orphaned children of the poor might be supported by the parish or sent into service to earn their keep.[38] It was not uncommon for young people to migrate from one part of Scotland to another in search of work, either temporary or permanent.[39] Many young people, the majority of them boys and young men, found opportunities for work outside the country, especially as mercenaries. In the first half of the seventeenth century, thousands of young men went to Europe for military service. The newly planted territories of Ulster, and towards the end of our period, the New World, also provided opportunities for these children, although emigration was not necessarily voluntary on their part.[40] The impact on the home society of such large-scale emigration by young men has still to be fully investigated.

Children and youth were not only valuable to and valued by their parents and families; they were also crucial to society and the state. Education and socialization were important in the creation of a new generation which would carry on the ideals of society and those characteristics which made up its identity.[41] The portraits of elite families of the eighteenth century proclaimed an identity at once British and Scottish, comfortable in the Union of 1707. Many of the children of the eighteenth-century elite were educated in London, where they learned English ways of speech and culture which they brought back to Scotland. Education could also be used to gradually eliminate other languages and cultures. Although debate continues over the actual short-term effectiveness of the Statutes of Iona of 1609, with their requirement that elite sons (and some daughters) be educated in Scots rather than Gaelic, the long-term effects of education

[37] Mullan, *Narratives*, 154–7.

[38] Helen Dingwall, *Seventeenth-Century Edinburgh: A Demographic Study* (Aldershot, 1994), 119. For poverty generally, see Cullen, 'Famine of the 1690s'; Rosalind Mitchison, *The Old Poor Law in Scotland: The Experience of Poverty, 1574–1845* (Edinburgh, 2000). For Europe see, for example, Joel Harrington, *The Unwanted Child: The Fate of Foundlings, Orphans, and Juvenile Criminals in Early Modern Germany* (Chicago, 2009).

[39] Ian Whyte and Kathleen Whyte, 'The Geographical Mobility of Women in Early Modern Scotland', in Leah Leneman (ed.), *Perspectives in Scottish Social History* (Aberdeen, 1988), 45–53.

[40] Steve Murdoch and Esther Mijers, 'Migrant Destinations 1500–1700', in Devine and Wormald (eds), *The Oxford Handbook*; Michael Anderson, 'The Demographic Factor', 43–4.

[41] See essays in Robert Anderson et al. (eds), *The Edinburgh History of Education in Scotland* (Edinburgh, forthcoming). Education is one area where the literature on the Scottish experience has been and continues to be extensive.

in another tongue would prove critical for the Gaelic language; the reluctance of young Archie Campbell to learn Gaelic was a real concern for his parents and foster family.[42] Children were the key to bringing about social developments: we need to have a better understanding of their lives in order to interrogate long-term continuity and change.

[42] For examples of the role of education as a sometimes contested tool of socialization, see Shona Vance, 'Godly Citizens and Civic Unrest: Tensions in Schooling in Aberdeen on the Eve of the Reformation', *European Review of History* 7:1 (2000), 123–77; Clotilde Prunier, '"They must have their children educated some way": The Education of Catholics in Eighteenth-Century Scotland', *Innes Review* 60:1 (2009), 22–40.

Part I

Experiences of Childhood and Youth

1

*A 'gret cradil of stait': Growing up with the Court of James IV**

Mairi Cowan and Laura E. Walkling

On the last day of April 1508, a gift of 3s was presented 'to ane pure barne that tuke the King be the hand'.[1] We know that the king and the child were in St Andrews, and we know that the king was James IV, king of Scots; we do not know the name, sex or age of the 'barne', nor do we know what kind of conversation, if any, happened between the monarch and his young subject. The one fleeting glimpse of this encounter is provided by the *Accounts of the Lord High Treasurer of Scotland*, in which someone recorded the poor child's holding of the king's hand.[2] In terms of monetary value, the king's gift of 3s was a long way from the lavish expenditures made for members of his own family, such as the sum of over £57 spent on the 'gret cradil of stait', a princely cradle covered with cloth of gold and lined with scarlet that was provided for James's infant son in February 1507.[3] Although the king's gift to the child who took his hand was much less extravagant than the 'gret cradil of stait', nonetheless, the record relating this moment of human contact between the most powerful person in the kingdom and a poor child remains a rather touching report of a young person's interaction with his or her king.

When records from the court of James IV are considered together, several notable aspects of childhood and youth emerge. The first is a lack of clear chronological boundaries denoted by the words used to describe childhood and adolescence. These words seem able, at least in some cases, to refer to a person of any age from before birth to approximately twenty years old, or older still when the child-related vocabulary associated with servile occupations is taken into account. Another notable aspect of childhood and youth to come to light is that the day-to-day experiences of young people differed significantly according to social status, and that social status was, in turn, influenced by a variety of factors including gender, place of origin, and publicly recognized parentage. In many

* We would like to thank editors Elizabeth Ewan and Janay Nugent for their support and encouragement, the anonymous reviewers for their remarks and suggestions, and our friendly ideal readers Whitney Hahn and Hilary Evans Cameron for their thoughtful questions and comments.

1 Thomas Dickson and J.B. Paul (eds), *Accounts of the Lord High Treasurer of Scotland* [*TA*], 4 vols (Edinburgh, 1844–1902), iv, 114.

2 *TA*, i, 200.

3 *TA*, iii, 273–4.

ways, therefore, the lives of the youngest people in and around the court of James IV were as varied as the lives of any other group there. However, the third feature of childhood and youth to appear in the records is that the lives of young people also shared a certain age-related commonality in spite of unclear chronological boundaries and multiple forms of social distinction. Childhood and adolescence were regarded as stages of life distinct from full adulthood, with their own expectations and realities, eliciting from adults an acknowledgement that the younger members of society required their own age-specific care that could transcend other social distinctions.

The Court and its Records

The royal court moved from place to place with James IV and was therefore defined not by its physical location but rather by its social formation around the person of the king. This particular king was highly energetic, travelling frequently around the kingdom on justice ayres and pilgrimages. He was also a gregarious person who surrounded himself with friends, courtiers, musicians, artists, poets, and entertainers of various sorts. James's 'glore of princelie governyng', in the words of poet Sir David Lyndsay, probably did make his court – to use an adjective often applied to Renaissance court culture – glittering.[4]

A good deal of information about the busy and boisterous life at court is contained in the treasurers' accounts, the records of the treasurers' management of royal revenue. These accounts list a very wide variety of expenditures, from armour worn by the king in tournaments, to food served at yuletide feasts, to pensions paid to court poets. Among the many items, a perhaps surprisingly high number relate to young people. In addition to these items in the treasurers' accounts, this study also draws upon letters to and from the king, reports from visitors to court, and even the personal reminiscences of one of Europe's most famous writers, Desiderius Erasmus of Rotterdam. Mention of young people is for the most part brief and from an oblique angle, as if the children and adolescents were but incidental: the writers were usually not writing about young people because they wanted to say something about this group in particular, but rather because they were recording some other aspect of court life and the young people happened to be there. Even so, the sources provide enough information to permit a description of the lives of several individual children and adolescents in considerable detail, and to observe, at least for a moment, the presence of others in and around the court.

An important early step in this discussion is the seemingly simple one of establishing parameters around the categories of 'childhood' and 'adolescence', as well as some procedures for determining whether a given individual fits within these parameters. The distinctiveness of childhood in the life cycle of medieval

4 Norman Macdougall, *James IV* (East Linton, 1997), 292.

and early modern Europeans is generally well established.[5] Many scholars also accept that medieval and early modern Europeans recognized a distinct stage of life between childhood and adulthood, lasting from the early teens to the early twenties, and usually called 'adolescence' or 'youth' in the modern literature.[6]

A potentially good method for finding children and adolescents in the records is to look for age-specific words being used to describe particular people, and then to look also for hints of youthful behaviour. Clear indicators of sub-adult age include the Latin *puer* (for 'boy')[7] and *impuber* (for 'youthful', 'not yet grown up'),[8] as well as the Scots 'bairn' (for 'child') and 'boy' (for a male child).[9] Other words may indicate sub-adult age, but with less certainty. 'Cheld', for example, could simply mean 'child', but it could also mean a young servant.[10] Several people are described as 'little', though not all of these were necessarily sub-adult in age. 'Maister Laurence Tailfeir, the litil doctor', for example, was presumably not young in age but perhaps small in stature.[11] By contrast, one instance when 'littil' does occur in association with a young person is in 1513, when 6s was given 'to litill Trumbull' to buy him 'stikis' (wooden sticks of some form). It can quite confidently be assumed that Trumbull was young, for only two months earlier the sum of £5 was to be provided to a schoolmaster in Edinburgh for 'ane boys burd callit Trumbule', that is, the boarding costs of Trumbull living at school.[12] Further words suggesting but not confirming sub-adult age include 'lad', 'lass', and 'maidin'.[13] Less reliable as indicators are words in the

5 For example, Nicholas Orme, *Medieval Children* (New Haven, 2001); Margaret L. King, 'Concepts of Childhood: What We Know and Where We Might Go', *Renaissance Quarterly* 60:2 (2007), 371–407.

6 Kim M. Phillips, *Medieval Maidens: Young Women and Gender in England, 1270–1540* (Manchester, 2003), 4–5; Konrad Eisenbichler, 'Introduction', in Konrad Eisenbichler (ed.), *The Premodern Teenager: Youth in Society 1150–1650* (Toronto, 2002), 2; Barbara Hanawalt, 'Historical Descriptions and Prescriptions for Adolescence', *Journal of Family History* 17:4 (1992), 351–76; Ilana Krausman Ben-Amos, *Adolescence and Youth in Early Modern England* (New Haven, 1994); Orme, *Medieval Children*. For an argument considering the age of adolescence, starting in about the year 1500, see Don Romesburg, 'Making Adolescence More or Less Modern', in Paula S. Fass (ed.), *The Routledge History of Childhood in the Western World* (Abingdon, 2013), 229–32.

7 *Puer* is normally translated as 'male child' or boy, but may occasionally have meant 'young man' or an adult with childish characteristics. See '*puer*' in Charlton T. Lewis and Charles Short, *A New Latin Dictionary* (New York, 1891); Gary Dickson, '*Rite de Passage*? The Children's Crusade and Medieval Childhood', *JHCY* 2:3 (2009), 315–32.

8 *Puber* is one who is grown up. See '*pubes* and *puber*' in Lewis and Short, *A New Latin Dictionary*; '*impubes*' as 'youthful, beardless, under age, below the age of puberty' in Leo F. Stelten, *Dictionary of Ecclesiastical Latin* (Peabody, MA, 1997); '*impubertas*' as 'youth' in R.E. Latham, *Revised Medieval Latin Word-List from British and Irish Sources* (London, 1965).

9 'Barne, Bairn, Bern' and 'Boy' in *DSL*; 'Bairn' in *Oxford English Dictionary*.

10 'Cheld' and 'Child' in *DSL*.

11 *TA*, iii, 153.

12 *TA*, iv, 404, 410.

13 'Lad', 'Las', in *DSL*; 'Maidin' in *DSL*; Phillips, *Medieval Maidens*, 42–3. For examples of how the terminology functioned in England at about the same time, see P.J.P. Goldberg, 'Childhood and Gender in Later Medieval England', *Viator* 39:1 (2008), 249–62.

various languages for 'son' and 'daughter', since these terms designated familial relationship regardless of age.[14]

Some ambiguity must be acknowledged in the usage of terms that would seem on the surface to denote a child or adolescent, and it is likely that the court's scribes themselves were not always especially precise in their terminology. Over a short period of time, the pre-pubescent treble singers of church choirs were referred to by a variety of words, including 'boyis', 'barnis', 'childir', and 'laddis'; as if to confirm the interchangeability of terms, an entry from 1507 speaks of 'the barnis quarter fee to thre childer' of the chapel.[15] Indeed, even if there are cases where an individual person's calendrical age can be known, medieval and early modern sources disagree among themselves about when exactly a person moved into a particular stage of life. The 'ages of man' or 'ages of life' genre of literature discussing the individual's passage through stages of the life cycle provides a variety of options for beginning and end points to childhood and youth. Augustine of Hippo distinguished the stages of infancy, boyhood and adolescence, but did not attribute to these stages specific years of an individual's life. Isidore of Seville determined that infancy lasted to age seven, childhood to age fourteen, and adolescence to age twenty-eight, but other writers chose different ages at which a person moved from one stage to the next.[16] The fifteenth-century Scottish poem *Ratis Raving* articulated seven stages in the life cycle, including the first stage lasting for the first three years, the second from when the child is three to when the child is seven, the third from the age of seven to the age of fifteen, and the fourth from the age of fifteen to the age of thirty. Even at thirty a person is perhaps not completely mature according to this poem, for the time of full reason commences only after that year.[17]

Clearly, the boundaries around childhood and adolescence were often imprecise for writers, and this imprecision can lead to considerable ambiguity for historians. The case of Margaret Tudor, daughter to King Henry VII of England and Elizabeth of York, and wife to James IV, illustrates how it can be difficult to place an individual person on any precise point in the life cycle. Her marriage to James would seem to suggest a certain maturity and ability to give the rational consent required to make a legal union. Canon law stipulated that the minimum age for marriage was twelve for females (fourteen for males),[18] and, in fact, at thirteen Margaret was only just over the minimum when, in August

[14] 'Son' and 'Douchter' in *DSL*.

[15] *TA*, iii, 134, 145, 158, 186, 331, 336, 400, 415; *TA*, iv, 68, 96.

[16] Augustine of Hippo, *De Diversis Quaestionibus LXXXIII*, Bk 1, Qu. LVIII, cited in J.A. Burrow, *The Ages of Man: A Study in Medieval Writing and Thought* (Oxford, 1988), 199–200; Isidore of Seville, *Etymologiae*, Bk XI, Ch. 2, in Burrow, *The Ages of Man*, 200–1; Deborah Youngs, *The Life Cycle in Western Europe, c. 1300–c. 1500* (Manchester, 2006), 20–3, 39–40, 71–2, 96–7.

[17] *Ratis Raving* in R. Girvan (ed.), *Ratis Raving and Other Early Scots Poems on Morals* (Edinburgh, 1939), ll. 1104 ff. For this poem, see also Chapters 10 and 11 in this collection.

[18] Youngs, *Life Cycle in Western Europe*, 133.

1503, she wed the Scottish king, who was then thirty.[19] Certain aspects of their relationship may suggest that James did not regard his bride as fully mature, whatever canon law had to say on the matter. She did not bear her first child until February 1507. Thereafter she had children in fairly quick succession (her second in July 1508 and her third in October 1509), suggesting the two were a fertile pair.[20] The absence of any child earlier in the marriage may indicate that Margaret was not yet able to conceive or that the two did not consummate their union for several years, perhaps waiting until one or both of them decided that Margaret was sufficiently mature. If they were delaying a sexual relationship, they were certainly in keeping with others' opinions on the matter of too early a consummation.[21] Margaret's grandmother, Margaret Beaufort, had been married to Edmund Tudor at the age of twelve and gave birth to her first child, the future Henry VII of England, at the age of thirteen. The difficult birth may have led to permanent physical damage to the mother impeding her later fertility, or at least to increased anxiety about pregnancy, and she opposed the marriage of her granddaughter to James IV because she worried that James would not wait until Margaret was a suitable age before trying to consummate the union.[22] James did provide his wife with New Year's gifts of a gold coin and sapphire rings in 1504, and he showed special concern for her health later that year by transporting her away from Dunfermline when plague arrived in the town. The couple also played cards together during the winter of 1505/1506. The two of them may have got along, but Margaret's ambiguous placement in the life cycle – within 'childhood' according to the 'ages of life' literary tradition; within 'adulthood' according to canon law; probably immature according to social conventions of sexuality – meant that they did not act as fully married.

Sons and Daughters of the King

Of all the young people at the court of James IV, the best documented are the king's own sons and daughters. They certainly received thoughtful, age-specific training to help prepare them while young for the roles that lay in their future. Although the king's 'legitimate children' – the heirs to the throne – enjoyed the most luxurious material culture of any children at court, his 'natural' children (his children with mistresses) were treated very well and their illegitimacy was not a complete bar to their social advancement.[23]

19 *TA*, i, 412, 463; TA, iii, 180–1.

20 Richard Glen Eaves, 'Margaret (1489–1541)', *ODNB*.

21 Phillips, *Medieval Maidens*, 38–43. For further discussion of the issue of consummation of child marriages see Chapter 10 in this collection.

22 Michael K. Jones and Malcolm G. Underwood, *The King's Mother: Lady Margaret Beaufort, Countess of Richmond and Derby* (Cambridge, 1992), 40.

23 James had at least five children outside of marriage. See Macdougall, *James IV*, 98, 113–14, 162–3, 286, 310 n. 14.

James's first child in the records is Alexander Stewart, who was born about 1493 to Marion Boyd, daughter of Archibald Boyd of Naristoun and Christina Muir, and regularly referred to as the king's son.[24] As a young child Alexander was cared for by a nurse in Ayr, whose salary was paid as a royal expenditure,[25] and dressed in sumptuous clothing.[26] One lot purchased in February 1503 included a satin-lined gown costing more than £8 and a velvet gown costing more than £25.[27] From an early age, Alexander was being prepared for a career in the Church. In 1497 the king obtained for him papal dispensation for illegitimacy, and in 1504 Alexander was provided with the archbishopric of St Andrews. As for intellectual training, Alexander was given a first-rate education. He was sent to Stirling and taught by James Watson, a graduate of the University of Louvain, and later was tutored by the king's secretary and renowned classical stylist, Patrick Paniter. He attended the faculty of arts at the University of St Andrews, and then, in 1507, he went to the Continent to study first with Raphael Regius and then with one of Europe's leading intellectual figures, Desiderius Erasmus.[28] He studied with Erasmus every morning, and in the afternoons he played music on the monochord, flute and zither. Erasmus reported that Alexander devoted any remaining time to the reading of historians, since history was his favourite subject. Alexander made a very favourable impression on Erasmus. Writing after Alexander's death at the Battle of Flodden in 1513, Erasmus described Alexander's dignity and quiet temperament, his gentleness of nature and fairness of mind, and also his aptitude for scholarship. Remembering his tutoring of Alexander in rhetoric and Greek, Erasmus lauded his pupil's quick mind 'ready to follow any clue' and 'capable of grasping many things at once', and Erasmus also praised Alexander's religious devotion as being without a trace of superstition. Erasmus summed up by saying that 'no one, in a word, was ever more worthy to be a king's son and the son of that king'.[29]

James's first daughter in the records is his child with Margaret Drummond, a girl referred to in the treasurers' accounts as Lady Margaret. Her care and upbringing had much in common with that of her half-brother Alexander. She too had acknowledgement of the king's paternity, being called 'the Kingis dochtir'.[30] Like her half-brother, Margaret was very well dressed. One lot of clothing from December 1504 included a gown of velvet lined in ermine cost-

24 *TA*, ii, 58, 154, 156.
25 *TA*, i, 378.
26 For example, *TA*, ii, 58.
27 *TA*, ii, 303–4.
28 Trevor Chalmers, 'Stewart, Alexander (*c.* 1493–1513)', *ODNB*; *TA*, ii, 123; Robert Kerr Hannay (ed.), *The Letters of James the Fourth 1505–1513* (Edinburgh, 1953), 92, 103.
29 Desiderius Erasmus, *Adagia* II.v.i 'Spartam nactus es, hanc orna', ll. 136 ff. in *Opera Omnia Desiderii Erasmi Roterodami* II-3 (Amsterdam, 2005), 402–6; Desiderius Erasmus, *Collected Works of Erasmus: Adages II i 1 to II vi 100*, trans. R.A.B. Mynors (Toronto, 1991), 241–3; Desiderius Erasmus, *The Adages of Erasmus*, trans. William Barker (Toronto, 2001), 188–90.
30 *TA*, ii, 330, 478.

ing in excess of £25, and another lot from just three months later included a damask gown bordered in velvet for more than £13.[31] In early January 1506 she was given the costly gift of twenty-two gold beads.[32] She too was under the care of a nurse for several years. At the end of 1504 the nurse was discharged and Margaret's care was transferred to the wife of the captain of Edinburgh Castle.[33] Margaret would have been about seven-years-old at the time, a pivotal age in several examples of the 'ages of man' literature including *Ratis Raving*, when the child moves from a stage characterized by play to one characterized by the beginnings of discretion and reason.[34] Like Alexander, Margaret's education was transferred from a nurse to another authority, but unlike Alexander, Margaret remained in Edinburgh Castle for her tutelage. Her education was less bookish than that of Alexander, but perhaps better suited to the expected life of a courtly lady: she was trained in dancing by one of the court musicians.[35]

Alexander and Margaret were provided with care by nurses, accommodation in royal castles, beautiful clothing, and education to prepare them for a career in the Church or for courtly marriage. In short, they were furnished with material comforts and training befitting the offspring of a king and, moreover, they were publicly acknowledged as the king's children. But whatever their talents and skills, whatever the affection they inspired in the king, they were not heirs to the Scottish throne. Those children who were the heirs were provided with even more luxurious trappings and louder acclamations of the king's paternity.

The birth of Prince James, the first child of James and Margaret, took place on 21 February 1507.[36] The happy event was announced far and wide. James was informed by a lady who 'brocht tithingis to the King of the Prince birth', for which service she was paid the very handsome reward of £90 and a great cup of silver;[37] James then sent word of the birth to the king of England.[38] The successful delivery must have been cause for celebration at court, for the king gave to 'Guilliam', one of the court musicians, £4 4s 'for making of ane dans the tyme of the Princes birth'.[39]

The material conditions of life for this little prince were of a very high standard. Even before his birth, preparations were begun on his luxuriously appointed nursery featuring taffeta from Florence, woollen curtains, and ten tapestries from Arras costing £50.[40] The baptism of the two-day-old heir to the throne was also sumptuous, with the infant being carried on a cloth of gold lined with ermine

31 *TA*, ii, 330–1; *TA*, iii, 93–4.
32 *TA*, iii, 178.
33 *TA*, ii, 376, 470; *TA*, iii, 361.
34 The pivotal nature of the age of seven is also discussed in Chapter 3 in this collection.
35 *TA*, iii, 117.
36 *TA*, iii, 287.
37 *TA*, iii, 369.
38 *TA*, iii, 369.
39 *TA*, iii, 371.
40 *TA*, iii, 272, 274, 275.

that cost the astonishing sum of more than £62.[41] He had a nurse from his first days, and her living conditions were also well looked after. Her bed had a canopy, and she was assisted by 'rokkaris', women to rock the cradle.[42] It was for this prince that the 'gret cradil of stait' was made; in addition he had a 'litill cradill' covered in scarlet with green ribbons, bordered with ermine, decorated with black fur tips, lined with soft cotton, and containing several blankets and sheets. Even the infant prince's cushion was luxurious, made of purple velvet and filled with feathers.[43]

No expense, however, could guarantee health or happiness. Of James and Margaret's six children, only one lived beyond early childhood. Their first three died in infancy. James, who was born in February 1507, died in February 1508. Their second child, a daughter (unnamed in the treasurers' accounts), was born in July 1508 and died the same day. Their third, Arthur, was born in October 1509 and died in June 1510. Their fourth child, also named James, was born in April 1512. Perhaps this pregnancy had been especially difficult, for in its final month the king sent one of the officers of the wardrobe to fetch a relic – the shirt of St Margaret – for the queen.[44] This baby lived and, in time, acceded to the throne as James V. A girl was born after James and died probably in early 1513. James and Margaret's last child, Alexander, was born in April 1514, seven months after King James died at the Battle of Flodden. It is unlikely that James ever knew of his wife's pregnancy, and the child Alexander died before his second birthday.

Any effort to make a direct comparison between the 'natural' and the 'legitimate' children of James IV is hindered by the very small size of the sample. Only one legitimate child, the second James, survived infancy. No female child of James and Margaret Tudor survived whose life could be compared against that of Lady Margaret, and the one legitimate child who did survive was crowned king at just seventeen months of age. Being king, this boy could hardly be sent overseas to study with great Continental humanists, and his father could not take any direct interest in the child's upbringing, because he was deceased. Therefore, if later reports of James V's somewhat disappointing erudition suggest that he lacked the intellectual sparkle of his half-brother Alexander, such may be due to circumstance as much as aptitude. All the acknowledged children of the king were provided with age-specific care, but the details of what was included in this care certainly depended on the child's sex and legal status, only possibly on the child's disposition. Alexander Stewart was fortunate to have had access to education that suited his temperament; had he been born a different sex or without the acknowledgement of royal paternity, he likely would not have had the same opportunities for intellectual development.

41 *TA*, iii, 272–3.
42 *TA*, iii, 273, 275, 276.
43 *TA*, iii, 273–4.
44 *TA*, iii, 334.

From Far and Near

Many children at the court were born locally, but some came from abroad and not all of these travelled to Scotland of their own volition. Several arrived from the Continent, with or without their guardians. The 'boy of the Franch leiches' (a doctor's boy) and the 'spelar boy' (likely an actor or acrobat) 'callit Francis de Luca' were mentioned in April 1502.[45] 'Litill Martin the Span[y]art' first appears in the records in 1506 when he was given a yellow coat, a doublet and hose, and he continued to be provided with clothing regularly until the end of May 1513. That he was a child at his first appearance in the records is suggested by his presence among the 'Kingis hensmen', the pages or boy attendants of the king, starting in September 1511.[46] Since a 'henchman' was always young – a servant of high rank serving the king and young in age – then Martin must have been really quite young five years before taking up that position.[47] Often associated with Martin in the accounts is a French boy named Baroun, who may have been the boy left behind by a French knight in January 1507. He was given very similar clothing to Martin at similar intervals, and he too joined the henchmen of the king by the autumn of 1511.[48]

A Danish boy named Christopher or Christian was especially well looked after.[49] He first arrived in Scotland as 'Christofer the barne' in February 1505, when he was given a set of expensive clothing including a damask coat and two other coats, a gown, a velvet doublet, a hat and a hood. He was also provided with a feather bed, blankets and linen sheets.[50] Subsequent records indicate that Christopher continued to be provided not only with luxurious clothing,[51] but also with medical care when needed: on 28 November 1505 a payment was

45 *TA*, ii, 14, 145, 153.

46 *TA*, iii, 300–19 passim, 353, 356, 364, 366, 368, 370, 380, 381, 382, 386, 392, 396, 399, 404; *TA*, iv, 49, 50, 53, 63–6 passim, 72, 82, 130, 243, 367–8, 427, 434.

47 'Hensman' in *DSL*; Nicholas Orme, *From Childhood to Chivalry: The Education of the English Kings and Aristocracy 1066–1530* (New York, 1984), 51–2.

48 *TA*, iii, 314–17 passim, 320, 322, 366, 374, 376, 398, 401, 403, 404, 414, 415; *TA*, iv, 49–65 passim, 76, 82, 86, 130, 235, 236, 315, 317.

49 It is not entirely clear who this Christopher was. The editor of volume 3 of the *Treasurers' Accounts* says he was the heir apparent to the Danish throne, the son of Princess Elizabeth and nephew of King Hans (John), and that he would later succeed as King Christian II. See *TA*, iii, pp. xc–xci. The editor of *Letters James Fourth* agreed. Recent histories of Denmark say that Prince Christian was sent to Norway in 1502 and there assisted in raising a siege and halting a rebellion, and he was also sent to Norway in 1506 as viceroy. See Jens E. Olesen, 'Inter-Scandinavian Relations', in Knut Helle (ed.), *The Cambridge History of Scandinavia, Volume I* (Cambridge, 2003), 710–70, especially 763–4; Thomas Riis, 'The States of Scandinavia c. 1390–c. 1536', in Christopher Allmand (ed.), *The New Cambridge History of Medieval Europe, Volume VII* (Cambridge, 1998), 671–706.

50 *TA*, ii, 332, 478.

51 For example, *TA*, iii, 103, 105–6; see also 92–3, 95–100 passim, 102, 111–16 passim, 155, 182, 206, 300–4 passim, 314, 316–22 passim, 333, 334, 337, 343, 345, 351, 363, 370, 385, 395, 396.

recorded 'to leich Cristoferis hede'.[52] James wrote to King John of Denmark to report on the progress made by Christopher at court. In April 1505, he said that boy of his (*puer ille tuus*) was liked and doing well, that among the pages at court he was proving his noble lineage and showing promise.[53] The boy may also have attracted the personal interest of the king for reasons both of kinship and of international relations. James's mother was Margaret of Denmark, and her marriage to James III in 1468 brought with it full diplomatic alliance between the two countries. King John of Denmark seems to have respected the judgement of the king of Scots in matters pertaining to the boy, for in 1508 he consulted James about arranging the boy's marriage. Though he was hearing much about various daughters of princes, John said that he would not take any steps without first asking James's advice.[54]

Each of these children was far from home, and may have been brought to Scotland to suit adult interests rather than the child's, but each found a network of care at the Scottish court. Some children from abroad arrived under circumstances that made them much more vulnerable to neglect and abuse. In 1505 a payment of £12 was made for the transportation over water of a Portuguese horse, a civet cat, a small Spanish horse, and 'the Moris', or Moors.[55] The timing and contents of this shipment strongly suggest a connection between the court of James IV and the nascent Atlantic slave trade. By the later fifteenth century, Portuguese ships were bringing people directly from Sub-Saharan Africa to be slaves in Europe,[56] and in the late fifteenth and sixteenth centuries some members of the upper echelon of European society were intent on procuring black African slaves for their retinues, most often to serve as court musicians or personal attendants.[57] The presence of a black African slave, whether child or adult, was considered advantageous to a court, indicating the court's power and ever-expanding influence.[58] The vogue of acquiring black African slaves seems also to have taken hold in the court of James IV.[59] Several people variously described as 'Moor' or 'black' appear in the records, including a Moor taubronar,

52 *TA*, iii, 173.
53 *Letters James Fourth*, 4.
54 *Letters James Fourth*, 118.
55 *TA*, iii, 148.
56 David Northrup, *Africa's Discovery of Europe 1450–1850*, 2nd edn (Oxford, 2009), 1–7.
57 The demand for, and resulting increase of, black African slaves in European courts is recorded in the visual culture of Renaissance Europe. See Annemarie Jordan, 'Images of Empire: Slaves in the Lisbon Household and Court of Catherine of Austria'; Paul H.D. Kaplan, 'Isabella d'Este and Black African Women'; and Kate Lowe, 'The Stereotyping of Black Africans in Renaissance Europe', all in T.F. Earle and K.J.P. Lowe (eds), *Black Africans in Renaissance Europe* (New York, 2005). For more on child slaves in Scotland and in Scottish portraiture, see Chapter 7 in this collection.
58 Jordan, 'Images', 156, 179; Kaplan, 'Isabella', 139; Milton Meltzer, *Slavery: From the Rise of Western Civilization to the Renaissance* (New York, 1971), 239.
59 Mairi Cowan, 'In the Borderlands of Periodization with 'The blythnes that hes bein': The Medieval / Early Modern Boundary in Scottish history', *The Journal of the Canadian Historical Association* 23:2 (2012), 159–66.

Peter the More, and two Moor lasses. There was also a group of women whose exact identities are unclear but who seem to have included: one 'blak lady' who participated in two tournaments with the king and who may or may not have been one of the 'lasses'; a second black lady; and the named figures of Ellen or Helen More and Margaret Moire, who may or may not have been among the unnamed lasses and/or ladies. In keeping with the fashions of the Continent, the Moor taubronar, or tabor player, was a courtly musician, entertaining the king during both public and private events.[60] He was well paid for his services, usually on a par with, and sometimes in excess of, other musicians at court. Like the taubronar, Peter the More was a member of the king's entourage, also well paid, and probably a personal attendant accompanying James on his travels, whether in short excursions to Stirling or on pilgrimages to Tain.[61] Of particular interest for this investigation are the two girls who lived in Edinburgh Castle with Lady Margaret.[62] It was likely in accordance with the customs of courtly women elsewhere seeking black children – as young as four years of age and with skin as black as possible – that King James procured the 'tua Moor lasses' for his daughter's retinue. A payment of 10s 8d on 7 November 1504 for their freight and ferry to the king in Inverkeithing marks their arrival at the Scottish court, probably to live as attendants to the young Lady Margaret whose nurse had recently been dismissed.[63] Membership in Lady Margaret's retinue had its advantages. Living expenses for the group totaled £100 per year,[64] and clothing was richly provided. The Moor lasses received tailored dresses with Holland cloth collars, 'blak gray' lined 'russet' gowns and 'red carsay ... kirtillis' with velvet detailing,[65] in addition to shoes, boots, stockings and chemises.[66] The finery of their clothing, while not as lavish as the damask and velvet worn by Margaret, was appropriate to the lasses' status as members of the Lady's retinue.[67]

However involved in daily life at court, the children identified as Moors were also marked as being different from other children. Even when baptized, and therefore initiated into the Christian community, a child's Moorish identity was noted by the scribe who recorded the sum given for the candle on 11 December 1504 'quhen the More las wes cristinit'.[68] A still stronger marker of difference

[60] For public performances (Easter, Yule and Shrove Tuesday), see *TA*, ii, 427, 472, 477; *TA*, iii, 132, 190. For non-public, or private, performances throughout Scotland, see *TA*, ii, 439, 444, 451, 457–9, 461–2, 464; *TA*, iii, 163, 182.

[61] *TA*, ii, 97, 99, 415–16, 420, 432, 434–5, 442, 444, 449.

[62] The Moor lasses are only ever found in Edinburgh and in the company of either Margaret Stewart and/or members of her retinue. *TA*, iii, 93–4, 100–1, 113–14, 154–5, 172, 175, 182, 310–11, 336, 361.

[63] *TA*, ii, 465, 470.

[64] *TA*, iii, 175, 361.

[65] *TA*, iii, 94, 101, 310–11, 321–2; *TA*, iv, 59.

[66] *TA*, iii, 114, 154–5, 172, 182, 336, 370–1, 387, 409; *TA*, iv, 51, 82, 100, 116; *TA*, iii, 113; *TA*, iv, 51, 62; *TA*, iv, 61.

[67] For reference to materials used for Margaret Stewart's clothing see *TA*, iv, 93. For the distinction made between the two Moor lasses and Margaret Stewart's servants see *TA*, iii, 175.

[68] *TA*, ii, 469.

was recorded in February 1506, when an infant was presented as an object of exotic interest to the king, who paid 28s 'to the nuris that broucht the Moris barne to see'.[69] In spite of such markers of difference, basic human consideration might sometimes have prevailed, as indicated perhaps by the payments made to the wife and child of the Moor taubronar after his death around the spring of 1507.[70] Whether because of their skin colour, their origins in lands distant from Scotland, their religious identity, or a combination of all three, the Moor children were treated differently from other children at court in some ways, but nonetheless were still recognized as having the same needs for companionship and basic material support. The extent of their personal freedom, either while children or after reaching adulthood, is unclear, but one enigmatic entry from the treasurers' accounts suggests the possibility of self-determination: Peter the More was paid the substantial sum of £3 'for to pas his way for evir', perhaps indicating that he left the Scottish court a free man to pursue his interests elsewhere.[71]

Birth and Death

Transcending nearly every marker of social status for children and adolescents at the court of James IV were the basic experiences of coming into life and, occasionally, falling into death. In at least one instance, the mysteries of the pre-natal period were harnessed by the king to satisfy his interest in games as he bet on the sex of an unborn child; such mysteries were beyond even his royal ken, for James lost the bet.[72] Midwives are mentioned a few times, suggesting the likelihood that they were regular attendants at births, and valued ones too.[73] The midwife who attended the queen in her first delivery was paid the very handsome sum of ten French crowns (£7).[74] Baptism was normally administered during infancy, and there are numerous references to gifts from the king at these ceremonies, sometimes when he was acting as godparent.[75] Baptism was a rite both of initiation into life and a spiritual rebirth in preparation for the afterlife,[76] and death was not far away for many of the youngest at court.

Children sometimes survived injuries that tell of childish activities, such as the 'lad that lap [leapt] in the stank [pond]' in the yard of the abbot of Holyrood on

69 *TA*, iii, 182; Mary E. Robbins interprets this event as showing that the Moor drummer shared a 'familiarity' with the king: 'Black Africans at the Court of James IV', *ROSC* 12 (1999), 40–3. Cf. Cowan, 'In the Borderlands of Periodization', 162–3.

70 *TA*, iii, 197, 206, 330, 377, 388.

71 *TA*, ii, 450.

72 *TA*, ii, 140.

73 *TA*, ii, 47; *TA*, iii, 371; *TA*, iv, 185.

74 *TA*, iii, 371.

75 *TA*, i, 120, 182; *TA*, ii, 97, 404, 478; *TA*, iii, 175, 364, 365–6, 384; *TA*, iv, 104–5, 109, 185.

76 Mairi Cowan, *Death, Life, and Religious Change in Scottish Towns c. 1350–1560* (Manchester, 2012), 95–6, 129, 160.

the last day of March 1502 and 'ane other boy' who fell in the same pond the following day, or the boy who broke his leg from a fall in the hall of Holyrood.[77] Sometimes the children did not survive. The cause of death is rarely recorded, but violence was involved at least once when, in 1508, a gift of 28s was made 'to the woman that hed hir barne slane in Stretherdill'.[78] A death recorded in the autumn of 1503 may well have been that of one of James's children, based on the interest he seems to have taken. In September, one of the king's officials rode to Edinburgh to 'warne the King of the deing of ane of the barnis', then in October more than £6 was paid as fee to 'the [y]ongest nuris quhen the barne wes dede ... be the Kingis command', and a winding sheet was purchased for the infant's body.[79] James showed an awareness of the precariousness of neonatal life in his letters to the king and queen of Denmark in April 1512, informing them that the Scottish queen had recently given birth to a son. He expressed hope in signs that the baby would live (*insignitus spem vitae*) but also conveyed a sense of caution lest the baby not survive (*modo vivat*).[80] James wrote another letter to King John in November of that same year, with different and sadder tidings: a few days earlier the queen had given birth prematurely to a son and he had died soon after baptism.[81] Infant mortality was high at all social levels in fifteenth- and sixteenth-century Europe, and Scotland was likely no exception. Even the original occupant of the 'gret cradil of stait' could not escape the sad fate of infant death.

In spite of high rates of infant mortality, attempts were regularly made to meet the particular demands of the early years of life. Sufficient nutrition for infants was ensured by the hiring of nurses, including at least once in January 1513 with special consideration for a baby's illness when an Irish nurse was paid £4 4s 'that gaif my Lord Prince sulk the tyme he wes seik'.[82] Indeed, without access to human milk an infant was likely doomed to an early death.[83] Abandoned children would have been especially vulnerable, and the woman who was paid 10s in 1512 'for nurising of ane fund barne' was probably saving a young life.[84]

Cultures of Childhood at Work and Play

Once they grew beyond infancy, young people still occupied a designated place within society. This is not to say that they were isolated from the world of adults, but age-specific concessions made to children and adolescents demonstrate an

[77] *TA*, ii, 142; *TA*, iii, 143.
[78] *TA*, iv, 131.
[79] *TA*, ii, 298, 394.
[80] *Letters James Fourth*, 243–4; *Epistolae Jacobi Quarti, Jacobi Quinti, et Mariae, Regum Scotorum* (Edinburgh, 1722), 141–2, 150.
[81] *Letters James Fourth*, 273; *Epistolae Regum Scotorum*, 167.
[82] *TA*, iv, 403.
[83] For wet-nurses in the French court, see Susan Broomhall, *Women's Medical Work in Early Modern France* (Manchester, 2004), 186–213.
[84] *TA*, iv, 182.

understanding that their youth in and of itself could be reason for differential treatment in training and work.

The vocabulary of childhood and youth could be used to refer to a person physically mature but still in a subservient social position. For example, 'Thom Barkaris man and his cheld' went to Melrose to repair wheels and purchase coals, and 'Sande Law and his cheld' were falconers, although it is not at all clear that any of these people were sub-adult in age. Other workers described as 'childer' were to be found alongside timber merchants, employed with a mason, and on board ships looking after the king's horse and watching over the vessel.[85] These 'childer' may well have been young men, but other labourers were more likely pre-adult, such as a boy looking after the hounds of the king, a boy who 'kepit the gait', and the 'boyis' and 'litill cuke laddis' of the kitchen.[86] One child at least was involved in possibly the most eccentric project of James's court: 'the boy that kepis the quinta essencia'.[87] Headed by the French (or possibly Italian) alchemist John Damian and funded by revenues from the abbey of Tongland in Galloway, the search for 'quintessence' – the fifth element and elixir of life – involved furnaces at Stirling and Holyrood, alum, quick silver, salt and eggs, and large quantities of whisky.[88] A frequently recorded task for boys was as runners, usually with letters to or from the king.[89] Most of these jobs were probably done by males, but in Stirling a 'madin', likely a young woman if not a child, made gloves for the king for which she was paid handsomely on several occasions.[90]

Many people described using words associated with children brought small food gifts to the king as he travelled from town to town. Common in the summer were fruits such as cherries, pears and apples, as well as fruit jelly.[91] Occasionally, the gifts of food would extend beyond fruit. A girl referred to as 'Stobois [Stobo's] madin' brought capons from at least 1501 to early 1507,[92] and 'ane madin of William Hakirstounis' also brought capons – though hers were described as 'fed' or fattened.[93] Two 'laddis' brought live young roe deer to the king in 1501, and two 'childer' brought large pike in 1507.[94] Most of these food gifts were fairly little in size, as might be suitable for the small stature of the givers, though the fattened ox brought to the king in 1508 certainly belies the trend.[95] All these gifts led to rewards from the king, ranging in value from the 2s 8d given to the two

85 *TA*, i, 290, 292, 352, 380, 391; *TA*, ii, 48; *TA*, iii, 199.

86 *TA*, iii, 174, 353, 376; *TA*, iv, 75.

87 *TA*, iv, 77.

88 For example, *TA*, ii, 359, 361, 362, 393; *TA*, iii, 183, 188; *TA*, iv, 79–80, 85, 96; John Read, 'A Flying Alchemist', in John Read, *Humour and Humanism in Chemistry* (London, 1947), 16–36.

89 For example, *TA*, i, 321; *TA*, iv, 89, 102, 373.

90 *TA*, iv, 134, 163.

91 *TA*, i, 96, 180, 200, 309, 329.

92 *TA*, ii, 105, 106; *TA*, iii, 176, 178, 181.

93 *TA*, ii, 146, 378.

94 *TA*, ii, 110; *TA*, iii, 377.

95 *TA*, iv, 135.

children who brought pikes and the 3s given to a child who brought pears, to at least 14s bestowed on each of the maidens who brought capons.

The court also hosted or interacted with several children and adolescents who were in formal training. Some were in academic studies. The scholarly career of Alexander Stewart has already been discussed, and other examples of scholarly activity can be found in closer physical proximity to the court. January seems to have been a significant back-to-school month for boys, several of whom (including Walter Steward, Sande Kenedy, Symon Graham, the son of 'Baille Veris', and the boy named 'Trumbule') went at that time of year in 1512 and 1513 to school in Edinburgh and paid to the schoolmaster there £5 10s, a sum that covered both board and 'scolage' (the fee for instruction) for six months.[96] At least one student received from the royal household not only his tuition but also fashionable clothing for his schooling, being given three ells of 'Franche claith of the new mylk and wattir' (a cloth blueish white in colour) to be for him a coat 'to syt in the scoile'.[97]

Some children were trained as musicians. In 1512 the king gave more than £26 to 'foure scolaris menstralez' to purchase instruments in Flanders and to help with their expenses and passage.[98] Child musicians were also paid for their performances, such as the four boys who played on shawms in 1505–6.[99] Other young performers included various maidens who danced for the king, as well as an 'Italien las that dansit' and received not only the very large sum of 30 French crowns (£21) but also blue damask to make a gown worth a further £6.[100]

Concessions were made to young minds as well as young bodies. Perhaps a child-like forgetfulness was at the root of a payment for a hat to Alexander Stewart in 1503, 'quhen he tynt [lost] his aun hat'.[101] Alexander offers a particularly interesting case for the special considerations due to youth. Aged only about eleven years when he became archbishop of St Andrews, Alexander was certainly young for the role, and his youth was repeatedly acknowledged and accommodated. When James wrote to the pope in 1505 about the grant of the archbishopric, he described his son as 'not yet grown up' ('vel impuberi'). Intending that St Andrews should be administered with care, and also that the pope not regret the promotion of Alexander, James requested that an experienced Dominican theologian be appointed to serve the archbishop. James also mentioned the young age of Alexander to the cardinal of St Mark, who had assisted with obtaining the position for him.[102] By 1508, Alexander himself was recognizing the possible weakness attending his youth, acknowledging in a letter to the cardinal that his

96 *TA*, iv, 240, 242, 246, 404.
97 *TA*, iv, 245.
98 *TA*, iv, 338.
99 *TA*, iii, 179, 180, 183, 189, 307, 379.
100 *TA*, ii, 395, 401, 463.
101 *TA*, ii, 303.
102 *Letters James Fourth*, 16–17, 19, 136–7; *Epistolae Regum Scotorum* (Edinburgh, 1722) 3, 5–6, 9.

age did not permit his full defence of the liberty of the Church.[103] James IV also considered Alexander's young age in his deliberations on which location would be most suitable for his son's studies. The secretary to the cardinal of St Mark thought that Alexander was doing quite well at Padua but that he would do better still at Rome, where the pronunciation of Latin and Greek was better and where there was more of life to be seen and more experiences to be gained. James responded that he was grateful for the help, but that Alexander was too young for the city at that time, though perhaps he could visit Rome later.[104] Thus did James and Alexander both demonstrate an awareness of the limitations to the authority of a young person, and a concern for the implications of such limitations for the leadership of the Church. Erasmus too conceded Alexander's youth in writing of how his student was unusually mature for his years. He characterized him as a young man (*iuuenis*) but lacking no quality of a full man (*consummati viri*), thereby contrasting youth with full adulthood. Furthermore, Erasmus said that even though Alexander was a very young man (*adolescentulus*) of scarcely more than eighteen years, he had followed so much in each kind of study as you would wonder at in any man (*in quouis viro*), again making a distinction between adolescence and adulthood.[105] Erasmus was aware of the limitations of youth, and from his perspective the fact that Alexander had surpassed the normal intellectual expectations for people of his age was a sign of uncommon maturity.

Work and training were important parts of daily life for many young people, but the most characteristically childlike activity at court was surely that of play. A few tantalizing hints at toys are provided in the treasurers' accounts, such as when, in February 1508, a 'hurle stule' was given to the prince. This device was covered in fabric and decorated with ribbons, and it was placed on painted rolls.[106] It may have been some kind of small cart or walker, a very age-appropriate item for a one-year-old infant. The pair of carving knives given to the prince in December 1507 seems less appropriate as a baby's toy, though perhaps it was meant to be saved for a later time: the cost of £3 does suggest high quality.[107] More frequent than toys in the records are indications of games and sport. In Stirling, a boy brought balls to the king for a game of 'cach', which might have been a game of hand-tennis.[108] Boys also helped the king with his sport of hawking, and they chased ducks in pools.[109] The childishness of children at play was especially sought in festivities associated with the feast day of St Nicholas, patron saint of children. Each year on or around this day (6 December), the king donated money to the boy bishops in various towns, and sometimes also to

103 *Letters James Fourth*, 132; James Gairdner (ed.), *Letters and Papers Relating to the Reigns of Richard III and Henry VII* (London, 1861), 273.
104 *Letters James Fourth*, 136–7.
105 Erasmus, *Adagia* II.v.i, ll. 137–8, 159–61; Erasmus, *Collected Works of Erasmus*, 241–3; Erasmus, *The Adages of Erasmus*, 188–90.
106 *TA*, iv, 33. For more on children's toys, see Chapter 4 in this collection.
107 *TA*, iv, 33.
108 *TA*, i, 277.
109 *TA*, i, 277, 288, 305, 366.

their servants disguised as devils.[110] Children were the best agents of misrule for activities carried out in celebration of their own saintly patron.

These children, of course, formed a varied group. Rich and poor, male and female, from near and far, the young people in and around the court of James IV were diverse according to most conventional markers of the time. However, in spite of the variety among them, they were nonetheless a group by virtue of the commonality of age. Their shared youth placed them within an age category that was recognized as distinct from adulthood, and this recognition of distinctness helped shape experiences and expectations at work, in training, or in play, and possibly even strengthened a young person's claim to care from his or her elders. The royal court that provided a 'gret cradil of stait' for an infant prince was also an environment where a poor child could take the hand of a king, and even be rewarded for the gesture.

110 *TA*, i, 183, 239, 307, 370; *TA*, ii, 128, 349, 350, 409–10; *TA*, iii, 175, 176, 356; *TA*, iv, 87, 88–9, 179, 180.

2

A Perl for Your Debts?: Young Women and Apprenticeships in Early Modern Edinburgh

Cathryn R. Spence

The importance of apprenticeships in the medieval and early modern world has long been acknowledged. The role played by these relationships in shaping the lives of early modern European boys and the men they would become has been well documented. In addition to teaching a trade, these apprenticeships provided young men with a master who would monitor their behaviour and keep them from trouble and harm. However, work on apprenticeships has predominantly focussed on boys and men, rather than girls and women. Given the prevalence of male apprenticeships in extant documents, this is perhaps understandable. The training in which women partook has also been discussed, but more with regard to its ambiguity than what it meant for a woman's life and future. Women in the early modern period, it is accepted, tended to work in whatever trade or occupation was practised by their husbands. Although they might engage in their own trade, or in any number of by-employments, while carrying out their roles as wives and mothers, they tended not to develop a strong occupational identity of their own. As a result, girls were not usually entered into formal apprenticeships by their parents, and instead learned a variety of skills that would stand them in good stead for their anticipated future role of wife and helpmeet to a husband.

There were exceptions to these rules. Caroline Barron argued that single women in London in the late fourteenth and early fifteenth centuries could become apprentices.[1] Historians have uncovered a number of apprenticeship contracts for girls in medieval London, and the apprenticeship arrangements of girls have also been discussed for England more broadly by others.[2] Elsewhere in

[1] Caroline M. Barron, 'The "Golden Age" of Women in Medieval London', *Reading Medieval Studies* 15 (1989), 39–41, 45–7.

[2] Barbara Hanawalt, *Wealth of Wives: Women, Law, and the Economy in Late Medieval London* (Oxford, 2007), 39; Caroline M. Barron, 'The Education and Training of Girls in Fifteenth-Century London', in D.E.S. Dunn (ed.), *Courts, Counties and the Capital in the Later Middle Ages* (Stroud, 1996), 139–53; Stephanie R. Hovland, 'Girls as Apprentices in Late Medieval London', in M. Davies and A. Prescott (eds), *London and the Kingdom: Essays in Honour of Caroline M. Barron* (Donington, 2008), 179–94; Cordelia Beattie, 'Single Women, Work, and Family: The Chancery Dispute of Jane Wynde and Margaret Clerk', in M. Goodrich (ed.), *Voices from the Bench: The Narratives of Lesser Folk in Medieval Trials* (Basingstoke, 2006), 187–9; Kim M. Phillips, *Medieval Maidens: Young Women and Gender in England, 1270–1540* (Manchester, 2003).

Europe, female apprenticeships seem to have become somewhat more common by the early modern period, as work on France and Germany illustrates.[3] In Bristol in the 1530s and 1540s, girls were often apprenticed to seamstresses. Two-thirds of female apprentices were apprenticed to seamstresses or housewives, who were themselves the wives of masters.[4] Ilana Krausman Ben-Amos, in her investigation of female apprentices in the trades and crafts of early modern Bristol, noted that in the seventeenth century almost all women who entered apprenticeships (which differed from service contracts in that apprentices paid a fee to assume those positions) took on positions in domestic service, or else positions that combined a craft and household service.[5] As a result of these positions, she argues,

> women who married after several years in domestic service could offer invaluable household skills such as sewing, knitting, brewing, cooking, washing, and rearing children; they could contribute small dowries they had saved; and they could also provide practical understanding in managing small trade, in supervising apprentices, offering advice, and managing shops when occasion required.[6]

Sometimes, such positions and the duties associated with them were spelled out in contracts or indentures.

For Scotland, there has been little discussion of apprenticeships, either male or female. The relationships of male apprentices and journeymen were discussed in a study of the master and servant relationship in an introduction to Scots law for historians in 1958.[7] Articles by other historians have also discussed Scottish apprenticeships and indentures, but only in the seventeenth and eighteenth centuries.[8] There has been even less consideration of apprenticeships for girls in Scotland. Elizabeth Sanderson, in her exploration of women and work in eighteenth-century Edinburgh, found evidence of fifty-nine apprenticeship contracts for girls in the eighteenth century, but noted that 'since there are no apprentice registers for girls in Scotland it is impossible to judge the scale of

[3] Merry E. Wiesner, 'Spinsters and Seamstresses: Women in Cloth and Clothing Production', in M.W. Ferguson, M. Quilligan and N.J. Vickers (eds), *Rewriting the Renaissance: The Discourses of Sexual Difference in Early Modern Europe* (Chicago, 1986), 191–4; Natalie Zemon Davis, 'Women in the Crafts in Sixteenth-Century Lyon', in Barbara Hanawalt (ed.), *Women and Work in Pre-Industrial Europe* (Bloomington, 1986), 170–1.

[4] Ilana Krausman Ben-Amos, 'Women Apprentices in the Trades and Crafts of Early Modern Bristol', *Continuity and Change* 6 (1991), 229–30.

[5] Ben-Amos, 'Women Apprentices', 233–4.

[6] Ilana Krausman Ben-Amos, *Adolescence and Youth in Early Modern England* (New Haven, 1994), 154.

[7] T.B. Smith, 'Master and Servant: Further Historical Outlines', *Juridical Review* 3 (1958), 215–29.

[8] T.M. Devine, 'The Merchant Class of the Larger Scottish Towns in the Later Seventeenth and Early Eighteenth Centuries', in G. Gordon and B. Dicks (eds), *Scottish Urban History* (Aberdeen, 1983), 92–111; Diane Baptie, 'Apprentices in the North-East of Scotland', *Scottish Archives* 9 (2003), 37–44. See also, for a British perspective on apprenticeship, W.W. Knox, 'British Apprenticeship, 1800–1914', unpublished Ph.D. thesis, University of Edinburgh (1980).

female apprenticeship'.[9] Female apprenticeship contracts like those found for England and Europe do not seem to exist for seventeenth-century Scotland, save for one example involving two sisters who were apprenticed to a perling worker in 1638. This apprenticeship contract involved the two daughters of John Eiston, a maltman burgess of Edinburgh, and Robert Wilson and Marion Campbell, a merchant and his wife. Dated 5 August 1638, the contract stipulated that the two daughters, Janet and Elspeth, were to remain with their mistress for three and four years respectively to learn the 'art and calling of perling'. They were not to absent themselves from service and, if they did, after the conclusion of their contract they were to serve two days for every one day of work missed.[10] The lack of existing apprenticeship contracts, aside from this one example, means it is necessary to use other sources when seeking out evidence of apprenticeships in early modern Scotland.

This essay uses the Edinburgh burgh court records to reveal evidence of debt servitude contracts that operated as a form of training and apprenticeship in early modern Edinburgh. Within these records sixteen debt cases have been found that refer to repayment of a debt not through money, but through labour. In particular, this labour involved young, usually fatherless, women, who promised to perform the labour of perling to repay a debt of money. 'Perling' is another term for lace-making, as perling was a lace made of thread or silk which was used to trim garments. For example, Agnes and Katherine Jameson, daughters of the late William Jameson, borrowed from Helen Manuel, wife of William Glendinning, a saddler, the sum of £20. Agnes and Katherine promised to repay the sum by having Katherine stay and create perling for Helen. If Katherine had to be absent from the house, Agnes would take her place, and this arrangement would endure until the entire debt had been repaid.[11] It is difficult to determine how commonplace these arrangements were. However, it is reasonable to assume that only a small percentage would have found their way into the burgh court records. Thus far, no examples have been found outside of Edinburgh, but this may well be attributable to the lesser number of debt cases formally recorded in other Scottish communities. A more detailed exploration of these perling and debt contracts will be provided below.

Other evidence for apprenticeships emerges, not surprisingly, from an examination of guild records, although women appear infrequently. Apprenticeships provided the workforce for guilds through a rigorous process of training in which the apprentice learned to master the complicated techniques required by the craft. The crafts were highly specialized, and it was important that practitioners were adequately trained, undergoing the transition from apprentice to

9 Elizabeth Sanderson, *Women and Work in Eighteenth-Century Edinburgh* (Houndsmill, 1996), 87. Most of these apprenticeships were for shopkeeping, millinery, mantua-making, or a combination of several pursuits.

10 Edinburgh City Archives [ECA], Moses Bundles, 25:1033. This two-day clause was also common in apprenticeship contracts for boys, see Baptie, 'Apprentices in the North-East of Scotland', 38.

11 NRS, B22/8/30, 25 April 1638.

journeyman to master, and thereby earning their place in the guild. Guilds were a driving economic force across the entirety of Europe by the mid-sixteenth century. In Scotland guilds were present by the time of the *Statuta Gilde* of Berwick, which dates from 1249 to 1295.[12] By the fifteenth century, many burghs had a merchant guild, and the establishment of craft guilds soon followed. Guilds were awarded monopolies within particular towns which allowed them to purchase raw materials and regulate trade. In this way, they minimized competition both between members of a community's guild and from external threats. They also protected their members from being underpaid for goods and services, and protected consumers from sub-standard products and fraudulent producers.[13] In Edinburgh, the skinners were the first to become an incorporated craft guild, in 1474, and by 1523 the town had fourteen craft guilds, some of which were conglomerate organizations.[14] The Edinburgh Incorporation of Hammermen, for example, represented trades that all dealt with an aspect of metalware production or hammered work, and included the blacksmiths, goldsmiths, lorimers, saddlers, cutlers, buckler makers and armourers, all listed in the original seal of cause in 1483.[15] Masters determined who was admitted to the guild and, as a result, who could practise the craft.[16] Through this patriarchal control, women were effectively excluded from most production intended for sale.

The guilds elected a deacon each year to act as the head of their craft and by 1551 had two seats on the Edinburgh town council. This rose to six seats in 1583, giving the crafts as many seats as the merchants in terms of ordinary councillors.[17] Yet, the growing political importance of the incorporated craft guilds was increasingly detrimental to the potential involvement of women in these guilds. While Maryanne Kowaleski and Judith Bennett noted that some guilds in England and Europe offered women (particularly the wives, daughters and servants of skilled tradesmen) the opportunity to be associated with the guild and its economic security,[18] they were, nevertheless, secondary members. In Edinburgh, women did not play significant roles in any of the incorporated crafts. Women were also barred from political processes and could not be elected to public office. As a result, they could not advance up the guild hierarchy, or hold offices of any importance.[19] Similarly, wives of guild masters in Scotland do not seem to have attained the rank of 'guild sister' like some wives did else-

12 Aaron Allen, *The Locksmith Craft in Early Modern Edinburgh* (Edinburgh, 2007), 2.

13 Allen, *The Locksmith Craft*, 5.

14 E.P. Dennison, 'Urban Society and Economy', in B. Harris and A. MacDonald (eds), *Scotland: The Making and Unmaking of the Nation, c. 1100–1707*, vol. 2 (Dundee, 2006), 148.

15 J.D. Marwick (ed.), *Extracts from the Records of the Burgh of Edinburgh*, vol. 1 (Edinburgh, 1869), 47.

16 Dennison, 'Urban Society and Economy', 148.

17 Michael Lynch, *Edinburgh and the Reformation* (Edinburgh, 1981), 16.

18 M. Kowaleski and J.M. Bennett, 'Crafts, Gilds, and Women in the Middle Ages: Fifty Years after Marion K. Dale', *Signs* 14 (1989), 475.

19 Mary Verschuur, *Politics or Religion?: The Reformation in Perth, 1540*–1570 (Edinburgh, 2006), 11.

where.[20] However, a widow could benefit from her husband having been a guild member, as widows and orphans in this position were sometimes eligible for pensions and charity provided by the guild.[21]

In Edinburgh, for example, the merchant widows enjoyed many of the same freemen privileges as had their husbands, and were allowed to engage in international trade, sell at the burgh market, and employ apprentices.[22] A widow of a guild master sometimes took over her husband's craft for a short period of time (suggesting she had worked alongside her husband before his death), as in the case of the widow of Thomas Short, deacon of the Incorporation of Hammermen. Short's widow ran his booth for a time after his death in 1544 during the 'Rough Wooing', when he was killed defending Edinburgh from an English raid on the Netherbow Port. His widow is listed on a role of masters of the hammerman craft in 1546, indicating that Short's servants continued to work for her after his death, but it is not known for how long this occurred.[23] Similarly, Robert McCauley, an armourer, was ordered in 1619 to pay to Agnes Annand, widow of Hew Gilmour, also an armourer, 20 merks. The debt is identified as a

> sum the said Robert by an ordinance of the deacon and brethren of the hammermen was ordered to pay to the said Agnes in contention of his service between Pasche [Easter] and Lambes [1 August] in 1617, at which time he should have served the said Agnes, together with £10 for the price of a sword bought by Robert from him.[24]

The debt implies that Agnes had continued her husband's armoury after his death, perhaps to the extent of overseeing apprentices. Robert was apparently not happy with this agreement, perhaps reflecting the attitudes of the time to women in these positions.

Generally, widows were only allowed to pursue or oversee the work produced in the booths of their deceased husbands until they remarried, a convention that mirrored practices elsewhere in Europe. Fourteenth-century European ordinances regarding guilds rarely mentioned widows, leading Merry Wiesner to speculate that a widow had unrestricted rights to run her husband's shop after his death (at least as long as she remained unmarried).[25] Ordinances from the

20 Kowaleski and Bennett, 'Crafts, Gilds, and Women', 478.

21 Allen, *The Locksmith Craft*, 6.

22 Martin Rorke, 'Women Overseas Traders in Sixteenth-Century Scotland', *JSHS* 25:2 (2005), 93.

23 John Smith, *The Hammermen of Edinburgh and their Altar in St. Giles Church* (Edinburgh, 1906), 130. Similarly, in an entry from 2 March 1678 in the *Minute Book of the Dunfermline Hammermen*, Robert Brown was booked as journeyman to Margaret Duke, the widow of John Stevenson, from Martinmas 1677 to Whitsunday 1678. John Stevenson died sometime in 1677. *Transcript of the Minute Book of the Dunfermline Hammermen* (Dunfermline Local History Library, DI/HAM). Thanks to Ms Sue Mowat for providing this reference.

24 ECA, Register of Diets, 1615–19, 6 February 1619. To make the text more accessible, spelling and notations in direct quotations have all been modernized.

25 Merry Wiesner, 'In Defence of Their Public Role', in M.B. Rose, *Women in the Middle Ages and the Renaissance: Literary and Historical Perspectives* (Syracuse, 1986), 7; Judith

late fourteenth century relating to the dyers' guild of York ordered that 'no woman of the said craft shall occupy the said craft after the death of her husband longer than a whole year unless her servant who shall occupy the craft is put by her to the franchise of the city'.[26] A selection of bequests made through wills in fifteenth-century York, however, indicates that widows took part in a host of crafts, including weaving, saddler work, mail work and bow work.[27] In some instances, widows of guild masters supervised workshops, hired apprentices and journeymen, and participated in guild celebrations; however, this was not the norm.[28]

In the mid-fifteenth century many European crafts began to impose limits on how long a widow could run her deceased husband's shop, stipulating that she could only do so for a few months or finish work that was already started, and could not take on apprentices, hire new journeymen, or buy raw materials.[29] In mid-fifteenth-century Shrewsbury, for example, it was decreed that 'no women shall occupy the craft of weaving after the death of her husband except for one quarter of the year, within which time it shall be lawful for her to work out her stuff that remains unworked'.[30] In circumvention of stipulations like this, Jeremy Goldberg has found early sixteenth-century evidence of widows who chose to marry their apprentices 'rather than be forced by guild and community pressures to give up control of the inherited workshop'.[31] Bennett, meanwhile, has found ordinances restricting the involvement of women in guilds in every century between 1300 and 1700, and so suggests that attempts to circumscribe women's work in organized guilds and crafts were ongoing, rather than attributable to one specific century.[32]

The role of women in early modern Edinburgh craft guilds seems to have been minimal and relegated to times of economic necessity, as in the case of Thomas Short's widow. In the 1540s, with the burgh and country under threat and the production of weapons essential, there was a distinct advantage to maintaining as many hammerman booths as possible, even those run by widows. At other times, the presence of women in the crafts was less necessary, and those women who do appear (such as Agnes Annand) are exceptions to a very stringent rule. However, one type of craftwork that does seem to have been dominated by women in Scotland during this period was perling. It seems clear that although women were not significant in the formal craft sector, they had an important role in the informal craft sector. A picture of women producing and selling this type of

Bennett, *History Matters: Patriarchy and the Challenge of Feminism* (Manchester, 2006), 100.

26 P.J.P. Goldberg, *Women in England: c. 1275–1525* (Manchester, 1995), 204.

27 Goldberg, *Women in England*, 199.

28 Kowaleski and Bennett, 'Crafts, Gilds, and Women', 478. For examples of widows who did continue to enrol apprentices see Mary Prior, 'Women in the Urban Economy: Oxford, 1500–1800', in M. Prior (ed.), *Women in English Society, 1500–1800* (London, 1985), 107–8.

29 Wiesner, 'In Defence', 7.

30 Goldberg, *Women in England*, 205.

31 Goldberg, *Women in England*, 20, 133.

32 Bennett, *History Matters*, 97.

craftwork emerges from individual debt cases. Christian Calquhoun, for example, sold two ells of perling to Mark Seyton for £4 in 1614.[33] John Scobie owed £4 to Katherine Sibbald, a wife, for perled overlays and hands.[34] While early debts for perling are few and far between (only five references to perling exist in the Edinburgh records between 1605, when it is first mentioned, and 1620), thirty-three debt cases mentioning perling appear in the Edinburgh burgh court records between 1621 and 1640. A further fifteen involved – as either the debtor or creditor – a woman identified as a 'perling weaver' or 'perling worker', even if the cases were not concerned with perling work and were instead debts for lent money, drink, food, merchandise or services. The first woman to be identified specifically as a perling worker was Jean Anderson in 1629. Jean owed Marion Boyd and James Christie, her husband, for beer and ale furnished to her by them.[35] The emergence in the early seventeenth century of the term 'perling worker' or 'perling weaver' to describe a woman engaged in perling, when such a descriptor or other evidence of this practice did not exist before, suggests that perling was gaining in popularity and visibility, perhaps because of a demand for locally produced lace. It is logical that Edinburgh, as Scotland's largest and pre-eminent town in this period, would have led that demand.

Many female perling workers seem to have been unmarried women, and were daughters, orphans or widows. In this, they were similar to lace-makers elsewhere.[36] Of all women who entered apprenticeships in Bristol between 1617 and 1628, nearly seventy per cent were fatherless, and virtually all were apprenticed into the clothing and textile trades (including lace-making).[37] Similarly, in Colyton before 1650, the death of a father was more likely to lead to a child being apprenticed than was a mother's death.[38] Furthermore, in Colyton between 1598 and 1740, 'the job descriptions of apprentices were not usually specific except in a gender sense, being "servant in husbandry" if they were boys and "housewifery" if they were girls'.[39] Pamela Sharpe speculates that it was likely apprenticeships for girls would include some training in spinning and lace-making.[40] Other women, typically young, used positions as servants in the lace-making industry as a way of repaying debts of money, a practice that also occurred elsewhere in early modern Europe.[41]

33 ECA, Register of Diets, 1612–15, 29 January 1614.

34 ECA, Register of Diets, 1615–19, 26 April 1617.

35 ECA, SL234/1/12.

36 Sheilagh C. Ogilvie, *A Bitter Living: Women, Markets, and Social Capital in Early Modern Germany* (Oxford, 2003), 200.

37 Ben-Amos, 'Women Apprentices', 233, 234, 236.

38 Pamela Sharpe, 'Poor Children as Apprentices in Colyton, 1598–1830', *Continuity and Change* 6:2 (1991), 262.

39 Sharpe, 'Poor Children as Apprentices', 256.

40 Sharpe notes that lace-making became a significant industry in Colyton, with an estimated twenty-one per cent of the population involved by the end of the seventeenth century. The sex ratio was heavily biased toward women, see Sharpe, 'Poor Children as Apprentices', 257–8.

41 Sara Mendelson and Patricia Crawford, *Women in Early Modern England, 1550–1720* (Oxford, 1998), 87–8; Ogilvie, *A Bitter Living*, 165.

There are a great deal of similarities between English apprenticeship contracts and the evidence found in Edinburgh. While these Scottish agreements were not identified specifically as apprenticeships, they did involve young women (many fatherless), lace-making, and strict terms of employment.[42] These terms included legally binding contracts, which stipulated that the training was to be supervised by an experienced practitioner, in an artisan or merchant household and workshop that was not that of the girl in question.[43] The only feature the Scottish agreements lacked when compared to similar English agreements was a fixed term of apprenticeship. As a result, they appear to have been de facto apprenticeships with one important difference: many such contracts were devised as a way of repaying a debt.

These agreements, which combine the repayment of lent money through service in the perling industry, begin to appear in the Register of Deeds for Edinburgh in 1630.[44] In all, sixteen contracts involving perling were entered, with contracts becoming more common in the mid-1630s and early 1640s. The latest contract dates from November 1642, after which no contracts appear through 1660, the last year examined. Recorded mainly in the 1630s, these perling contracts appeared in the same decade as another textile anomaly, that of the phenomenon of female spinners and weavers in Aberdeen, who attained what Gordon DesBrisay describes as 'a degree of economic security' by producing cheap woollen cloth that was sold to the Dutch for trade in their colonies.[45] Perhaps both the Edinburgh perling weavers and the Aberdeen spinners and weavers were able to recognize and capitalize on a previously untapped market, even if for a brief time. The Edinburgh contracts involved either entering a daughter into the training of perling, or using perling skills that had already been acquired, to pay a debt. The contracts typically followed a pattern whereby the debtor, usually identified as a daughter, but sometimes identified as the girl's parents or parent, borrowed a certain amount of money from another woman. The girl then worked for the creditor until the debt had been completely repaid. Of the sixteen contracts, eight involved a girl who was identified as the daughter of a deceased father, one involved a girl who clearly still had a living father, and

42 Ben-Amos notes that 'the proportions of women whose fathers were described as "deceased" rose dramatically from less than a fifth in the 1530s to nearly two-thirds in the 1600s': 'Women Apprentices', 233.

43 Hovland, 'Girls as Apprentices', 180; Phillips, *Medieval Maidens*, 76, 82–3, 134.

44 The reasons why debts involving perling and perling workers appeared as early as 1605 in the burgh court records, while perling agreements do not appear in the Register of Deeds until the 1630s, are unclear, but may have something to do with the nature of the courts. The burgh courts dealt with smaller, day-to-day debts, while the Register of Deeds was often concerned with larger obligations, contracts and other, more formal agreements. Perhaps early cases involving perling workers were less formal in the early seventeenth century and, as these arrangements formalized, it was seen as necessary to identify them in a more formal court.

45 Gordon DesBrisay, 'Aberdeen and the Dutch Atlantic: Women and Woollens in the Seventeenth-Century', in Doug Catterall and Jodi Campbell (eds), *Women in Port: Gendering Communities, Economies, and Social Networks in Atlantic Port Cities, 1500–1800* (Leiden, 2012), 69.

in seven cases it was unclear whether the girl was fatherless or not (i.e., her father was not mentioned in the debt, but neither was it explicitly stated that he was deceased).

While the creditors were sometimes married couples, the explanation for the debt, and the related perling agreement, always made clear that it was the wife who was responsible for teaching the debtor 'the art and craft' of perling. In early modern Scotland, wives were commonly named alongside their husbands in debt contracts if they had participated in the debt in question.[46] The debtor then promised to remain with the creditor and 'work in the vocation and weaving of perling until the debt is completely paid'.[47] Often provisions were made in anticipation of any days of missed work (on average, as noted above, every day of missed work resulted in two days of make-up work) and in anticipation of defaulting on the debt. Typically, if the woman absented herself from service or died before the debt was completely paid, the entire debt became due and had to be paid either by the woman's cautioner (the person who stood with the debtor and promised to ensure that the debt was paid) or her heirs. In this, these contracts were similar to the lone female apprenticeship contract found for Edinburgh in 1638, and to contracts for indentured servants bound for the Americas from England and Europe in the sixteenth century.[48] Unlike other apprenticeship contracts, there was no mention of an apprentice fee. Perhaps this was included in the original debt, or waived because the girl was already in debt to the person with whom she was to work.

Consider the case of Jean Anderson, a daughter of Thomas Anderson, who borrowed from Gilbert Oustian, a tailor, and Susanna Watson, his wife, a total sum of £12. To repay the debt, Jean promised to 'serve Susanna and Gilbert in perling weaving to the feast of Witsunday next'.[49] Jean was to work weekly for Susanna for 20s per week until she had completely repaid the first £6. Then, she was to work for 10s weekly until Susanna been had paid the other £6. Further, Jean promised that if she failed to repay the debt or

[46] It is noteworthy that women in late sixteenth- and early seventeenth-century Edinburgh were conspicuously active as creditors in debt contracts, whether those contracts involved the sale of goods or services, or moneylending. See Gordon DesBrisay and Karen Sander Thomson, 'Crediting Wives: Married Women and Debt Litigation in the Seventeenth Century', in Elizabeth Ewan and Janay Nugent (eds), *Finding the Family in Medieval and Early Modern Scotland* (Aldershot, 2008), 85–98; Cathryn R. Spence, '"To Content and Pay": Women's Economic Roles in Edinburgh, Haddington, and Linlithgow, 1560–1640', unpublished Ph.D. thesis, University of Edinburgh (2010).

[47] Examples of this type of debt and credit agreement can be found in the following cases: NRS, B22/8/26, fols 225r–v; B22/8/28, fols 253v–254r; B22/8/29, fols 332v–333r; B22/8/30, fols 101r; B22/8/31, fol. 35r; B22/8/31, fol. 185v.

[48] ECA, Moses Bundles, 25:1033; D. Eltis, 'Free and Coerced Transatlantic Migrations: Some Comparisons', *American Historical Review* 88:2 (1983), 251–80; David W. Galenson, *White Servitude in Colonial America* (Cambridge, 1981), 40–4; Abbot Emerson Smith, *Colonists in Bondage* (Chapel Hill, 1947), 16–20.

[49] NRS, B22/8/26, fol. 225r–v.

> absent myself from my said service between now and the said term, or otherwise not work with my said tack work, in that case I and my cautioner bounds and obliges us conjunctly and severally to content and pay to the said Gilbert and Susanna the sum of £6 more … and also serving as long after the said term as it shall happen to be absent and also making up of my work so much as shall be wanting.[50]

Jean's cautioner was Christian Young, a widow, indicating that Jean was fatherless (as fathers usually acted as cautioners for their daughters in these cases). Cautioners were common in debt proceedings, and the sex or age of the debtor seems to have had little bearing on whether or not a cautioner was utilized. In this case it is obvious that a debt of money was being repaid by a period of work, specifically the work of perling, or lace-making. An examination of all of the debt records entered into the Edinburgh court records between 1560 and 1640 reveals no other type of work used to repay a debt for money. This suggests that either these girls were especially vulnerable and had no other way to pay their debts, or that this type of work was especially desired and either the girls or the people who employed them were keen to capitalize on it. The strictures surrounding these arrangements, and specifically the stipulations that the debtor was to remain with the creditor for a specific time and create a specific product, indicate apprenticeship-like arrangements. Further, as will be shown, some women engaged multiple girls in debt-repayment perling contracts, one even going so far as to stipulate that these girls would work in her 'booth of perling craft'.[51]

Some perling agreements were quite detailed. Both the language used and the terms of service and accommodation mimic those found in apprenticeship agreements for girls in medieval and early modern England.[52] Margaret Houston, daughter of the deceased John Houston, entered into such a detailed agreement with Marion Boyd and her husband, merchant James Christie, on 18 March 1640.[53] Margaret owed £44 to them and promised to repay the amount under the following conditions:

> induring my health of my body so long as any part or portion of the principle sum shall happen to remain unpaid and wrought for in their service and art and craft of working and weaving in their booth of perling craft and calling as long as I am able in my health And farther I faithfully bind and oblige … that I shall diligently work to them in their booth in weaving of perling yearly, termly, quarterly, monthly, weekly and daily every day so long as I am owing them any part of the said sum, and will not remove nor transport myself from their service and lying in bed and remaining at night in their dwelling house so long as I am in their debt, but shall

50 NRS, B22/8/26, fol. 225r–v.

51 NRS, B22/8/31, fol. 129r–v.

52 For an English comparison see the indenture of apprenticeship of Katherine Nougle, 1392 in Hovland, 'Girls as Apprentices', 193–4.

53 Marion Boyd and James Christie are listed as marrying on 25 June 1607, see H. Paton (ed.), *The Register of Marriages for the Parish of Edinburgh, 1595–1700* (Edinburgh, 1908), 199.

> continue and remain with them until they be completely paid of all compts that they can lay to my charge.[54]

This case implies that Marion and her husband were using a debt owed by a young, fatherless daughter as a way to acquire labour. Certainly, perling stands alone as the only trade or craft used by creditors-cum-employers as a way for their debtors to repay their debts. Other debt repayment agreements tended to use provisions for the payment of interest on a debt, known as 'annual rent', in order to help ensure that the debt would be repaid.

What is not clear is how perling work was viewed by the debtors. Parents may have seen it as a viable and productive line of work for their daughters. On the other hand, it is possible that perling work was neither desirable nor well paid, which would explain why positions were readily available. Regardless, it is likely that young women who entered into these debt arrangements had little choice. A young woman was expected to help support her family, and her training revolved around the expectation that she would one day serve as a helpmeet for her own husband and household. Parents likely saw it as their daughters' duty to accept being entered into perling contracts to pay off debts, underlining that young, unmarried women were still under the control of their parents and, as a result, owed them certain responsibilities. While the idea that perling workers could absent themselves from their service does acknowledge some agency on the young women's part, the financial penalty involved significantly limited that agency.

Returning to Marion Boyd, she and her spouse acted as creditors in at least six cases involving perling workers. It is likely that it was Marion who taught these girls to perl, as her husband was a merchant and Marion was often named before her husband, indicating that she was the half of the couple to whom the debt was primarily owed.[55] These agreements correlate with similar agreements in England. Ben-Amos notes that most women apprenticed in Bristol from 1600 were trained in sewing, knitting, button-making and lace-making, and that 'the girls who were apprenticed in these occupations were taught by women, and in households in which the master, and perhaps other apprentices or journeymen, were often engaged in a separate craft or employment'.[56] The majority of young women to whom Marion and James lent money stayed within the couple's house and booth while engaging in perling to work off the debt (although presumably not all the women they lent money to were there at the same time). This may indicate that the word 'booth' in this case should perhaps be understood as 'workshop', and that Marion and James may, as a result, have been running a workshop specifically for the purpose of producing perling. This sounds similar

[54] NRS, B22/8/31, fol. 129r–v.

[55] For a discussion of women's roles in debt litigation in early modern Edinburgh, see Cathryn Spence, '"For his interest?": Women, Debt and Coverture in Early Modern Scotland', in Cordelia Beattie and Matthew F. Stevens (eds), *Married Women and the Law in Premodern Northwest Europe, 1200–1800* (Woodbridge, 2013), 173–90.

[56] Ben-Amos, 'Women Apprentices', 237.

to the schools and small workshops where girls were taught to sew, spin, and make lace in sixteenth-century Lyon, and which mimicked the apprenticeships offered to boys through other craft workshops.[57] Moreover, this workshop may have been able to accommodate a number of people, which was unusual at this time as the size of workshops in Edinburgh was theoretically restricted.[58] The employment of so many young women may indicate that Marion and James were running a type of early manufactory (with only the debt element of the labour relationship being different), likely with the goal of keeping production costs to a minimum by containing their workers in one place.

Sewing schools existed in Edinburgh by the early seventeenth century; a statute against them entered into the *Book of the Universal Kirk* on 15 August 1616 stipulated that because 'certain women takes upon them[selves] to bring up the youth in reading, sewing, and other exercises in schools it is not lawful for any person or persons to hold schools for the teaching of youth unless they have the permission of the bishop of the diocese'.[59] Yet lace-making does not appear to have developed into a significant market, as it did in England.[60] Instead, it remained the purview of young, fatherless women. By 1705, Hamilton in South Lanarkshire in the west-central Lowlands of Scotland, had a lace manufactory to provide work and care for twelve poor girls.[61] Perhaps the workshop run by Marion and James was an early version of this.

Another notable point stemming from the case between Marion and Margaret was the stipulation that Margaret was to stay either in the booth or house during her term of service. As their debtor, this allowed Marion and James to keep Margaret under their control until the debt she owed had been completely paid. Keeping Margaret there may also have been a way for James and Marion to control Margaret's sexuality while she was in their service. Perhaps her status as a fatherless daughter, which implies that she was a young woman, was cause for concern. Kim Phillips has noted that the medieval contracts of female apprentices elsewhere often ordered the girls to refrain from fornication both within and without the houses of their masters.[62] The requirement that a perling worker promise to stay within the confines of the house of her master or mistress was a way of controlling her behaviour in general, and her sexual behaviour in particular.

[57] Zemon Davis, 'Women in the Crafts', 170–1.

[58] 'Leges Burgorum', in Cosmo Innes (ed.), *Ancient Laws and Customs of the Burghs of Scotland* (Edinburgh, 1868), custom lxi, 29–30; Peter G.B. McNeill (ed.), *The Practicks of Sir James Balfour of Pittendreich*, 2 vols (Brussels, 1962), i, 69–70.

[59] Thomas Thomson (ed.), *The Booke of the Universall Kirk of Scotland*, 3 vols (Edinburgh, 1839–45), iii, 1120.

[60] Sanderson, *Women and Work*, 87.

[61] Dennison, 'Urban Society and Economy', 150.

[62] Phillips, *Medieval Maidens*, 83. Male apprentices were also usually required to refrain from fornication and marriage, as well as disreputable pursuits such as gambling, drinking and boisterous behaviour: see Ben-Amos, *Adolescence and Youth*, 85; Baptie, 'Apprentices in the North-East of Scotland', 38.

The perling contract between Elspeth Dalgleish, daughter to Robert Dalgleish, a bellman, and Isabel Cunningham, a widow, even took clothing as surety. Taking surety in a lending contract was exceedingly rare; debt cases tended to include a provision for the payment of interest if the debt was not repaid within the time agreed. Robert and Elspeth – with Elspeth's father named in the debt in the same way that a husband often was, in that he was named with her but she was the primary actor – had borrowed £24 from Isabel. In payment, Elspeth was to work in perling with Isabel until the sum was completely paid. Additionally, Isabel was to have control of a black satin gown with a red stemming wyliecoat (underskirt) owned by Elspeth. Elspeth was allowed to borrow the gown and underskirt from Isabel every Sunday (likely to wear to church), and the outfit would be returned to Elspeth once the debt had been paid in full. In the meantime, however, Elspeth was to deliver the gown and underskirt back to Isabel every Monday. Should she fail to return it as specified, Elspeth would owe another two days of perling work to Isabel. Moreover, every week that Elspeth absented herself from working for Isabel, the clothing would not be lent to her on the Sunday.[63] This degree of care and attention is much more indicative of an apprentice relationship than a relationship between a creditor and a debtor, or even an employer and employee.

Periodically, a perling worker was unable to complete her term of service or pay off her debt due to sickness or death. The debts of those who died sometimes fell to their surviving parents. This could indicate either that the parents had originally contracted the debt, or simply that they were responsible for the debt as their child's heirs. Janet Crawford and John Black, her spouse, were ordered by the court in 1636 to pay £3 6s 8d to Marion Vernor and her husband James Lyon, in complete payment of a greater sum delivered by Marion and James to Janet in the name of Janet's daughter, Annas Mitchell.[64] Annas was supposed to have engaged in the making, and then selling, of perling in Marion and James's service, but had died at the previous Easter. However, Annas had left 'much unwrought' perling work behind at the time of her death, and her mother was expected to cover the cost of the making and selling of that perling, which was perhaps left over from the debt she herself had incurred from Marion and James.[65] That Annas was also expected to sell the perling could, again, suggest more than a simple creditor–debtor relationship. This is not simply a quantity of work being done, but involvement in multiple aspects of a craft. The young woman was being trained not only in the art of perling, but also in the selling of that work, indicating a transfer of multiple skills. This could allow the debtor/apprentice to continue that work independently at a later date.

63 NRS, B22/8/31, fol. 185v.

64 Annas's surname, Mitchell, which does not match the surname of her mother or her mother's husband, indicates that John Black was not Annas's father. It is possible that Janet, Annas's mother, entered into a debt with Marion and James after the death of Annas's father, when Janet was a widow and before her marriage to John Black, which would correlate with the trend for perling workers to be fatherless daughters.

65 ECA, SL234/1/16.

Perling workers sometimes employed other perling workers. Katherine Scott appeared before the Edinburgh burgh court on 31 May 1631, owing a couple for lint. Two months later she appeared again, this time owing to Margaret Thomson, a daughter, £11 for Margaret's 'service in working of perling' from Martinmas 1630 to Whitsunday 1631.[66] Some established perling workers hired other, younger, women to work for them, indicating that the craft was pursued by older women and that part of their work was to teach younger women. In some cases, those young women who promised to perform perling weaving in order to pay off a debt continued to perl after their term of service had ended, sometimes teaching others the skill. On 26 October 1640, it was established that Mausie Dobie (daughter to the deceased John Dobie, a merchant burgess) owed £14 to Isabel Cunningham, a widow. In order to repay the sum, Mausie was to 'stay, serve and work perling to the said Isabel, conform to the order of the dealing, and until the sum be completely satisfied by work she shall serve two days for one absence'.[67] On 8 January 1642, Katherine Cruickshank, the orphaned daughter of the deceased Robert Cruickshank, was found to owe £40 to the same Mausie Dobie, who was still engaged in perling work. As in other perling cases, Katherine promised to remain with Mausie and conduct perling work until the £40 debt had been fully repaid.[68] On 3 November 1642, Katherine again appeared in the records. This time, she was found to have received 'in friendly borrowing' from her good friend Katherine McMullen and James Bynnie, McMullen's husband, the sum of £100. Katherine promised to deliver weekly to Katherine McMullen 20s worth of 'good and sufficient perling well wrought', until the £100 had been completely repaid.[69] Katherine therefore seems to have used her perling skills, once acquired, as a way of not only earning a living, but also as a form of in-kind trade to be used to repay other, later debts she incurred.

Edinburgh, then, seems to have been home to a growing opportunity for young women to learn the skilled craft of perling weaving over the course of the 1630s. While many of these girls were fatherless and did not have the means to repay debts apart from through lacework created by their own hands, they were nevertheless effectively apprenticed in organized workshops to a skilled trade that could offer them decent remuneration. Lace-making in Edinburgh in the seventeenth century seems to have had many of the attributes Kowaleski and Bennett associate with high-status work: valued skills, organized workshops, and apprentices.[70] What these Edinburgh perling workers might have lacked (and also shared in common with the French lace-workers discussed by Natalie Zemon Davis) was a 'precise work identity'.[71] Boys and men followed a ritual, and achieved at the end of their apprenticeships membership in a brotherhood

66 ECA, SL234/1/14.

67 NRS, B22/8/31, fols 186r–v. It seems very likely that the Isabel Cunningham mentioned in this case was the same Isabel Cunningham active in the case involving Elspeth Dalgleish.

68 NRS, B22/8/32.

69 NRS, B22/8/32.

70 Kowaleski and Bennett, 'Crafts, Gilds, and Women', 480.

71 Zemon Davis, 'Women in the Crafts', 171.

they would likely remain a part of for the rest of their working lives. Girls did not. In this, their experience was analogous to that of women engaged in similar types of work; perhaps the most comparable were the London silkwomen in the fifteenth century, who also left little evidence of a cohesive craft consciousness, such as ordinances or standards to which they needed to adhere.[72] However, a lack of documented ritual or formal recognition should not minimize the importance of this type of craft. As with any skilled endeavour practised by a subset of the population, a degree of self-recognition certainly existed. The hierarchical passing of knowledge would have further added to this awareness. That neither these young perling workers nor the women that trained them organized themselves into more workshops, or even a guild, speaks to the constraints faced by women who participated – or tried to participate – in organized craft production in early modern Scotland. The argument that women who engaged in a particular craft or trade did not form themselves into guilds because they lacked a strong occupational identity does not apply to these women, who identified themselves as perling weavers, created designated booths in which they performed perling work, and trained young women in the 'perling craft'. Similarly, the agreements made between the perling weavers and the young women who owed them money certainly give the impression of being apprenticeship contracts in all but name. While the initial relationship between the perling worker and the girl or young woman was built around a debt of money, rather than an intention to be trained in a craft, the commitment of the perling weaver and girl to live under the same roof and work in the same workshop, as well as the commitment of the perling weaver to provide clothing, all indicate a relationship like that of a master and an apprentice. It seems clear that these young women, trained in the 'art of perling', were providing themselves with not only a means of repaying their debts, but also with a way of earning money and perhaps a living through craftwork. That this work was potentially piecemeal and potentially low status does little to detract from the importance it played in the lives of these young women, or the glimpse it can give into a women-centred craft that was clearly important in early modern Scotland.

72 Marion K. Dale, 'London Silkwomen of the Fifteenth Century', *Economic History Review*, 1st ser. 4 (1933), 335.

3

'Your louing childe and foster': The Fostering of Archie Campbell of Argyll, 1633–39

Janay Nugent

Fosterage was a Celtic practice where children were sent from their natal family to be raised in another household. This differed from other early modern European alloparenting practices (such as wet-nursing, service, and apprenticeship arrangements) as 'fosterage was a socio-political arrangement often used by chiefs to ensure continuation of close relations with the head of a cadet branch, a neighbouring clan or one of his own *fine*'.[1] The resulting fictive kinship was intended to develop bonds of loyalty and friendship between families that benefited all of their members. One such bond began in March 1633, when arrangements for the fosterage of the four-year-old Archibald Campbell were negotiated.[2] Archibald was the son of Archibald Campbell, lord of Lorne, who later became 8th earl of Argyll and 1st marquis of Argyll.[3] The foster-father was a member of Lorne's *fine* (the principal men of the clan), a relation by the name of Colin Campbell, laird of Glenorchy. The Glenorchy Campbells were descended from the house of Argyll and therefore were part of Clan Campbell, yet they formed a distinct lineage, which Colin Campbell was careful to assert in his commissioning of George Jameson's unique portrait, 'The Campbell of Glenorchy Family Tree'.[4]

Ideologically, fosterage was about creating bonds of fictive kinship between families in clan society. These bonds had far-reaching political, economic, military and social implications for that society.[5] Very little research exists on Scottish

1 Alison Cathcart, '"Inressyng of kyndnes, and renewing off their blud": The Family, Kinship and Clan Policy in Sixteenth-Century Gaeldom', in Elizabeth Ewan and Janay Nugent (eds), *Finding the Family in Medieval and Early Modern Scotland* (Aldershot, 2008), 129.

2 Alexander O. Curle suggested that most fosterage arrangements were made for children at seven or eight years of age. See 'Notice of Four Contracts or Bonds of Fosterage: With Notes on the Former Prevalence of the Custom of Fosterage in the Scottish Highlands', *PSAS* 30 (1896), 16.

3 The lord of Lorne became the 8th earl of Argyll in 1638 towards the end of this fosterage contact. To distinguish between father and son, he is referred to as Lorne, or the lord of Lorne, while the young foster is referred to as Archibald or by his nickname Archie.

4 *CL*, 9; NGS, PG2167, oil on canvas painting by George Jamesone, 'The Campbell of Glenorchy Family Tree', 1635.

5 Peter Parkes, 'Celtic Fosterage: Adoptive Kinship and Clientage in Northwest Europe', *Comparative Studies in Society and History* 48:2 (2006), 375–9; Allan Macinnes, *Clanship, Commerce and the House of Stuart, 1603–1788* (East Linton, 1996), 11–14.

fosterage; the role that women and children played in the fosterage contract has been particularly neglected. Yet most of the actual experience of fosterage occurred far from the meetings of powerful clansmen, existing instead within the realm of women and the household. As women were almost solely responsible for the care and education of young children, especially those under seven years of age,[6] the success of the fosterage relationship depended to a significant degree on the actions of women. As Jane Dawson argued in her work on Clan Campbell, 'the political importance of a wife to her husband has been underestimated'.[7] Equally, it was real children who were removed from their homes; they were the glue that was to bond the two families together, thus their willingness and ability to connect with their foster family was significant to how successfully the families bonded. The political importance of Highland children has been undervalued within the historical literature.[8] This essay uses the fosterage correspondence in the Campbell of Glenorchy papers to demonstrate that Lady Margaret Douglas and her son young Archibald Campbell were not just pawns in the politics of clan business, but that they themselves helped ensure the socio-political success of a fosterage contract through cultivating and maintaining the bonds of fictive kinship between the two families.[9]

The Context of Lorne and Glenorchy

Archibald Campbell, 8th earl and 1st marquis of Argyll, is well known in Scottish history. Born in 1607, he became one of the most powerful men of his time. Chief of the Clan Campbell, he was also a significant political figure at the Scottish court. Before succeeding to his earldom at the age of thirty-one, Archibald Campbell, lord of Lorne, had already accrued much political power as a Privy Councillor and an Extraordinary Lord of Session. He became a key figure in the Covenanting movement, the War of the Three Kingdoms, and a celebrated foe to James Graham, marquis of Montrose. Argyll was important in the political government of Scotland during the civil wars; his power was best exemplified in the honour bestowed upon him of placing the crown upon Charles II's head at his 1651 coronation at Scone. He advanced to become the 1st marquis of Argyll, a title denied his heirs when his high-stakes political

6 Janay Nugent, '"The Mistresse of the family hath a special hand": Family, Women, Mothers, and the Establishment of a "godly community of Scots"', in Daniel MacLeod and Stuart Macdonald (eds), *Scottish Religion at Home and in the Diaspora* (Guelph, 2014), 56. After the age of seven, fathers were expected to take over the education of their sons.

7 *CL*, 22.

8 See also Cathcart, 'Inressyng of kyndnes'.

9 Cf. Anne Frater, arguing that Highland women had no political sway, 'Women of the Gàidhealtachd and their Songs to 1750', in Elizabeth Ewan and Maureen Meikle (eds), *Women in Scotland c. 1100–c. 1750* (East Linton, 1999), 69.

wrangling caught up with him in 1661 after the Restoration, and he was beheaded for treason.[10]

Not surprisingly, historians have paid a great deal of attention to the 1st marquis of Argyll and his high profile in political intrigue. The fostering of his son to the Campbells of Glenorchy is well known to researchers, as dozens of letters dealing with the fosterage are extant within the Breadalbane family papers held in the National Records of Scotland.[11] Argyll's biographer, John Willcock, argued that this 'little bundle of letters and accounts' can tell us much about life at Glenorchy and Inveraray.[12] The *Black Book of Taymouth* reproduced a handful of these letters in their entirety.[13] The socio-political bond of fosterage is a common side note, fitting well within the political narrative of Argyll and demonstrating his powerful position as chief of Clan Campbell, but not receiving much analysis in its own right.

The fostering of young Archibald Campbell also fits within the context of clan politics. As important politicians at court, leaders of the Reformation, and head of the powerful Clan Campbell that spanned both Scots- and Gaelic-speaking lands, the earls of Argyll relied upon their friends to support and maintain this massive network. Clan Campbell was on the rise in the seventeenth century, with one major ingredient being 'the solid and unchallenged power base established in the Campbell heartland of Argyll and the western Highlands'.[14] As 'fosterage was a useful way of maintaining good relations with political allies, neighbouring families, [and] cadet branches',[15] the fostering of young Archibald was important to reinforcing existing ties of friendship between the current and future earls of Argyll and their powerful kinsmen, the lairds of Glenorchy. Lorne looked to Glenorchy to help him maintain his standing within the clan and the wider political community in Britain. When Charles I visited Scotland in 1633, Lorne requested Glenorchy's support in fulfilling obligations of hospitality. In three separate letters he asked Glenorchy to send food that was in season, to send venison, and even asked to borrow Glenorchy's silver plates.[16] These were requests that Lorne could only have made to close friends. Scholars of early modern England have established the highly symbolic value of venison as a gift given amongst the elite to their closest friends, thus reinforcing their ties and

[10] For more on the biography and political career of Archibald Campbell, see Allan Macinnes, *The British Confederate: Archibald Campbell, Marquess of Argyll, 1607–1661* (Edinburgh, 2011).

[11] NRS, GD112/39/47–71.

[12] John Willcock, *Great Marquess: Life and Time of Archibald, 8th earl, and 1st (and only) Marquess of Argyll (1607–1661)* (Edinburgh, 1903), 26.

[13] C. Innes (ed.), *The Black Book of Taymouth: With Other Papers from the Breadalbane Charter Room* (Edinburgh, 1855), pp. xviii–xxii.

[14] Jane Dawson, 'Campbell Family', in Michael Lynch (ed.), *The Oxford Companion to Scottish History* (Oxford, 2001), 65.

[15] Alison Cathcart, *Kinship and Clientage: Highland Clanship 1451–1609* (Leiden, 2006), 81.

[16] NRS, GD112/39/48/21; NRS, GD112/39/49/8–9.

obligations to one another.[17] The loan of silver also symbolized a relationship of great trust. When Margaret returned the plates, she sent a letter outlining how carefully they had cared for the silver and tended to its safety.[18] It addition to obligations of hospitality, in 1634 Glenorchy lent Lorne 8,000 merks.[19] Later, in 1638, the laird held musterings and weaponschaws, forwarding lists of arms and men to Lorne in Inveraray who was deciding how he would respond to issues surrounding the National Covenant.[20] The retention of independent military capabilities through the seventeenth century set the groundwork for Campbell power on the national stage; much of this was due to their ability to raise a large and powerful army from their own supporters, such as Glenorchy.[21]

In return for his support, Glenorchy was drawn closely into Lorne's circle of friends, becoming a valued adviser to the future earl.[22] The Glenorchy family had risen in status during the tenure of the previous seven lairds, in large part due to the successes of Clan Campbell. Jane Dawson argued that they 'owed much to the strength of their wider kindred'.[23] In some fostering situations 'the whole family of the fosterer was under the protection of the chieftain and held in the highest esteem',[24] and Glenorchy certainly seemed to be treated in this way by Lorne. The benefits were economic, social and political, placing Glenorchy within a strategic position in the clan. In return for the loan in 1634, Lorne ordered his men not to meddle with Glenorchy or any of his tenants, and also granted him land. In reference to this land grant, Lorne wrote to Glenorchy that 'I wold not haue done for verie mutche if it var not to testifie the love that I beare unto yow'.[25]

Fosterage Contracts

Fosterage arrangements were typically made for a number of years, and included a significant financial commitment by the foster family. This included an

17 Emma Griffin, *Blood Sport: Hunting in Britain since 1066* (New Haven, 2007), 44–5; Felicity Heal, 'Food Gifts, the Household and the Politics of Exchange in Early Modern England', *Past and Present* 199:1 (May 2008), 55–62.

18 NRS, GS112/39/49/15.

19 *Black Book of Taymouth*, 77.

20 Cosmo Innes, *Sketches of Early Scotch History and Social Progress* (Edinburgh, 1861), 383 n. 2. By this point Lorne was de facto head of the Clan Campbell as his father, a Catholic convert, was living on the Continent. The National Covenant was a declaration which stated that King Charles I had broken his covenant to God and the Scottish people by trying to impose the Church of England Book of Common Prayer on the Presbyterian nation. The Covenant was signed by many Scots as copies of the document circulated around Scotland.

21 Dawson, 'Campbell Family', 66.

22 NRS, GD112/39/48/11; NRS, GD112/39/49/23; NRS, GD112/39/51/19; NRS, GD112/39/52/11. For additional examples of the types of political advantages that could emerge from fosterage arrangements, see Cathcart, *Kinship and Clientage*, 80–5.

23 Jane Dawson, 'Campbell Family of Glenorchy', *ODNB*.

24 Martin Rackwitz, *Travels to Terra Incognita: The Scottish Highlands and Hebrides in Early Modern Travellers' Accounts c. 1600 to 1800* (Münster, 2007), 243.

25 NRS, GD112/39/49/14.

obligation to support and educate the child, an exchange of property (particularly cattle), and the right for the foster to claim a bairn's part on the death of the foster-father.[26] Despite the significant financial obligation for the foster family, which was almost always of a lower social status than their foster,[27] clan gentry did not regard being a fosterer as a burden and indeed considered it an entitlement for the *fine*.[28] 'Its major function [was] to reinforce ties between kin, and the paradigm for fostering involves relatives pressing claims on the children of close kin.'[29] *Fine* members vied to become foster-fathers, as this position afforded them an opportunity to forge close personal bonds with the most powerful men in the clan.[30] The connections also passed to the next generation, with the bonds between foster and foster-brother(s) continuing to be close, yet Glenorchy did not have any children so this bond was not developed. As noted in the correspondence between Lorne and the laird, many of Lorne's friends had offered generous terms to foster the young Archibald.[31] Being chosen as the foster-parent was a great privilege, as Glenorchy acknowledged in 1633:

> that syndrie of your Lds friends wer most desyrous to have your Lds eldest sone fostering yet for divers respects your Ld wes better pleasit to have him brought vp with me. Quhich I acknowledge is a great testamonie both of your Lds taist [inclination/liking] and love and thes in god evir so to approve myself to be most willing & desyrous to deserve both.[32]

It is at this point that most historians end their discussion of fosterage, without considering how these fosterage arrangements actually built the intended bonds of friendship and loyalty. The letters of the lord of Lorne and his wife Margaret Douglas, drafts of letters to Lorne from the laird of Glenorchy, letters from Glenorchy's agent (another Archibald Campbell),[33] and eventually letters signed by the foster himself, offer insight into how these relationships were constructed and tested.

The setting up of the fosterage arrangement was usually negotiated by men as part of a political process.[34] Letters exchanged between Lorne and Glenorchy

26 Parkes, 'Celtic Fosterage', 363, 369, 375; Curle, 'Notice of Four Contracts', 13–22 (see NRS, GD111/4/11 for originals of these and other fostering contracts); Macinnes, *Clanship, Commerce and the House of Stuart*, 14; *The Black Book of Taymouth*, passim. For a ledger of expenses connected to the fosterage of Archibald Campbell, see NRS, GD112/1/496. For additional discussion of fosterage contracts, see Chapter 5 in this collection (n. 3 explains a bairn's part).

27 Curle, 'Notice of Four Contracts', 14.

28 Macinnes, *Clanship, Commerce and the House of Stuart*, 14.

29 Llinos Beverley Smith, 'Fosterage, Adoption and God-Parenthood: Ritual and Fictive Kinship in Medieval Wales', *Welsh History Review* 16:1 (1992), 6–7. My thanks to Rab Houston for this reference.

30 Parkes, 'Celtic Fosterage', 366.

31 NRS, GD112/39/47/12; NRS, GD112/39/47/14.

32 NRS, GD112/39/47/15, n.d.

33 *Black Book of Taymouth*, 80–1.

34 Cathcart, *Kinship and Clientage*, 82.

in March 1633 depict a negotiation between two members of the *fine*. Lorne wrote, he had 'resolveit fare rather to have him brocht up with yow [Glenorchy] for many respects as I have shawne'.[35] Yet, there are hints that this decision was not made only by the male heads of households. Lorne wrote to Glenorchy that 'otheris of my kinsmen hes dealt earnestlie with me *and my wyf* to have my sone brocht up at thame'. Further, he wrote that he had been assured that Glenorchy *and his lady* were desirous to have his young son as their foster.[36] Involving both the natal mother and foster-mother in setting the terms of care was critical, as Highland houses followed early modern trends where it was the wife who was primarily responsible for the day-to-day operation of the household, including caring for the children.[37] The *Black Book of Taymouth* noted that the foster-mother was '[e]ven more important in such a relation' than the foster-father.[38] Alison Cathcart has argued that although the mother's role in Highland society was not formally recognized, 'maternal influence was regarded as important'.[39] It was decided in the formal arrangements that Margaret Douglas and Juliane Campbell (Archibald's foster-mother), should meet to discuss the 'speciale care' of Archibald.[40] Glenorchy wrote to Lorne, 'as for the rest of the particulars conteinit in your Lords letter, I sall answer them at my wyfes coming to your lady [as she] hes desyreit'.[41] Unfortunately, details of this meeting between mothers have not survived.

Lady Margaret and Glenorchy

The maternal influence of Margaret Douglas continued beyond the initial drawing up of terms in March 1633.[42] When Archibald Campbell entered fosterage to Colin Campbell of Glenorchy, he was just over four years of age.[43] For the next six years Margaret mounted a prolific letter-writing campaign, sending dozens of letters to Glenorchy about the care and welfare of her young son. Many of these were short letters of only a few lines inquiring about Archibald's well-being or reporting on his health if he was visiting his natal home. Margaret almost always finished these letters with a formulaic declaration of her affection and friendship, reminding Glenorchy of the ties between their families. When Archibald was

35 NRS, GD112/39/47/12, 14–15.

36 NRS, GD112/39/47/14. Emphasis added.

37 Domhnall Uilleam Stiùbhart, 'Women and Gender in the Early Modern Western Gàidhealtachd', in Ewan and Meikle (eds), *Women in Scotland*, 234–5. Cathcart, *Kinship and Clientage*, 83–4 also suggests possible significance in the legal and economic obligations that foster-mothers may have inherited if their husband passed away.

38 *The Black Book of Taymouth*, p. xviii.

39 Cathcart, 'Inressyng of kyndnes', 137.

40 NRS, GD112/39/47/15.

41 NRS, GD112/39/47/15.

42 For a contemporary portrait of Margaret Douglas, see NGS, PG 1413, oil on canvas portrait by George Jameson, 'Lady Margaret Douglas, Marchioness of Argyll', 1634.

43 Archibald Campbell was born on 26 February 1629.

sick – with stomach problems and the measles – Margaret's gratitude for the care that Glenorchy showed Archibald drew the two families closer together. During these times of ill health, Margaret thanked Glenorchy for the care he showed the child and she asserted her willingness to use her position as future countess of Argyll to serve Glenorchy's interests: 'I shall be readie to requite it and other your favoures, as occasion shall offer'.[44] Some of Margaret's letters were a full page in length, and included reports on family news, Lorne's movements, and other items that might have interested Glenorchy. In particular, Margaret relayed important news about Lorne's whereabouts and when Glenorchy might expect to hear from him, thus serving to strengthen the connection between the two families. For example, in July 1635 she sent a letter asking Glenorchy to come to Stirling the following week for a rare meeting with both the lord of Lorne and his father, the earl of Argyll.[45] Although Margaret was clearly interested in advancing the connections between their families, as with other letters written by mothers about their children in early modern Europe, her letters mainly focussed on the health and education of young Archibald,[46] as well as negotiating visits to his family home. As Linda Pollock suggested, elite reliance on correspondence 'presents an opportunity to investigate their emotional world'.[47] This documentation, as articulated in the *Black Book of Taymouth*, 'serves better than formal contracts to show the feelings of two families of the same lineage drawing closer the bonds of kindred by the still more tender relation of fosterage'.[48]

Presumably Juliane Campbell, foster-mother, also played an important role in the constructing and maintenance of this close relationship with Archibald, but unfortunately her personal correspondence does not survive. As discussed below, she did receive letters from the young foster, but Juliane's correspondence was not collected as part of the family papers. Mention of the foster-mother beyond customary salutations is fleeting in the extant correspondence. Margaret Douglas may well have corresponded with Juliane Campbell about the day-to-day care of the foster, but there is no suggestion of this in the surviving correspondence to Glenorchy, so her role in the successes of this arrangement is largely invisible to modern eyes.

Much of the extant correspondence about Archibald's fosterage was shaped by the emotional turmoil of Lady Margaret. This is first evident when, discussing the date at which the bairn would be handed over to Glenorchy, Lorne exclaimed, 'I shalbe doeing my best to spennie [divide or wean] him fra his

44 NRS, GD112/39/60/17. See also NRS, GD112/39/50/6; NRS, GD112/39/59/8; NRS, GD112/39/62/18; NRS, GD112/39/62/20.

45 NRS, GD112/39/55/30.

46 Jane Couchman, '"Our little darlings": Huguenot Children and Child-Rearing in the Letters of Louise de Coligny', in Naomi Miller and Naomi Yavneh (eds), *Gender and Early Modern Constructions of Childhood* (Farnham, 2011), 104–10.

47 Linda Pollock, 'Anger and the Negotiation of Relationships in Early Modern England', *The Historical Journal* 43:3 (2004), 571.

48 *The Black Book of Taymouth*, p. xviii.

mother qhm I know it wilbe some diffacultie'.[49] Margaret struggled with this separation throughout the fosterage. In 1637 Lorne explained to Glenorchy why Archibald's visit to his natal family had been extended, 'the fondnes of ane mother to hir child hes mad you want your foster so long'.[50] In the final year of the fosterage Lorne wrote to Glenorchy that 'his Mothers contined in hir longing desyr to see him'.[51] The love and protection that Margaret felt for her child, as well as her desire to be with him proved to be dominant themes in the fosterage of Archibald Campbell throughout 1633–39. The lens of maternal love, loss and fear, sheds light on the human and familial element of fosterage and how it affected the people who were actually involved. These emotions were strong and shaped Archibald's experience of being fostered. Far from being a simple political pawn, the fostered child was both loved and missed, and his well-being was constantly on his mother's mind. Glenorchy came to share these emotions, thus providing Archie with two doting families. This was a complicated relationship, as the shared commitment to Archibald's well-being was also a point of tension between the two families.

Much of the tension surrounded issues of the boy's precarious health. Margaret delayed the initial handing over of Archibald to Glenorchy in 1633 as during the previous few months he had been suffering from what they believed to be 'the gravell'.[52] This provided Margaret with the pretence for regularly checking in with Glenorchy and asking him to report on the care of her child. Fear for her son's life meant that she struggled not only with letting the child go to the care of another family, but she and Glenorchy were often in conflict over decisions made about Archie's health. Two months after Archibald finally arrived in Glenorchy's household, his natal parents visited and brought Dr Arnott with them to examine the child. This visit was at the beginning of August 1633, and on 27 August Margaret made it very clear that she expected Glenorchy to keep them up-to-date on his progress. She boldly asked that the bearer be allowed to look in on the child so he could report back to her on Archie's health. She also beseeched Glenorchy to acquaint her with Archibald's well-being by letter.[53] In addition to the underlying message that Margaret did not trust Glenorchy's word about

49 NRS, GD112/39/47/14. That parents experienced deep love for their children and were grief-stricken at the loss of a child has been widely demonstrated in the early modern Scottish literature. For grief and loss at the death of a child, see David Mullan, 'Parents and Children in Early Modern Scotland', in Ewan and Nugent, *Finding the Family*, 74–5; Nugent, 'The Mistresse of the Family', 59–60; Frater, 'Women of the Gàidhealtachd', passim and Chapter 5 in this collection. For more on children and emotion in early modern Europe, see Claudia Jarzebowski and Thomas Max Safley (eds), *Childhood and Emotion: Across Culture 1450–1800* (London, 2014), and Katie Barclay, Ciara Rawnsley and Kimberely Reynolds (eds), *Small Graves: Death, Emotion and Childhood in the Early Modern Period* (forthcoming).

50 NRS, GD112/39/63/10.

51 NRS, GD112/39/71/2. Lorne affectionately called his son Archie, NRS, GD112/39/57/19.

52 A condition similar in symptoms to kidney stones.

53 NRS, GD112/39/49/24. There were numerous other requests for news of his well-being in subsequent years, including NRS, GD112/39/53/7, 8 October 1634 and NRS, GD112/39/61/2, 14 October 1636.

the health of her child as she needed another's affirmation, such a request also interfered in Glenorchy's household by saddling him with the indignity of allowing a bearer to enter his home to examine his charge. Margaret also interfered in Glenorchy's care by installing a woman to serve the foster.[54] Glenorchy did initially work with Margaret's instructions, by engaging Dr Arnott in the treatment of the child and accepting his instructions for care such as keeping the child warm and moving him up and down.[55] In fact, Dr Arnott's presence almost became a form of surveillance as Lord and Lady Lorne regularly had him check in on young Archibald at the Glenorchy castles.[56] In a letter written in autumn 1633, Margaret gave all credit for Archibald's well-being to Arnott:

> I can not bot rander yow many thankes for the great caire wch ye tak of the bairne and in acquenting me of his weilfaire at all occasionns and specialle at this tyme be doctour arnottis lre (to quhome ye ar obleiged) ffor the same hes gevine me great contentment. So not doubting bot ye will continue still cairfull of the bairne as ye have began.[57]

As Glenorchy complied with Margaret's demands, she was relieved for her son's health and considered herself in Glenorchy's debt: 'Lowing frind the keindnes which I heir yow wes my sone with mak me that I can not bot at eury occasion randar yow thanks with ascouranc that ye shall euer feind me redei to expres my self in any thing that concarns you.'[58]

Margaret and Glenorchy's concerns were understandable. Considering the history of young Archibald's health, neither could be blamed for fretting over the child. Child mortality rates in the pre-industrial period were high. Although we do not know the child mortality rates of Scotland in the early seventeenth century, Peter Laslett found that, in the period 1600–49 in England, twenty-seven per cent of children died by the age of ten.[59] Parents feared for their children's health; death was a very real possibility. For a child who had been fostered, this fear was likely compounded for the natal mother as she was unable to act as a nursemaid. Women were trained and expected to care for the medical needs of their families, and noble women were even encouraged to bring these skills to their community.[60] Caring for a sick child was a symbol of a mother's duty, love, and care for her children, and Margaret had been denied this small comfort. Glenorchy likely dreaded Archibald's death in the early years of the fosterage as this would have resulted in the loss of his privileged connection to Lorne, as well

54 NRS, GD112/39/60/15 and NRS, GD112/39/62/15.

55 NRS, GD112/39/49/12–15; NRS, GD112/39/50/14.

56 NRS, GD112/39/50/12; NRS, GD112/39/50/13; NRS, GD112/39/55/17; NRS, GD112/39/62/22.

57 NRS, GD112/39/50/15. For stylistic reasons, 'y' is not modernized to 'th' for the word ye.

58 NRS, GD112/39/50/6.

59 Peter Laslett, *The World We Have Lost: Further Explored* (London, 2000), 112.

60 Susan Broomhall, *Women's Medical Work in Early Modern France* (Manchester, 2004), 137–8.

as the loss of the resources he had invested in the foster-child. As time passed, his own emotional connections to young Archie grew, and three years after the child's arrival at Balloch Glenorchy spoke of him with much affection and real concern for his well-being: '(as your Lord knows) that altho your sone be of ane quick and good spiritis (God blesse him) Yit he is weak and tender in the constitutioun of his bodie'.[61]

Despite periods of tension, Glenorchy and Margaret were mutually invested in the health of young Archibald, and often worked together for his welfare. When Archibald was ill with the measles, Glenorchy informed Margaret that he had summoned Dr Arnott. Knowing of the doctor's unavailability, Margaret sent Glenorchy a stone remedy that could be used if the measles became worse or reappeared.[62] Glenorchy then enlisted the support of Margaret's sister to help care for Archibald, an action which was met with great approval by Margaret as the sister had much experience in nursing her own children through the disease. Demonstrating her concern for Glenorchy as well, Margaret cautioned him not to harm himself in providing care for the child.[63]

Another collaborative effort between foster-father and natal mother emerged when Archibald resisted his Gaelic education. The Campbells, like other Highland clans, sought to preserve their Gaelic identity throughout the seventeenth century.[64] As heir to the Argyll earldom, Archie would become chief of the powerful Lowland and Highland Campbells, an important Scottish politician, and a British statesman. Strong English skills were admirable within Gaelic society,[65] but to not speak Gaelic would estrange him from a shared identity with his clansmen, who clearly saw themselves as distinct from Lowlanders.[66] Archie's fluency in both Scots and Gaelic was critical to his future political career, from which both the Lorne and Glenorchy families would benefit. Margaret and Glenorchy understood the importance of his education and language training, and worked together to ensure Archie's successes. Lorne and Glenorchy agreed in the fosterage negotiations that Archie's nurse was to speak both Irish and English.[67] When Archie resisted his formal Gaelic language studies four years later, Margaret asked Glenorchy to stand his ground.[68] Glenorchy complied and sent a message to Lorne demonstrating that he had found the child a new tutor – an excellent scholar – who was well versed in both English and Gaelic.

Despite the collaborative efforts of Margaret and Glenorchy over the foster's health and education, a point of contention was the annual struggle to have the child come and visit his natal family at Rosneath Castle (in Argyll and Bute on

61 NRS, GD112/39/59/5. Balloch was one of the Glenorchy castles in Perthshire.
62 NRS, GD112/39/62/22.
63 NRS, GD112/39/62/23.
64 Silke Stroh, *Uneasy Subjects: Postcolonialism and Scottish Gaelic Poetry* (Amsterdam, 2011), 81; Macinnes, *The British Confederate*, 66–7.
65 Stroh, *Uneasy Subjects*, 103.
66 Stroh, *Uneasy Subjects*, 94–5.
67 NRS, GD112/39/47/15.
68 NRS, GD112/39/64/16.

the Firth of Clyde) during the summertime. These visits were a critical time for young Archibald to connect with his parents and it was also an important opportunity for Lorne and Margaret to check on his progress. Also of significance were visits with Archibald's powerful grandparents. One year after Archibald's fostering, on 15 March 1634, Margaret summoned her son as his maternal grandmother would be visiting Rosneath the following week.[69] In July 1635, after the child's visit with his paternal grandfather, Lorne's kinsman (another Archibald Campbell) wrote to Glenorchy stating that 'the Earl of Argyll is to send your foister baicke againe to you – with quhome he is exceiding weill pleassit, And thinks hime self farre obleist to you for the caire ye have of him'.[70] Despite his son's very recent recovery from the measles in 1637, Lorne requested that Archie be sent to visit the earl of Morton (Archie's grandfather). Glenorchy acquiesced to the request, but wrote to Margaret of his reluctance as the boy was still 'tender' after the sickness.[71]

Glenorchy appeared to be agreeable to Archibald leaving to visit his family in the first year. These inspections reflected positively upon the care he had provided for Archibald and brought him into the good graces of the powerful earls of Morton and Argyll. As these visits to family were often extended well beyond what had been agreed upon, however, this became a point of contention. In 1634, when the annual visit had been extended beyond a month, Lorne felt the need to explain that Archie had to stay longer as Lorne had been summoned to Edinburgh and they could not yet leave Rosneath; moreover, his grandfather, the earl of Morton, was scheduled to visit. Beyond the explanation, Lorne reassured Glenorchy of Archibald's devotion by peppering the letter with declarations of Archie's love. 'I will assoor you your foster longs very muche to see you and doetlie not dar to tell he had rather be thair nor her and I assoor you he shall heaue his choice.' Furthermore, if the earl of Morton changed his plans, he 'shall immediatelie heaue him (as Archie calles it) home'.[72] These were messages of reassurance to Glenorchy that the bonds of loyalty and fictive kinship were strong, and that these would continue to grow and flourish once the child was returned to his foster-father. At times Margaret took a similar tack, such as when she wrote to Glenorchy during an extended visit in 1636, 'I assure yow hee longs greatlie to goe to yow and shall haue his desyre so soone as wee goe to Inveraray.'[73]

Despite the constant reassurances of loyalty by Lord and Lady Lorne, as well as the reiterations of Archibald's love for his foster-father, Glenorchy often resisted Archibald making such visits. Although the reasons for his hesitations

[69] NRS, GD112/39/51/21.
[70] NRS, GD112/39/56/7.
[71] NRS, GD112/39/63/6.
[72] NRS, GD112/39/52/4.
[73] NRS, GD112/39/57/20. For a similar example see GD112/39/59/8. Cf. Archibald's biographer, who noted that Archibald's view of Balloch being his home was met with amusement by his parents. John Wilcox, *A Scots Earl in Covenanting Times: Being Life and Times of Archibald 9th Earl of Argyll (1629–1685)* (Edinburgh, 1907), 7.

are not explicit, the letters suggest that his concerns were multifaceted. The most explicitly articulated concern was of the toll that travel would take on the child's health. Glenorchy did not want to risk his investment dying from an illness caught through the hardships of travel, and he genuinely feared losing the child he cared about. The child's poor health, combined with unseasonable weather, was ostensibly Glenorchy's main reason for keeping Archibald under his roof.[74] Yet there are hints that Glenorchy was also concerned that losing possession of the foster would stunt the growth of Archibald's love for his foster-father, thereby threatening the successes of the fosterage contract in which he had heavily invested for the family's future. In April 1635, when the weather was still poor, Glenorchy tried to dodge Margaret's request to allow Archibald to join her when she was visiting nearby 'St. Johnstone'. He suggested that she come instead to Balloch, where he would delay his own journey so that he could most 'heartle welcome' her.[75] This arrangement had the dual advantage of assuring his influence over the child and allowing him to show her hospitality, thus strengthening the connections between himself and the lord and lady of Lorne. Margaret turned down his offer as she was travelling to attend to her sister's delivery.[76] She made arrangements to have Dr Arnott attend to the child when he arrived to meet his mother in Perth, in the hope that this would make Glenorchy 'the willinger to let him come for this schort tyme'.[77] Ultimately the child was sent to briefly join his mother. Margaret, clearly annoyed by the struggle she had to undertake to see her child, returned Archibald with a letter stating, 'seiing I haue sent him bak, I hope ye will mak no ceremonie to let him come at anny other occasione qhen I send for him'.[78] Despite Glenorchy's best attempts, the lord of Lorne was his superior, Margaret Douglas was the child's natal mother, and despite poor weather and/or health, he could not deny their requests to visit with their son.

In 1636, the annual struggle for Archie to visit his natal family reached epic proportions. The initial setting up of the visits leaves one with the impression of a game of cat and mouse between Glenorchy and Margaret Douglas. Lorne's status and his gender kept Glenorchy from challenging Lorne too overtly, so most of his struggles were directly with Margaret. Yet, Margaret's status as Archibald's mother and as the wife of the future earl of Argyll made her a worthy adversary for Glenorchy when their interests clashed. In February 1636, multiple letters were exchanged between the pair, with Margaret Douglas wanting Archibald to come for a visit and Glenorchy resisting. Glenorchy even went so far as to appeal to Lorne for the well-being of his foster-son, convincingly writing:

74 NRS, GD112/39/55/11; NRS, GD112/39/57/34; NRS, GD112/39/57/35; NRS, GD112/39/59/5; NRS, GD112/39/62/18; NRS, GD112/39/63/6.

75 NRS, GD112/39/55/11.

76 NRS, GD112/39/55/12.

77 NRS, GD112/39/55/17.

78 NRS, GD112/39/55/18. For other instances where Glenorchy was given assurance that Archie would be returned to him after visiting his natal family, see NRS, GD112/39/59/1 and NRS, GD112/39/60/18.

> Your la knowes that this is ane verie vnseasonable tyme of yeir for your la sone to travell in sa that to my opinion my lord & and your la cannot do better, nor to suffer him to byde still with me qll [until] s'mer & fair weather, as qll tyme I hope in God your Lady will be able to come & sie him qr [where] my Lord & your La salbe heartlie welcome. For I know gif he travell this tyme of yer that may doe him skaith.[79]

This rationale won out, as young Archibald's health would have been unnecessarily risked by having him undertake a long journey across the Highlands in February.[80] In defeat, Margaret declined the invitation to visit, instead sending a bearer to check on Archibald's health.[81] When she took ill weeks later, she demanded to see the child despite Glenorchy's objections. With his wife's health failing, Lorne supported Margaret's request. Margaret wrote with apparent impatience to Glenorchy, 'I hop yea ar resolved or now to lett my sonne com heir and sie me, since I am not able to com and sie him. Qrfor I will writ no moir of it.' She then concluded the letter stating that she was waiting until Lorne returned from Edinburgh so that he could send for the child.[82] Glenorchy, questioning this directive, demanded to 'know that his Lo mynd to bring home his sone and the caus of it', stating that he was 'weill content' to keep the child at his house. Failing this, he beseeched them to wait until fairer weather.[83]

Despite the foster-father's objections, Archie was sent to his mother and Glenorchy was left to de-escalate tensions and salvage the bonds of loyalty between the two families. He drafted at least two letters to Lorne where he drew attention to the great care that Archibald had been receiving. He described the boy to be 'ane good and perfyte chyld (God blesse him) and the best schollar of his age in this kingdome'.[84] Glenorchy also commented that he hoped Lorne and his wife found the child well and were pleased with the care he had received. Glenorchy was clearly fretting lest Lord and Lady Lorne would not 'be pleased to send him to me again'.[85] These insecurities were resolved when Glenorchy received assurance that the child was to be returned shortly.[86] However, young Archibald was in Rosneath for most of the summer, staying nearly five months from the end of March until the middle of August.

As summer wore on, tensions persisted between the two families. One particularly fascinating point of contention surrounded Archibald's clothing. Archibald

79 NRS, GD112/39/57/35.

80 Even the ministers and elders in Argyll recognized the difficulties and hazards of travel in the winter months and successfully petitioned the Synod to accommodate them with a decreased meeting schedule. Jane Dawson, 'Calvinism and the Gaidhealtachd in Scotland', in Andrew Pettegree et al. (eds), *Calvinism in Europe, 1540–1620* (Cambridge, 1994), 246.

81 NRS, GD112/39/58/4.

82 NRS, GD112/39/58/9.

83 NRS, GD112/39/58/16 (this letter appears in the GD112/39/58 file, but is misnumbered as GD112/39/57/16).

84 NRS, GD112/39/58/24/2.

85 NRS, GD112/39/58/24/1. See also GD112/39/59/2.

86 NRS, GD112/39/59/1.

had now reached the age of seven, and his mother apparently thought it time that he left behind the skirts of infancy.[87] Archibald Campbell, Glenorchy's relation, wrote to the laird that he was concerned that 'theu [Margaret] vare taiking of sume thinges to mak shoirt clois'. As he explained to Lorne, 'I knew ye wald not be content, bot that theis thinges sould be on yor charges being the first shoirt clois that ever he had worne'. The significance of this ritual, and how important it was that this honour be bestowed on the foster-father as a symbol of his role in the child's life, was not lost on Lorne, who did 'tak in verie gud pairt Thairfoir I [Archibald Campbell] went to James Rae and desyreit him to give aff sicke thinge and war givine him in wol for ye bairnes his wse which I hoip ye will approve'.[88] The elaborate details of cloth, silk stockings, perling, points, silver buttons, scarlet French steinyng (a woollen cloth often used for hose), and other materials purchased to outfit the seven-year-old Archibald were meticulously recorded by Glenorchy in his ledger.[89]

Archie and Glenorchy

The fosterage relationship was intended to produce deep ties of affection and loyalty between the two families.[90] In part, this was meant to bond the heads of households together as close kin and allies. Yet the advantage that the foster family gained was not just from Lorne; the development of deep emotional bonds with the foster-child also brought them closer to the child and the future that he represented.[91] As Jane Dawson noted, it was a commonplace belief that '[a] nobleman's foster-family was as close as, if not closer than, his blood kin'. The remainder of this essay explores what we can ascertain about these connections.[92]

In Chapter 5 of this collection, Anne Frater examines Gaelic songs to persuasively argue for the strong emotional bonds between foster-mothers and their foster-children; the letters concerning the fosterage of Archibald Campbell also indicate a deep tie of affection forming between the foster and his foster-father. As future head of the clan, Archibald's love, affection and loyalty could bring great advantages to the Glenorchy branch of the family.[93] The fosterage arrangement allowed the growth of these emotional connections through shared time and space, with co-residence facilitating mutual experiences, an intimate knowledge of one another, and ultimately the development of something like a father–son relationship between the child and foster-father.

87 For more on children's clothing see Chapters 1 and 6 in this collection.

88 NRS, GD112/39/60/11.

89 NRS, GD112/1/496.

90 For more on children and emotion see Chapter 8 in this collection. See also Chapter 10 for more on the use of children to build connections between elite families.

91 Curle, 'Notice of Four Contracts', 17.

92 *CL*, 9. See also Curle, 'Notice of Four Contracts', 17.

93 For examples of how this loyalty could result in strategic political and military action, see Macinnes, *Clanship, Commerce and the House of Stuart*, 14.

During Archibald's extended visit to his natal home in 1636, when tensions were high, the boy entered the historical record as an important actor in the fostering process. Letters were sent to Glenorchy and ostensibly signed by Archibald himself. Upon first glance it appears that this is evidence of a child's voice surviving through the centuries, yet he was only a child of seven so it is questionable whether Archibald had composed such articulate and socially aware letters himself. The signatures also appear to be in a different hand than the body of the letters, suggesting perhaps that it had been written by an adult and signed by the child. As is common in the historical record, access to the child was mediated through adult voices that 'shape[d] or characterize[d] the young' and the question arises whether the child has himself acted, or been acted upon.[94] Despite these issues, it is clear that the foster-child's voice (to whatever extent it was shaped by adults) was believed to be critical in the socio-political relationship of fosterage. Archie assured Glenorchy of his health and of the strong bonds of affection that he had for him, while also seeking to smooth over tensions with his mother.

> Honorable and Loueing foster father. My loue being remembered wit that I am in good health (blessed be God) and nothing the worse for my travell. Doctor Arnot is to be here shortlie, qrfore advertise mee how yow are in health, and at what ease for the paine of your sore legg, and then I will try of the doctor what may doe yow good to release yow of your paine, I will no wayis forget it. I know yow will send to sie how I doe, and with all occasions I will wryt to yow till I goe there my selfe qlk I hope shall be shortlie. Thus remembering my loue & heartlie comendations to your selfe and the Ladie I rest
> Your louing childe and foster
> A Campbell
> Rosse ye 2 Aprile 1636.
> Ladie Minnie remembers her commendation to yow, for she might not wryt her selfe.[95]

People not only felt emotions, but employed them.[96] This letter was clearly a demonstration of Archie's love and concern for his foster-father and appears to have functioned as a note of conciliation to Glenorchy for the extended visit. Emotions are, in part, socially constructed and therefore across the chasm of time they 'do not map exactly onto modern definitions of "emotions"'.[97] What we can say about Archie's feelings for his foster-father must be viewed through this lens. Yet, there is knowledge about what ails his foster-father and a genuine attempt to try to alleviate Glenorchy's discomfort. This concern demonstrated to Glenorchy that Archibald was committed to his foster-father's well-being and that he was

94 Mary Jo Maynes, 'Age as a Category of Historical Analysis: History, Agency, and Narratives of Childhood', *JHCY* 1:1 (2008), 117–18.
95 NRS, GD112/39/59/2. Archibald referred to his mother as Lady Minnie and his father as Lord Deddie.
96 Pollock, 'Anger and the Negotiation of Relationships', 590.
97 Philippa Maddern, 'How Children Were Supposed to Feel; How Children Felt', in Jarzebowski and Safley, *Childhood and Emotion*, 122.

bothered by the pain of Glenorchy's gout, thus reassuring him of their connection despite the lengthy separation.[98] Children were both emotionally driven and emotionally driving.[99]

As Archibald grew older, many similar letters were sent to his foster-father when he was away. Throughout the lengthy visit of 1636 discussed above, the young foster-child became the conduit of information between his natal and foster families, bearing news about when he would or would not return to Glenorchy. By delivering details and explanations about each extension to the visit, Archibald served as a shield for Margaret Douglas from Glenorchy's frustration, thus protecting the fictive kin relationship that they were building between the two families. By demonstrating Archibald's bonds of affection for Glenorchy, the author of the letter sought to quell the mounting tensions. Regardless of whether Archibald wrote the letters himself, he was a political actor in the fosterage relationship as his love and loyalty were critical to the successes of the fosterage contract. His emotions were constantly tested and needed affirmation. On 24 April, a letter from young Archie reassured his foster-father that 'Lord Deddie' and 'Lady Minnie' were pleased to send him back to Glenorchy and that he longed to see him. The outside of this letter was addressed to his loving foster-mother, which suggests that there was a similar letter of assurance and declaration of love enclosed to Lady Glenorchy that has not survived.[100] On 30 May 1636, young Archibald wrote to Glenorchy explaining that Lorne had been summoned to Edinburgh by Traquair, thus delaying his return to Inveraray.[101] Despite the delay, Archibald reinforced his affections and commitment to his foster-father, 'these delayis mak mee still long more and more to sie you and wish my returne home may be shortlie'.[102] On 28 June, Archibald explained again his inability to return. '[I] long verie much to sie yow, but I must of necessitie comport wt all delayis, till Lord Deddie goe to Inverary of whilk wee are as yit incertaine.'[103]

The tensions between Glenorchy and Margaret Douglas threatened to boil over at various points, which would certainly have damaged the fostering contract. But the relationship was salvaged by the intercession of Lorne, his kinsmen Archibald Campbell, and the young foster-child himself. Indeed, finding ways to make the dynamic work between Margaret and Glenorchy may have actually drawn the *fine* closer together as they were required to consistently demonstrate

[98] NRS, GD112/39/58/17 explains that Dr Arnott diagnosed the problem as gout.

[99] W.M. Reddy, *The Navigation of Feeling: A framework for the History of Emotions* (Cambridge, 2001).

[100] NRS, GD112/39/59/8.

[101] For a discussion about the challenges of travel to Argyll see Roxanne Reddington-Wilde, 'The Power of Place: Spatial Analysis and Social Organization of the Campbells in Early Modern Argyll', unpublished Ph.D. thesis (Harvard University), 1995, 146–7.

[102] NRS, GD/112/39/59/17. Again, who wrote the letter is in question, but the power that Archibald's voice was believed to have is still of great interest.

[103] NRS, GD112/39/60/8.

their allegiances to one another. Eventually Margaret reached out to Glenorchy to acknowledge the tensions and reassert her loyalty.

> I kno ye well think it my plot that your foster coms not so shoun as was feirst promesed bot when ye have considered the caus of his stay is that he may sei my father heir if it pleas god he com hom at this tym I hap ye well no construck it to any on gratitud in me for your former keind ushag of him bot well stell iudg of me as of on who shall all ways apru them self to be your most aschured friend to pour. Margrat Douglas.[104]

Conclusions

Although the details of Archibald Campbell's fosterage experience are limited, this case study illustrates that women and children made important contributions to the creation of fictive kinship and to ensuring the political and social successes of the fostering arrangement. The reality of emotional connections between natal parents and their children, as well as between the foster and his/her foster family brought both complications and solutions to the tensions that might arise.

This study also allows us to begin to piece together the experience of fosterage for the foster-child. As heir to the earldom of Argyll, Archibald had a privileged childhood. He wore fine clothing, was educated by private tutors, and received his own toys. For example, in October 1634, Archibald Campbell, Glenorchy's agent, wrote to Glenorchy that he had not yet been able to secure the byas [bias] bowl (bowls used in bowling) that Juliane had ordered for Archie, but promised to send them to her with the next bearer.[105] The foster's educational experience was constructed to ensure he was equipped with the tools necessary to step into the role of earl of Argyll. Although his natal and foster-parents made the decisions about what his education entailed and how it was carried out, Archibald could resist subjects which he did not enjoy, such as Gaelic.

As a foster, Archibald spent much of his childhood travelling around the Highlands and Lowlands of Scotland, shifting residences between his natal and foster families. He grew up in the luxurious castles of Inverarary, Rosneath, Balloch and Kilchurn. The trips between these castles were long, and complicated by elements of Scottish geography and climate, yet Glenorchy's ledger indicates the foster-father took on many expenses to protect his investment and ensure the child's safety and comfort as he travelled with an entourage between locations.[106] Beyond spending time with his parents and siblings, extended family visits with both paternal and maternal grandparents punctuated Archibald's summers. Aunts also entered into his experiences, with one coming to nurse him when

104 NRS, GD112/39/59/20.
105 NRS, GD112/39/53/11.
106 NRS, GD112/1/496.

he was ill, and he visited another while his mother was tending to her sister in childbed.

Archibald also faced many of the regular realities of childhood in the early modern period. His health was fragile. He faced chronic gastro-intestinal disease, as well as the ravages of epidemics such as measles. Like every other child, Archie passed through socially recognized stages of childhood, such as the important ceremonial shift out of the skirts of infancy. He was also loved by his parents and in turn held strong affections for his family, both natal and fictive. Despite Archie's extraordinary status as heir to the earldom of Argyll, it was these commonalities of childhood that shaped his experience of fosterage, bringing both tensions and cohesiveness to the two families that were being drawn together through the relation of fosterage.

4

Work and Play: The Material Culture of Childhood in Early Modern Scotland

Stuart Campbell

In 1612, *The Book of Customs and Valuation of Merchandises in Scotland* listed among the imported goods a gross of 'Babeis [dolls] or puppettis for childrene' at a total value of £3.[1] References to toys appear occasionally in merchants' records of the period, but the bare facts of the ledger leave several questions unanswered; where these objects came from, who used them, and why they were desired remain elusive. Beyond their monetary value, such objects have remained frustratingly invisible to the historian, unless they are captured for posterity in contemporary portraits. This source of information is inherently partial in the society it depicts, fulfilling perhaps the preconception that toys and play were the preserve of leisured and moneyed households. That imported goods were widely available to those who could afford them is of course no surprise.

An increasing awareness of children and their material culture is part of a wider archaeological interest in the early modern period. Children's toys are increasingly being identified both in the British Isles and further afield. This study has been aided by a greater appreciation of the potential of metal-detected finds, with the majority of artefacts discussed in this essay having been found in this manner. As a complement to both documentary and pictorial evidence, it is clear that the childhood of early modern Scotland has a distinct archaeological signature and involves objects that are largely invisible to documentary sources. As objects that belonged to or were used by children, they do not feature in the wills, testaments, and inventories that list and categorize adult and household possessions. It is clear also that many of these objects were made for households of low or modest incomes, those social groups whose private and domestic lives are less prevalent in documentary sources of the period. Recent archaeological theory has been critiqued for viewing toys solely as an appropriation of childhood by the adult world, with toys seen as tools to mould children to adult preconceptions of gender or class.[2] This essay argues for a much more complex

[1] *The Book of Customs and Valuation of Merchandises in Scotland* A.D. *1612*, in C. Innes (ed.), *Ledger of Andrew Halyburton: Conservator of the Privileges of the Scotch Nation in the Netherlands 1492–1503* (Edinburgh, 1867), 288.

[2] For example, L. Wilkie, 'Not Merely Child's Play: Creating a Historical Archaeology of Children and Childhood', in J.S. Derevenski (ed.), *Children and Material Culture* (London, 2000), 100–13.

and dynamic understanding of the role that toys played in children's lives in early modern Scotland.[3]

Toys fit into a broader understanding of the raising of children in early modern Scotland. In Scotland, as elsewhere in Europe, a considerable body of written work regarding the raising of children has survived. Within the Scottish historiography, historians of childhood have largely focussed on the written record, exploring concepts of family and childhood as articulated through a wider Protestant culture.[4] Other works have examined the seminal role education played, not merely as a means of instruction but also with regards to the moral elements of childhood and how children were to be raised; crucially this included the importance of leisure and play.[5] While the written record inevitably defines our understanding of childhood, there is a considerable gap in the experiences it records. Individual accounts of childhood experience have survived, for example the play and instruction of (mainly elite) teenage boys.[6] Also studied are the most general and philosophical ideas of the nature of childhood and education at a European level.[7] Between these poles of individual experience and general philosophy, there remains a vast gap of what might best be termed a national or socially specific experience of childhood. This essay focuses on this gap by analysing a distinct category of children's toys whose use, manufacture, and purpose can be clearly deduced from the archaeological record.

By examining toys from the perspectives of production, trade, and as objects of purpose and play, an understanding of childhood which bridges the gap between individual experience and the most general of models begins to emerge. The objects discussed raise questions of class, affordability and aspiration, as much as they illustrate the ideal of childhood. They also provide a useful ambiguity as to the nature and purpose of childhood; the pioneering work of Iona and Peter Opie has meant that often childhood games are viewed as having a rationale and justification in themselves.[8] Many of the toys discussed here offer a more complex model; while clearly objects of play, they are unmistakably those which also

3 For a comparative critique see Eleanor Gordon, 'The Family', in Lynn Abrams et al. (eds), *Gender in Scottish History Since 1700* (Edinburgh, 2006), 237 on gender historians who view the family or household solely as an area of oppression for women rather than dissecting the economic and cultural complexity of gender and family.

4 David Mullan, 'Parents and Children in Early Modern Scotland', in Elizabeth Ewan and Janay Nugent (eds), *Finding the Family in Medieval and Early Modern Scotland* (Aldershot, 2008), 73–83; James Kirkwood, *The True Interest of Families: or, directions how parents may be happy in their children, and children in their parents* (London, 1692).

5 Craig Beveridge, 'Childhood and Society in Eighteenth-Century Scotland', in J. Dwyer et al. (eds), *New Perspectives on the Politics and Culture of Early Modern Scotland* (Edinburgh, 1982), 265–90.

6 J. Morice, *Two Students at St. Andrews, 1711–1716*, ed. William Croft Dickinson (St Andrews, 1952).

7 Naomi Miller and Naomi Yavneh (eds), *Gender and Early Modern Constructions of Childhood* (Farnham, 2011), passim. For more on the philosophical nature of childhood see Chapter 6 in this collection.

8 I. Opie and P. Opie, *Children's Games with Things* (Oxford, 1997).

reference and reflect the adult world. With this qualifier in mind, this essay also relies upon the concept of 'ludic decorum', that games created their own reality and rules while also referencing and allowing engagement with real-world roles and behaviours.[9] Childhood does not exist as a pure and untrammelled experience, but rather reflects a wider culture. The young in early modern Scotland were not just children, and growing up did not consist of a smooth – or abrupt – transition from childhood to adult life. Rather, experiences ranged from apprenticeships or service, to scholastic initiation. Childhood was, like adulthood, part of a wider culture, a distinct and separate antechamber to adulthood rather than an experience diametrically opposed to adult life. In short, childhood experience is not merely about being a child, but often occupies a middle ground between childish wants, daily experience, and necessity. Indeed the image of the unruly and riotous apprentice, a staple of the early modern period in both comedy and fact, attests as much.[10]

By considering the material culture that fed into these formative experiences, this essay takes a considered approach to both the objects themselves and the society that used them. As with the dissonance between expectation and reality, it is crucial to draw a distinction between the actual experience of children in the period and what society thought was childhood. The archaeological evidence suggests that toys tell us more about the latter than the former, although we should not discount the active role children played in acquiring and lending meaning to this material. These objects can tell us how society saw children and its desired ideal of what these children would become; the artefacts also suggest how children saw themselves, and how they navigated this wider society on their way to adulthood.

Toys Produced Outside of Scotland

It is the objects themselves that take these considerations of what toys can tell us about early modern childhood from the abstract to the particular, objects such as the remains of a bronze rattle intended for an infant, which was found near Elgin (Plate 4.1). Intact small bells were attached to the four loops at the base, with a fitting for a suspension attachment at the top. Two complete examples were recovered from the wreck of the Dutch East Indiaman Kennemerland which foundered off Shetland in 1664, and another example was excavated from a seventeenth-century context in Amsterdam.[11] These rattles were a simplified version of the elaborate silver and coral examples found in many museum collections,

9 K.R. Larson, '"Certain childeplayes remembred by the fayre ladies": Girls and their Games', in Miller and Yavneh (eds), *Gender and Early Modern Constructions of Childhood*, 72–3.

10 For example see Robert Darnton, *The Great Cat Massacre and Other Episodes in French Cultural History* (New York, 1984).

11 The Kennemerland finds are held by Shetland Museum. The Dutch example is in E.A. van de Baart, *Opgravingen in Amsterdam: 20 Jaar Stadskernonderzoek* (Amsterdam, 1977), 469.

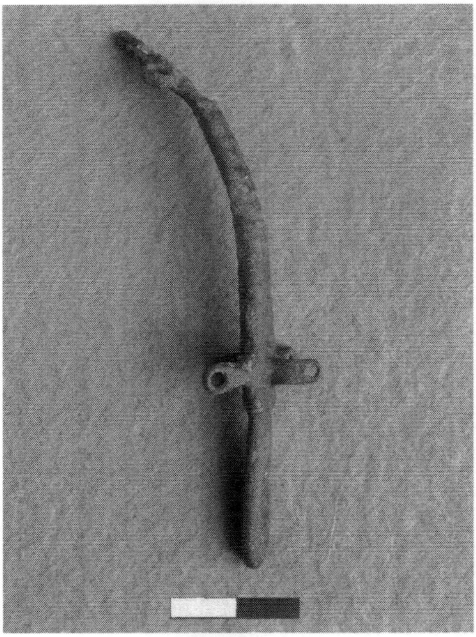

4.1 Seventeenth-century Dutch rattle found near Elgin, Elgin Museum.

and which can be seen around the necks of infants in portraits of the period. One example is the portrait of the four-month-old Charles II painted in 1630 and now held by the National Portrait Gallery, London.[12] An identical and later example was draped over the chair in Hogarth's *Marriage A-la-Mode: 4, The Toilette*, in the collection of the National Gallery, London. The smooth lobate terminal on the bronze examples bear close resemblance to the coral teething piece on these other types, although it seems unlikely to have offered the same practical and tactile comforts to the teething infant. Simply cast in bronze, these rattles seem intended as an affordable version of the elaborate and costly items used by the upper classes, and it is natural to ask who was the intended market. Together, these rattles suggest cultural references to childhood which extended throughout society; the effectiveness of a skeuomorphic object relies of course on familiarity with, or at least awareness of, the real thing.

A less genteel evocation of childhood experience can be seen in a diminutive Jews' harp found near Doune (Plate 4.2). Full-size instruments were common across Europe and appeared to have been manufactured in considerable numbers, presumably because they were an affordable instrument which a foundry could manufacture cheaply in quantity.[13] By comparison with full-size versions it is remarkably small, but was clearly fitted with the iron lamellar that made

[12] NGS, NPG6403, oil on canvas painting, unknown artist, 'King Charles II', 1630.
[13] Gjermund Kolltveit, *Jews Harps in European Archaeology* (Oxford, 2006).

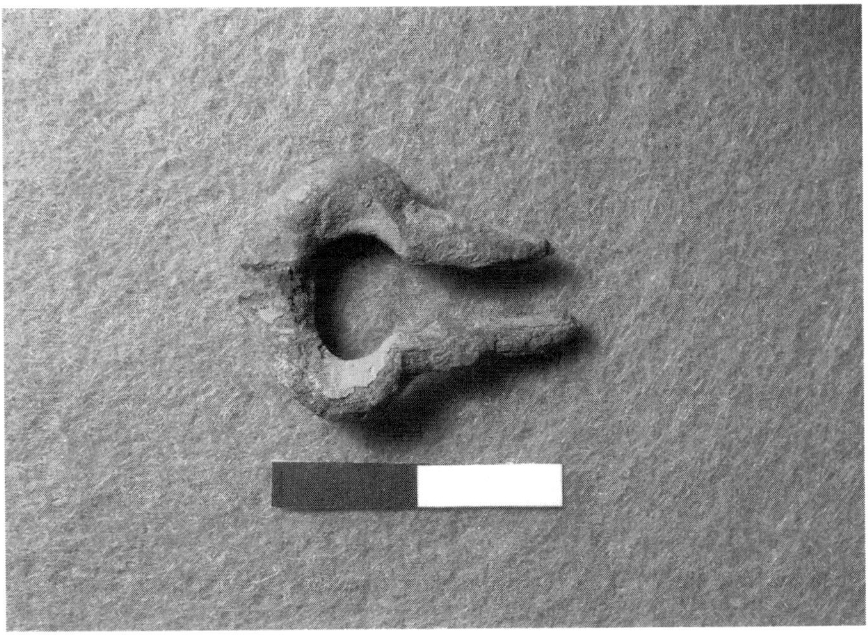

4.2 Miniature Jews' harp from Doune, NMS.

it a functional instrument. Its size is such that it could only have been played by a child, the dimensions suggesting a child of two to three years of age. The comparative simplicity of the instrument made it an ideal choice for a child, and it is tempting to see this as a natural progression from a rattle, which required only the incidental movement of the child to create a musical diversion. What is striking about both finds is that they understand the needs and skill of the child; they are made by adults for the requirements of an infant.

In both cases the use of bronze or brass betokens the work of a foundry rather than casual manufacture; they are both mass-produced, or at least as near as the artisans of the period could manage. The needs of children were recognized not just by parents or local artisans, but by a larger and more expansive industry. While it might be reasonably expected that toys were simple and home-made (examples are discussed below), the opposite also appears to have held true; it was profitable and feasible to mass-produce toys not just for the upper classes or the middling sort, but for a wider range of society. The two objects discussed above belong to a larger category that had reached its floruit in the later seventeenth century, comprising a variety of toys and miniatures intended for children. The archaeological record indicates that these were produced and traded on both a British and European level, and in Scotland these imports were augmented by local production. The majority of these toys are not those associated with children's games and pastimes, such as the balls, spinning tops and whirligigs often seen in genre paintings. Neither are they objects intended for children's games (although these do appear in the archaeological record). Rather, they are miniatures of adult objects or figures representing real life trades or occupations. They referenced the adult world rather than specific childhood experience.

The sudden appearance of these objects has proved a significant development in post-medieval archaeology, and clearly requires an explanation. A recent and authoritative study of English examples suggested that the population (particularly in London, where such objects are found in quantity) had increased to the level where commercial production was financially viable,[14] and a comparison of English and Scottish finds lends weight to this explanation. A comparison can also be made with the material that was found in the holds of the Kennemerland alongside the children's toys. In that ship, and indeed in the holds of other contemporary Dutch wrecks, were objects ranging from knives, costume jewellery and tobacco boxes, to a variety of trinkets and affordable objects. Trinket is perhaps an insubstantial word for objects that had clear purposes and uses, but it seems apposite in the sense that these objects were desirable rather than necessary. The concept of a consumer society has been thoroughly explored for the prosperous mercantile classes,[15] but objects like these indicate the power of the consumer at a lower and widespread level of society. It is natural to ask who these objects were intended for, or more simply, who might have afforded them. That it was profitable to trade objects intended for children is instructive and this theme of consumer choice, and the ready availability and import of goods, are recurring themes in this study. However, the ready availability of toys is not by itself an explanation of how they were used. The toys and other objects created for, and used by, children were informed by a social knowledge that distinguished the acquisition of these purchases from pure materialism.

Typical toys of this class appear in a group of objects from Fife, small figurines depicting a flat two-dimensional figure of a woman cast in lead alloy (Plate 4.3). The surviving examples comprise two incomplete figures from Falkland and Lundin Links (both examples now lack the upper body), and a third figure from Crail of which only the head survives. These artefacts belong to a wider category of similar figures found across Britain. Many were rather schematic in their details, but all portrayed a fashionably dressed woman in a bodice and a flaring skirt. Comparison with real-world fashion and hairstyles indicate a class of object which flourished from the very late sixteenth century until the very early eighteenth century.[16] Like the majority of contemporary toys, these were cast in cut-stone moulds, the flat design requiring a bare minimum of metal in comparison to a fully rounded figure. The Falkland and Lundin examples are identical and were clearly cast from the same mould. The production and distribution of these objects can be further elucidated, as a similar group of figures –

[14] H. Forsyth and G. Egan, *Toys, Trifles and Trinkets: Base Metal Miniatures from London 1200 to 1800* (London, 2005), 41.

[15] Lorna Weatherill, *Consumer Behaviour and Material Culture in Britain 1660–1760* (London, 1988).

[16] Forsyth and Egan, *Toys, Trifles and Trinkets*, 152.

4.3 On the left, eighteenth-century figure of a falconer from Culross, NMS. On the right, fragments of seventeenth-century toy dolls from Crail (top) and Falkland (bottom), Fife Cultural Trust.

not from the same mould but otherwise almost identical in style and appearance – have been discovered around Whitby in Yorkshire, with further similar types being found in Lincolnshire and elsewhere in Yorkshire.[17] The Fife figurines were clearly imported, and the cluster of figures from the eastern English seaboard suggests the most likely source. By comparison with other examples, these toy figures were clearly the cheapest and simplest of their type, and it is significant that they can be found so far from their area of manufacture. These objects have often been interpreted as toy dolls for girls, and while this should never simply be presumed, the subject matter of these and other finds does represent a fairly clear division on gender grounds.

What appears to be a particularly male toy-type can be seen in a pair of toy lead-alloy pocket watches, one found in Kelso, the other near Hawick. These are exact copies of the type of pocket watch common in the late seventeenth century (Plate 4.4). They can be directly compared with a well-known group from London that were made in the city,[18] with such similarities that it seems certain these Scottish examples also came from London. Again, these were simply cast,

17 Geoff Egan, *Playthings from the Past* (London, 1996), 5–6.
18 Forsyth and Egan, *Toys, Trifles and Trinkets*, 337.

4.4 Two late seventeenth-century toy watches from Roberton (left) and Kelso (right), NMS.

a single piece of metal with an imitation dial on the front face. Like the toy dolls these were the cheapest of their kind, there being rather more elaborate – and expensive – types that do not appear in Scotland, or indeed, very much at all outside London. Nevertheless, that toys were distributed and sold so far from their point of manufacture is instructive. While the rattles previously discussed could be seen as part of a wider category of affordable trinkets, it seems remarkable that it was considered profitable to transport and sell both these dolls and watches some distance from the point of manufacture. It suggests that the wish to purchase toys was widespread throughout the social scale, and that people had the financial means to do so.

The subject matter of these toys is also intriguing. For the period in question, pocket watches were still a novelty for even the prosperous middle classes. At the social level at which these toys must have been popular, it seems unlikely that anyone would have owned a real watch, although the desirability of such toys has been suggested as an instinctive attraction to an object at the forefront of technological innovation.[19] This certainly seems the case, but objects like this point perhaps to something else in terms of what their adult counterparts signified; like the rattles which mimicked those in silver, these toy watches relied on

19 Egan, *Playthings*, 12.

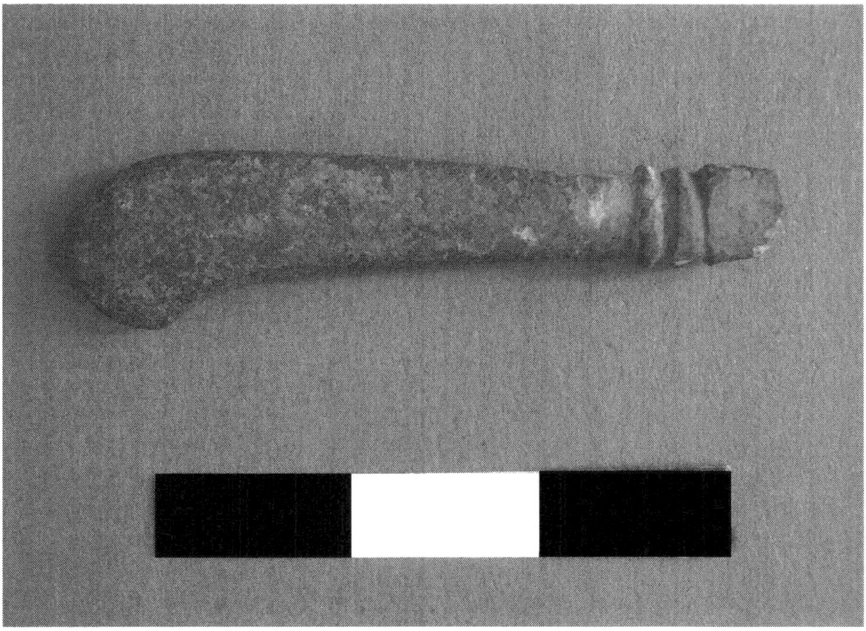

4.5 Fragmentary bronze table knife from Fortrose, Groam House Museum.

knowledge of the real thing for their effectiveness. Both types of objects reference a social milieu to which their users may not have belonged but which they (or their parents) recognized. To the adult males who carried them, a pocket watch was a symbol of social and financial status, a reference which would have been highly effectively articulated in the 'ludic reality' of child's play.

While toy dolls appear to have been the playthings of younger children, watches suggest something different, objects associated with older children who were aware of the adult world that they were soon to join. More specifically, they were objects associated with particular adult roles or behaviours. These same social concerns can be seen in a toy knife from Fortrose, recovered as part of a wider collection of post-medieval refuse (Plate 4.5). Made from copper alloy, it is an accurate depiction of cutlery from c.1750 and a rare and unusual survival; only three others are known from London, and toy cutlery itself rarely appears before this point.[20] Such objects appear to belong to a wider category of miniature household goods, items that were manufactured throughout the early modern period and that seem to have been intended as playthings for girls. Other examples include miniature kitchen implements and assorted domestic miniatures. A group of girls are depicted playing with similar items in a Dutch

[20] Forsyth and Egan, *Toys, Trifles and Trinkets*, 135.

print of 1625.[21] However, these artefacts that reflect the domestic arena can also be considered within a broader context, for we should note that miniature cutlery of this type could be easily used to teach table manners to both genders.[22] The appearance of these toys mirrored the wider use of individual knives and forks (and the necessary mores and manners), which became increasingly common from c.1725 onwards.[23] In this context, this knife is not so much a simple instructional toy, but – as new goods became increasingly available – one freighted with aspirations of class and consumer society.

Toys Produced in Scotland

Beyond toys manufactured in London or on the Continent, there is also some evidence for toy production in Scotland in the seventeenth and eighteenth centuries. This comprises objects while if not distinctly Scottish, are unusual and cannot be paralleled anywhere else in the British Isles. An example of this is a flat figure of a man with a falcon found in Culross, Fife (see Plate 4.3 above). The figure is damaged but is fashionably dressed in a hunting coat, the style of which – with buttoned back lapels and turnbacks on the skirts – indicates a date c.1750; the cross-hatching on the rear of the coat was likely an attempt to emulate the lace fashionable on contemporary hunting coats. The figure is not a triumph of the mould-cutter's art, and it can be seen where the maker tired of the intricate detailing of the body and depicted the arm as a simple right angle, the bird bearing more resemblance to a sickly pigeon than a bird of prey. More importantly, it is an unusual subject, rural rather than urban, and, as a type not paralleled further afield and not professionally made, it suggests production by a jobbing artisan to appeal to a local milieu. As both a rural subject and one that depicted the genteel (and perhaps, aspirational) pastime of falconry, the object was perfectly at home amongst the burgesses of Fife.

A similarly singular toy is a lead alloy mount from Ayr that imitates the firing mechanism for a flintlock gun, intended to be fitted to a wooden stock to make a toy gun (Plate 4.6). The mount is an accurate representation of a flintlock mechanism at full-cock, with the frizzen and pan closed and ready. An unusual feature allows this example to be dated closely; the sharply angled face at the rear of the cock is characteristic of a doglock, a variation of a flintlock with a simple external safety catch that was in use in the seventeenth century, principally by cavalry during the War of the Three Kingdoms. This is the only example of this toy known, but it can be paralleled by a series of similar finds in England, copper alloy miniatures of contemporary firearms that were designed to fire a small

21 This engraving by Jacob Cats is in the possession of Museum Boijmans Van Beuningen, Rotterdam and is reproduced in Forsyth and Egan, *Toys, Trifles and Trinkets*, 187.

22 Forsyth and Egan, *Toys, Trifles and Trinkets*, 134.

23 Weatherill, *Consumer Behaviour*, 35–6.

4.6 Lead alloy doglock from a seventeenth-century toy gun found in Ayr, North Ayrshire Museum Service.

charge of gunpowder and that date to the early to mid-seventeenth century.[24] From the medieval period onwards, military toys were mainly restricted to depictions of knights and a chivalric ideal. These more utilitarian implements of warfare, however, largely coincided with a period of civil conflict. Of all the toys discussed here, this toy gun seems perhaps the most timeless, yet also one that references directly the weapons that adult males used in contemporary warfare.[25] Both the Scottish and English examples are largely concerned with doglocks and pistols, technically advanced weapons that were the preserve of elite troops such as cavalry, which may have served as an additional cachet to those who played with them. While the ludic reality of play may have helped children live through a period of conflict, the existence of such toys might also reflect the idea of a popular engagement with the politics and causes of the war, an area that has been of increasing interest to historians.[26] Both the Culross figure and the Ayr

24 Forsyth and Egan, *Toys, Trifles and Trinkets*, 87.

25 For a discussion of medieval English children's battles and games during the civil unrest of Simon de Montfort versus the Lord Edward, Richard II versus Henry IV, and Wyatt's rebellion during Mary's reign, see Clare Valente, 'Children of Revolt: Children's Lives in the Age of Simon de Monfort', in J.T. Rosenthal (ed.), *Essays on Medieval Childhood: Responses to Recent Debates* (Donington, 2007), 94.

26 David Underdown, 'The Problem of Popular Allegiance in the English Civil War', *Transactions of the Royal Historical Society*, 5th ser. 31 (1981), 69–94.

4.7 Wheel from a locally made imitation of a London toy from Culross, Fife Cultural Trust.

doglock are single finds, but it is clear that they too must have been produced in some numbers. It is possible to say this as the details of both objects make it clear that they were cast from a cut-stone mould like the artefacts previously discussed. This investment of effort would only have been worthwhile if the intention was to manufacture a small production run of objects, perhaps a few hundred, as a case of local artisans responding to local needs and desires.

That other imported toys were in circulation can be seen from another find from Culross, a copy of a well-known class of London toys. Comprising now only a solitary carriage wheel (Plate 4.7), this was a rather crude copy of a series of toy carriages and chasses of late seventeenth- and eighteenth-century dates, usually depicted with a fashionably dressed occupant.[27] As with the watches, the real-world coach belonged to a distinct and separate social sphere from those who would have made and played with its toy replicas, but such finds illustrate a continuing interest with that which was modern, desirable or aspirational. In that sense the carriage wheel might be said to be a fitting companion to the figure of the falconer discussed earlier.

Another instance of local production can be seen with a pair of toy soldiers recovered in the area between Fort George and the nearby village of Ardersier (Plate 4.8). Both figures have been cast from the same mould, and are a detailed,

[27] Forsyth and Egan, *Toys, Trifles and Trinkets*, 316.

4.8 Two mid-eighteenth-century toy soldiers from Ardersier, Inverness Museum and Art Gallery.

though amateurish, depiction of British Army uniform from c.1750 until the late 1760s. The attention to detail is such that the soldiers are depicted with clubbed hair – which only became fashionable in the 1750s – and they are shown in the drill position, 'Under Arms', familiar from manuals of arms of the period. It is perhaps no coincidence that the uniform is one that was worn when construction first started at Fort George. Soldiers would have been a natural source of interest in the immediate area. That the toys date from the same time as the construction, and that they are found only in the immediate area of the fort, suggests strongly that they were intended to meet a very sudden and very local need. Their accurate depiction suggests first-hand familiarity with the subject matter and an expectation that those who played with them were equally discerning. Their appearance indicates they were made by pressing a carved wooden master-figure into a clay mould, suggesting opportunist production by a local or perhaps a soldier. In this case, the relative crudity raises the possibility of home-made toys for those who could otherwise not afford them.

Although primarily a local product, these military figures parallel a wider British trend. Toy soldiers began to appear in quantity in the eighteenth century.[28] Although quaint to contemporary eyes, these figures depicted a modern British army, having shrugged off the last vestiges of Marlburian drill and dress

[28] Forsyth and Egan, *Toys, Trifles and Trinkets*, 143.

after Culloden. They appear as the army did at its greatest public triumphs of Minden, Quebec and Plassey. This by itself might suggest the popularity of such toys, but the Scottish context is particularly interesting. None of these examples depict Highland or Scottish soldiers, but content themselves with standard British uniform. Preconceptions aside, there seems no reason why redcoats should not have been popular toys in Scotland. The British army had neither the manpower nor the political taste to be an instrument of repression in Scotland,[29] and authors like MacKillop have usefully analysed the relationship between the Highlander and the army as one of mutual opportunity rather than repression.[30] A military career was far from the stereotype of a last resort for the desperate, shiftless and criminally disposed; nor should we make the assumption that the civilian population regarded the army as a hostile and alien presence.[31] At Fort George in particular, there are records of interaction and commerce between the garrison and the local population.[32]

A final category of toy to be considered is remarkable not just for uniformity of type, but in having a distribution that covers Scotland from the south-west maritime Lowlands to the northern Highlands. These objects consist of a class of miniature tools, mainly axes, and are also exceptional in that all show evidence of amateur production; they were made in an open mould by creating the shape of the toy in clay or sand and simply pouring in lead to form the object (Plate 4.9). This is a marked contrast with the objects discussed previously; it was awkward, slow, and could only produce objects one at a time. The mode of production was also simple and required no specialist skills; it is likely these objects were produced by family members for their children. That these objects were not produced or traded in large numbers makes their ubiquity and uniformity of distribution all the more remarkable.

The evidence for a class of miniature tools is unique to Scotland – they appear hardly at all elsewhere, with finds from London being restricted to a saw and a pair of shears.[33] It seems that this class of objects was home-made precisely because similar toys were not produced in the wider (either European or British) context. The rationale of these objects can be seen clearly in a miniature hammer from Linlithgow; with a flat octagonal face, ball peen, and large swelling handle, it would be recognizable amongst the artisans of the burgh economy (Plate 4.10). It is an accurate representation of the standard metalworkers' hammer depicted on the arms of the guilds of hammermen. Equally, the range of axes represented can be paralleled to the broader categories of post-medieval tools and include

29 Victoria Henshaw, 'A Reassessment of the British Army in Scotland, from the Union to the '45', *Northern Scotland* 2:1 (2011), 1–21.

30 A. MacKillop, *More Fruitful than the Soil: Army, Empire and the Scottish Highlands, 1715–1815* (East Linton, 2000).

31 Stuart Campbell, 'Defence and Defensibility: The Material Culture of the Volunteer Movement in Scotland 1794–1815', *ROSC* 23 (2011), 72–93.

32 J. Sinclair (ed.), *Statistical Account of Scotland* 21 vols (Edinburgh, 1791–9), iv, 91.

33 Forsyth and Egan, *Toys, Trifles and Trinkets*, 312.

4.9 Home-made lead axe from New Galloway.

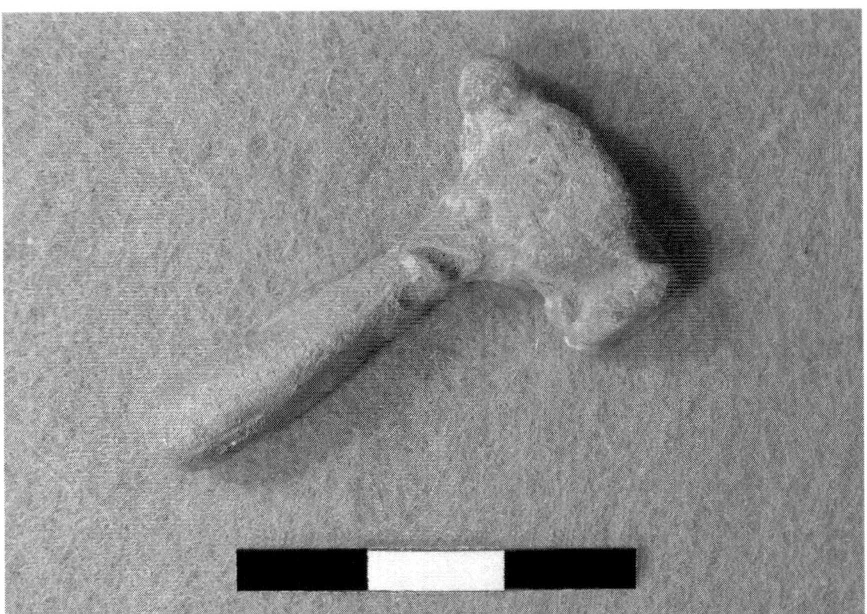

4.10 Home-made lead metalworker's hammer from Linlithgow.

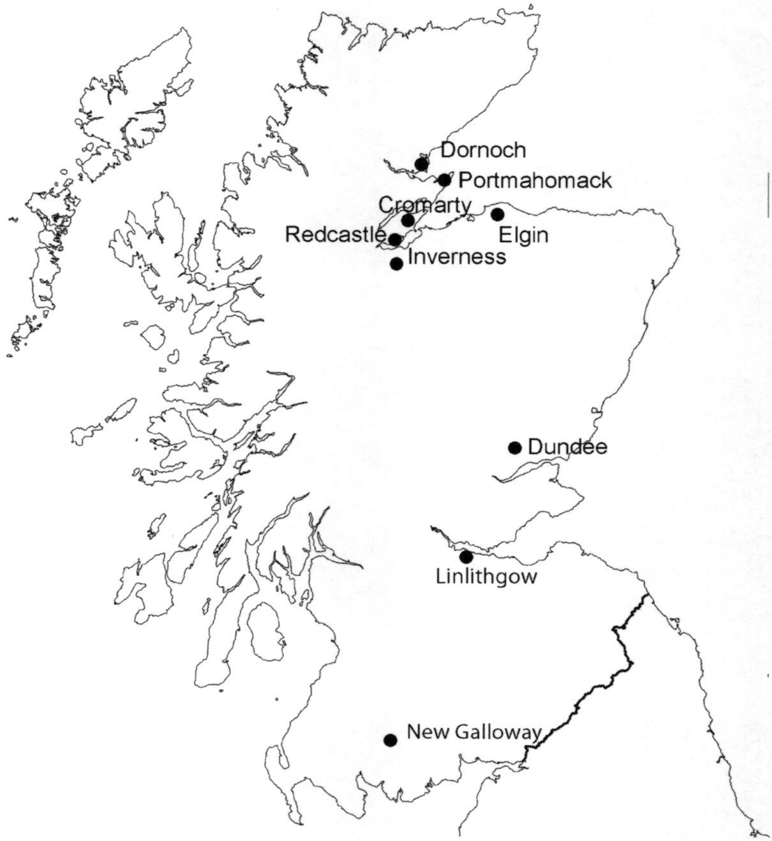

4.1 The mapped findspots of home-made lead alloy toys.

those associated with skilled workmen, such as coopers' axes.[34] Overall, this class of artefact corresponds to those objects associated with the skilled trades and crafts of the period.

It seems no coincidence that the findspot of these objects correlates to the seventeenth-century distribution of burghs (Map 4.1).[35] It certainly seems the case that these toys appear in those areas where the attraction of apprenticeship and entry to a skilled trade were most obvious. These were clearly not functional tools any more than toy watches could tell the time, but the symbolic value is equally

[34] Useful comparative sources for dating and identifying these are the tools and symbols used on the armorial bearings and other regalia of the guilds and Incorporations. There are also sources that provide a useful snapshot into the appearance of 'pre-industrial' tools, such as R.A. Salaman, *Dictionary of Tools Used in the Woodworking and Allied Trades, c. 1700–1970* (London, 1975).

[35] Some caution is required here, as by this point burghs were widespread.

powerful; they represented an aspiration, not least by associating certain skills or behaviours with an adult ideal. They were as attractive to a male child who lived in the vicinity as they were suggestive to hopeful parents. With an emphasis on work and skills they conceivably speak to a work ethic, and in a minor way they might indicate one change a burgh had on the culture of its hinterland, a social rather than primarily legal or economic relationship.

There is also a marked distinction between these home-made toys and the commercially produced examples whose analysis has comprised the bulk of this essay. Those commercially produced objects are almost always socially aspirational, referencing the possessions and behaviours of those who were at least notionally well-to-do. These home-made tools on the other hand were strictly vocational, referencing the skills or professions that would have ensured social mobility from the lower rungs of the social ladder. In itself, this distinction is perhaps the most useful resolution of the question for whom these objects were made and intended, and who might have wished or afforded them. It should be remembered also that the only other toys that were home-made are the toy soldiers from Ardersier. These objects reflected the premodern culture in which they were produced by emphasizing the traditional routes of apprenticeships, guilds or military service as an escape from labouring or agricultural work.

Conclusion

The exploration of children's material culture adds depth and complexity to our understanding of consumption and the circulation of goods within the Scottish economy. Overall, the primary evidence suggests that for the early modern period children's playthings were reasonably common, whether they were imported from Europe or elsewhere in the British Isles, copies of imports, or items produced to meet local demands. The preponderance of examples from Fife (and particularly Culross) may be representative rather than coincidental (Map 4.2). As an area of well-known historic importance, it has attracted a particular intensity of metal-detecting and the examples discovered seem typical of a reasonably prosperous area. That parents wished to procure toys for their children and had the means to do so might by itself be a useful antidote to the still-common idea of the Scottish seventeenth century as uniquely gloomy and bloody. It is necessary, however, to temper this picture; as was mentioned previously, far more elaborate versions of some of the toys here are known from London and elsewhere, and include three dimensional toy watches and dolls with moving parts. These are wholly absent from Scotland, as are the more elaborate and, one presumes, costly toys such as the miniature working firearms. The most persuasive explanation for such toys being made and sold in London is that by the seventeenth century the city was of a sufficient size and prosperity to merit it. By contrast, the simpler toys found in Scotland, most particularly the dolls and watches, are of the type commonly found in less prosperous and rural areas of England. This point can be developed further: while the seventeenth century might be said to represent

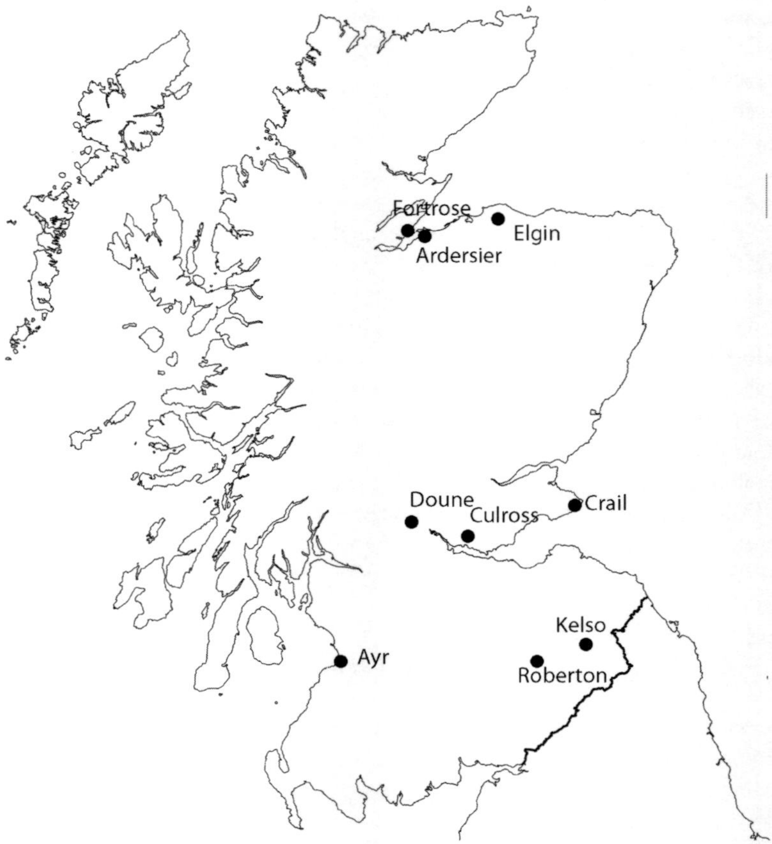

4.2 The mapped findspots of imported and professionally made toys and objects discussed in the text.

the point where these toys appear in Europe in large numbers, manufactured toys are known well before this point and can be traced to the late fifteenth and sixteenth centuries. None of these earlier toys are known from Scotland, and as can be seen here, the earliest examples appear when a wider category of consumer objects became tradable and affordable. This is not to retreat to the cliché of early modern Scotland as a wretched and poor place, but rather to make a wider point that toys were part of a larger category of consumer goods from tobacco boxes to hair pins. While many of these objects were caught up with social and material aspiration, the same object which may have been common in prosperous circles might also have been occasionally within the means of poorer families. Certainly when considering finds like the dolls or toy watches it is hard to see how they could have been made cheaper to produce, in terms both of the minimum metal or effort expended by the maker. The gross of dolls that was listed in the *Book of*

Customs and Valuations at the start of this chapter had a total value of £3. This works out to 5d per doll, and given what we know of both wages and the cost of basic items of sustenance in seventeenth-century Scotland, it is a challenge to assert that such objects were available only to those of a certain class.[36] It might be more accurate to say that these were objects designed to be affordable to as wide a range of people as possible, and in their basic complexity and type they appear to represent objects aimed at a spectrum of tastes and means.

While the survival of such fragile objects is inevitably patchy, they are generally of a type that would only have been profitable to make or trade in quantity. The findspots of many of these toys are associated with burghs or their hinterlands, and it seems fair to assume that they were imported and sold through local traders. The two identical dolls from Falkland and Lundin suggest that a further means of distribution was sale by itinerant peddlers and at market sites. These distributions tally well with what we know of such activity in Fife.[37] The toy soldiers from Ardersier were produced for an immediate local market, a resolutely working class milieu which did not involve burghs or a prosperous middle class. All told then, it seems that toys of this nature could be both affordable and widespread.

In addition to enriching our understanding of consumption, an examination of children's material culture has much to offer our understanding of the experiences of childhood and parental expectations of children. Toys were playthings, but they were also desired as educational tools. The early modern period witnessed a wide range of both Scottish and European writings concerned with religious or moral instruction, the practical aspects of education, and the wider concerns of how children were raised within the family. While historical work has naturally focussed on the literary traces of this debate, physical evidence of this instructional culture also survives. An example is the fifteen miniature bronze guns cast for the future King Charles II in 1638 and 1639 and now held by the Royal Armouries in the Tower of London. Like the pistols mentioned earlier, these were functional miniatures, and were intended to interest and instruct the future king in the arts of war.[38] Miniature cannon do appear as Scottish finds; many are slightly later than the scope of this volume, yet they do also have reasonable seventeenth-century precedents as toys, although those which can be identified would clearly have been expensive pieces.[39]

How such toys were used and the wider purpose behind them can be seen also with an unusual suite of toys from the castle of Middelburg-in-Flanders, which consists of a set of imitation sacramental items including chalice, paten, incense burner and holy water stoup. There are a number of other sets known

[36] A.J.S. Gibson and T.C. Smout, *Prices, Food and Wages in Scotland 1150–1780* (Cambridge, 1995).

[37] A. Fenton and R. Leitch, 'Itinerant Traders in Scotland', *ROSC* 22 (2010), 18–35.

[38] A.V.B. Norman and G.M. Wilson, *Treasures from the Tower of London: An Exhibition of Arms and Armour* (Norwich, 1982), 105.

[39] Van de Baart, *Opgravingen in Amsterdam*, 469.

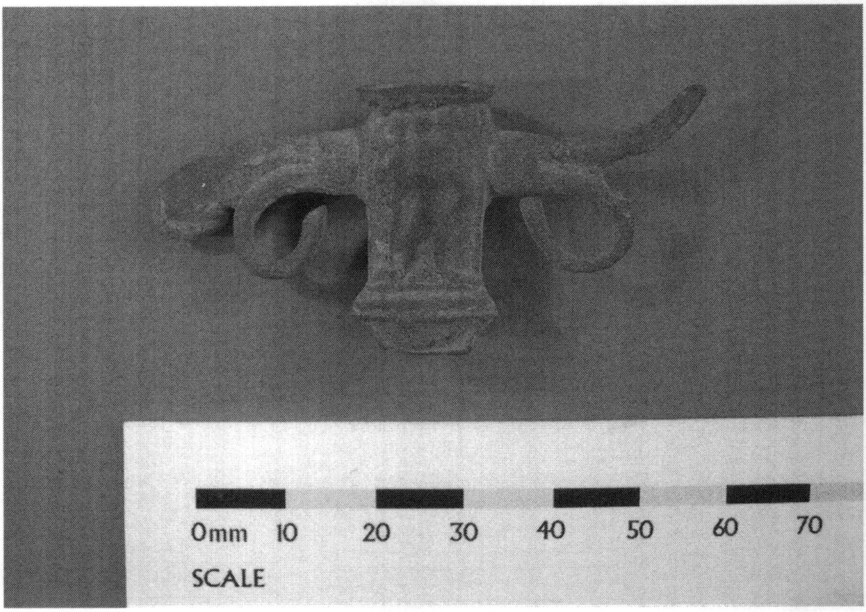

4.11 Hilt from a miniature sword, Culross, Fife Cultural Trust.

from Flanders and their use is described in accounts which indicate they were common toys in Catholic families, where children were encouraged to play with religious toys and mimic the rituals of the sacraments.[40] This is a clear case where miniature objects have an intrinsic educational aim. Granted, children might not intellectualize their play, but the value of the repetitive nature of play in providing training and instruction was widely recognized and practised in early modern Europe.[41] Overall these objects point to a process of learning through play, seen perhaps as an effective way to teach children on the cusp of the 'age of reason'. By using play to encourage and develop reflexive interests and behaviours, one can train up children in their adult roles.

Beyond specific examples of toys, other objects for children had a similar intention. One particular item which crosses these categories is another find from Fife, the remains of a small sword now comprising the cast brass hilt of a style that dates it to around 1730 (Plate 4.11).[42] The hilt has been designed to accept

[40] W. de Clerq et al., 'Living in Times of War: Waste of c. 1600 from Two Garderobe Chutes in the Castle of Middleburg-in-Flanders (Belgium)', *Post Medieval Archaeology* 41:1 (2007), 32–3.

[41] Larson, 'Certain childeplayes', 69.

[42] J.D. Alward, *The Small-Sword in England, its History, its Forms, its Makers, and its Masters* (London, 1946), 63.

the tang of a metal blade, meaning it was once a functional and accurate weapon. However, the overall size leaves no doubt that this must have been intended for a child. This is a comparatively simple weapon, and the construction was certainly within the means of any cutler or metalsmith. Similar swords were used as dress accessories for young males, not least to accompany the ritual of breeching when they abandoned the dress of infancy for conspicuously male attire.[43] The use of these miniature swords can be compared to another item of dress equally lacking in practical function, namely the codpieces frequently worn by adult and pre-pubescent males in the sixteenth century. With no practical function, they could denote a nascent social and gender identity that was distinct from the gender neutral garb of the early modern infant.[44] In this sense the sword was the badge of a man as well as an implement whose use demanded the bearer acquire certain behaviours and skills. This aspiration to the status of a man has some bearing on the other objects discussed, for if a small sword was an attractive symbol to a young male then it is likely that a toy watch was also appealing, representing the same mix of cultural knowledge and attendant aspiration. Or indeed, for either sex, miniature cutlery was a symbol of culture and manners. This is not to suggest these objects functioned as a crude imprinter of gender specific behaviour, but rather that they had a more metaphysical role, concerned with a wider social ideal of gender and aspiration that bridged the gap between social behaviour and formal education.[45] Just as play could occupy a liminal zone between real life and a ludic (and lucid) reality, so these objects could act as symbols in that similarly transitional zone between adulthood and infancy.

Like the writings of the period, these objects show a concern not just for children's needs, but also a concern with the adults that they would become. It is simplistic to define this as merely learning through play, for items like miniature swords suggest instead a wider concept of using material culture to socialize through behaviour. One can imagine also that display of these objects in public play bolstered the image of the family as a whole. This may be related to what overall seems a very materialist culture, where rattles and toy watches reference both the actual toys of upper-class children and the expensive possessions of their parents. Nevertheless, the concept of learning through play or imitation suggests a profound understanding of children's needs far removed from any conception of them as miniature adults, although they are clearly being treated as adults-in-waiting. This seems not so much an adult annexing of play for the sake of

43 The Victoria and Albert Museum has a similar sword in silver, accession number 141–1889. For further discussion of the custom of young children wearing skirts regardless of gender and the significance of older boys wearing breeches, see Chapters 3 and 6 in this collection.

44 C.C. Frick, 'Boys to Men: Codpieces and Masculinity in Sixteenth-Century Europe', in Miller and Yavneh (eds), *Gender and Early Modern Constructions of Childhood*, 157–9.

45 For a discussion of the role of material culture, education, and aspiration for the later eighteenth century, see Deborah Simonton, 'Economy', in Elizabeth Foyster and James Marten (eds), *A Cultural History of Childhood and Family: In the Age of Enlightenment* (Oxford, 2014), 64–7.

education, but – as with the objects from Middelburg-in-Flanders – a recognition that both education and play were natural outlets for children.[46] While it is natural to assume that these were items bought by parents for their children, it is clear also that these were objects intended to be attractive to children. Given the age at which children might start working, and the age at which many of these objects might prove attractive, it is worth raising the question of whether children might buy these objects for themselves, thus cutting out the arbiter of parental approval.

All the objects explored in this essay blur the boundaries between work, education and play, sharing the same philosophy of 'ludic decorum' regardless of which social class they may have been intended for. This by itself suggests that the wider concepts of childhood, play and education disseminated in writings of the period had found a fairly wide acceptance regardless of social class. This material culture evidence represents an engagement with a wider cultural ideal of what childhood was for and how it should be experienced. In particular, it might be said that society used childhood as a vehicle to articulate wider cultural ideas and concerns. These cultural ideas were given literal form via the material fruits of cheaply obtained and manufactured goods. As well as the European aspects there are also specifically Scottish concerns, and the toys found are distinct in reflecting what was a major focus in the immediate life of many families, the burgh economy, and the skilled trades that sustained them and their economic and social hinterlands. At the same time, it suggests cultural concerns that were informed but not confined to the upper classes, and those toys that are most impressively out of place – such as the cutlery from Fortrose – are those most easily associated with middle-class aspirations. What is most obvious, perhaps, is that the type and form of toys suggest that the stark division between work and leisure which is clear to modern eyes did not exist in the early modern period, although the distinction between adult and child was easily marked. Most of all, these objects demonstrate a sympathetic understanding of childhood itself, by equipping children with objects that allowed them to interact with the adult world on their own terms. They were objects through which children mediated their understanding of the adult world and negotiated their entry to that same place.

46 For more on the perceived 'nature' of children, see Chapter 6 in this collection.

Part II

Representations of the Young

5

Clann *and Clan: Children of the Gaelic Nobility c.1500–c.1800*

Anne Frater

Childhood in Gaelic medieval and early modern Scotland was probably not substantially different to the rest of the country, in that access to education was very much dependent on both social class and gender. Those records that survive, even those from the oral tradition, tend to focus on the higher strata of society, and there is little, if any, evidence of the lot of a low-born child. However, sources such as the *Register of the Privy Council of Scotland*, and writers such as Samuel Johnson, give a glimpse of some specific areas where an aristocratic childhood north of the Highland line was significantly different from that of the Lowlands, even as late as the second half of the eighteenth century. The bonds of kinship, clan solidarity and cohesion, and continuity of the chiefly lineage are given prominence: the clan was the foundation on which Highland society was built, and the *clann*, or children, ensured its future prospects.

Muime to *Dalta*: Foster-Mothers to Foster-Children

One feature of Gaelic society that sets it apart is the tradition of fosterage. While this was mainly used as a means of cementing clan alliances or of ensuring loyalty within the clan, with the chief or clan noble entrusting the care and upkeep of his child to another, there is some evidence in Gaelic literature that the ties of fosterage sometimes superseded the ties of blood for those involved. Fosterage was no ad hoc, casual arrangement: '[It] was a socio-political arrangement often used by chiefs to ensure continuation of close relations with the head of a cadet branch, a neighbouring clan or one of his own *fine*.'[1] Contracts were drawn up which stated the rights and responsibilities of both parties in some detail. On 29 April 1510, the following contract was agreed:

> Obligation by Johne McNeill Vreik in Stronferna, and Gregoure his brother, to receive Coleyne Campbell, lawful third son to Coleyne Campbell, the oldest son and heir of Sir Duncan Campbell of Glenurquhay, knight, in fostering, and to give him a bairn's part of gear; and giving the said Sir Duncan and his heirs their

[1] Alison Cathcart, '"Inressyng of kyndnes, and renewing off thair blud": The Family, Kinship and Clan Policy in Sixteenth-Century Scottish Gaeldom', in E. Ewan and J. Nugent (eds), *Finding the Family in Medieval and Early Modern Scotland* (Aldershot, 2008), 129.

> bonds of Manrent [bond of loyalty and protection] and Calps [payment of cattle], that is, the best aucht in their houses in the times of their decease; the said Sir Duncan and Coleyne his son being bound to defend the said John and Gregour in the lands of Stronferna, and the rest of the 'rowmis' [landholdings] they possess, as law will.[2]

This was not an empty honour bestowed on a close ally or a faithful retainer. Moreover, the foster family was not always of the same social status as the child being fostered, but was often on the lower levels of nobility, or ordinary clan members.

The fosterers were obliged to provide for the child in their care, giving him his share of the 'bairn's part'[3] or portion of cattle, which was sometimes, but not always, matched by the parent, with the increase of the cattle also belonging to the foster-child. The above agreement also makes clear that the child is to receive the best of the foster-father's belongings after his death. In this case, what the foster-parents have to gain from the arrangement is protection. Other agreements have a gift of stock given by the child's parents, which had to be matched by the foster-parent, but always with the increase going to the child. It should be noted, in regard to some of the songs that will be discussed below, that the child's grandfather is mentioned in the contract, as he was evidently still alive and head of the clan when the contract was drawn up. The child is important as the grandson of Sir Duncan, and it is to Sir Duncan initially that the manrent and calps are to be paid.

A contract from 1580 is interesting in that the terms have been adapted to take account of the possible death of the child placed in fosterage. This implies that, to some extent, the children were not seen as individuals, but as interchangeable 'children of the chief', even across gender lines:

> Contract between Duncane Campbell fiar of Glenurchay on the one part and his native servant Gillecreist Makdonchy Duff V'Nokerd and Katherine Neyn Douill Vekonchy his spouse on the vther part whereby the said Gillecreist and his spouse bind themselves to take in fostering Duncane Campbell son to the said Duncane to be sustained by them in meat drink and nourishment till he be sent to the schools … and to sustain him at the schools with reasonable support, the said father and foster father giving between them of makhelve[4] guddis … the value of two hundred merks of kye and two horses or two mares worth forty merks; these goods with their increase to pertain to the said bairn … and in case the said

[2] C. Innes (ed.), *The Black Book of Taymouth; With Other Papers from the Breadalbane Charter Room* (Edinburgh, 1855), 179. This contract, which is said to be the oldest fosterage contract extant, is also discussed in W.S. Curle, 'Notice of Four Contracts, or Bonds of Fosterage', *PSAS* 30 (1896), 13.

[3] In Scots law, this is a share of the moveable estate of a deceased person that was divided between the children, Curle, 'Notice of Four Contracts', 15.

[4] The introduction to the *Black Book of Taymouth* (p. xvii) questions the meaning of the word 'makhelve', which occurs in many contracts of fosterage. Perhaps it is a combination of 'mac' and 'shealbh', son and possessions or goods, which would make sense in this context. Curle, 'Notice of Four Contracts', 14–15, defines it as a small herd of cattle.

bairn shall die before he be sent to the schools, his father shall send another of his children lass or lad to be fostered in his stead, who shall succeed to the first bairn's goods.[5]

There is also evidence of fosterage bonds continuing over two generations, as happened with Duncan Campbell of Glenorchy and Duncan Campbell of Dunstrone in 1584:

> … Duncane Campbell of Glenurquhay on that ain part and Duncane Campbell of Duntrone and Agnas Nikolleane his spouse … forasmekle as the said Duncane Campbell of Glenurquhay being of befoir foster son to the said Duncane Campbell of Duntrone … The said Agnas with express consent and assent of the said Duncane hir spouse presentlie has receaueit and receaueis Coleine Campbell sone and air to the said Duncane Campbell of Glenurquhay in fostering.[6]

This contract also serves to show that the bond between a foster-parent and foster-child was not considered to be merely a business arrangement, and that the ties thus formed were often as strong as those of actual kinship. Apart from written legal documents, evidence from Gaelic song shows that foster-parents cherished their fosterlings as if they were their own, showing pride in their later achievements and lamenting any misfortune that befell them. Most of the extant songs of this type were composed by the *muime* (foster-mother) to her *dalta* (foster-child).

Most numerous among such songs are laments, such as the poignant 'Cairistìona' (c.1600), which is unusual in that the subject is female rather than male.[7] The song begins with the bardess calling to the dead woman:

Nach fhreagair thu, Chairistìona?
Nach fhreagair thu, chuilein dhìlis?
Nam freagradh gun cluinninn fhìn thu.

Will you not answer, Christina?
Will you not answer, my faithful pup?
If you should answer I would hear you.[8]

Then she sets the scene for her lament:

Chì mi luingeas air Caol Ìle
Tighinn an coinneamh Cairistìona,
Chan ann gu banais a dhèanamh
Ach g' a cur san talamh ìseal,
Fo leacan troma gu dìlinn.

[5] *Black Book of Taymouth*, 223. See Chapter 3 in this collection for a later example of a seventeenth-century fosterage contract involving the Glenorchy Campbells.
[6] *Black Book of Taymouth*, 228. This contract is also discussed in Cathcart, 'Inressyng of kyndnes', who points out the fact that it is Agnes who is named as receiving the child.
[7] Examples of poems of this type addressed to a male subject are 'A Mhic Iain Mhic Sheumais' (1601) and 'Tàladh Dhòmhnaill Ghuirm' (c.1610).
[8] K.C. Craig, *Òrain luaidh Màiri nighean Alasdair* (Glasgow, 1949), 87.

I can see a galley on the sound of Islay
Coming to meet Christina,
Not to arrange a wedding
But to put her low in the ground,
Under heavy slabs forever.[9]

The identity of the composer of the song is in no doubt, or at least her relationship to Cairistìona is made clear by the words 'gura mi do mhuime chìcheadh' ('I am your wet-nurse'). There are not enough clues in the text of this poem to allow one to identify Cairistìona, although references to Glencoe and Islay would indicate that she was a MacDonald, and of an important branch of that clan. As far as I have been able to ascertain, this is the only song to a female *dalta* that has survived and, for this reason, as well as for the obvious tender emotion displayed by the bardess, it is worthy of note.

An undated later song that gives a telling insight into the relationship between *muime* and *dalta* is that composed by Màiri Nic Phàil to Eachann Òg Maclean of Tiree, who was drowned between Tiree and Barra. This song uses some of the formulaic imagery of bardic elegy, such as 'Chaill mi ùbhlan mo chrann' ('My tree has lost its apples'), but also contains some strikingly imaginative similes of the bardess's own:

Gun do sgaoil e mo shic,
'S tha mo chridhe 'na lic,
'S e mo ghnàths bhi air mhisg gun òl.

It has ripped my belly,
And my heart is a stone,
I go about as if drunk without liquor.[10]

What is most interesting about this poem, however, is not the imagery, but the fact that it was composed as a lament to her foster-son when her own son was drowned in the same incident. Although the song runs to nine stanzas, her own son is mentioned only in the very last one:

Gun robh cuilein mo rùin,
Fear na camagan dlùth,
'S e a' seòladh ri d' ghlùin,
Gus 'n do dhalladh a shùil
Ann am mire nan sùgh gun deò.

My beloved child,
He of the thick-set curls.
Sailing by your side,
Until his eyes dulled
Lifeless in the dancing billows.[11]

[9] The poem is given in Somhairle Mac Gill-Eain, 'Some Thoughts about Gaelic Poetry', *Transactions of the Gaelic Society of Inverness* [*TGSI*] 52 (1980–2), 303.
[10] A. Maclean Sinclair, *The Gaelic Bards from 1715–1765* (Charlottetown, 1892), 150.
[11] Sinclair, *The Gaelic Bards*, 150.

The loss of the young Maclean would undoubtedly have been seen by the clan and its followers as more important than the loss of Màiri Nic Phàil's son, but it is strange that the bardess herself seems to think in the same way; the primary subject of her lament is Eachann Òg, while the loss of her own flesh and blood is treated as being of only secondary importance. This maybe gives us insight into the importance of strong leadership to the clan as a whole, and how the collective need of the clan is given prominence over the personal needs of a mother, even by the mother herself.

Songs are a reflection of the society in which they were composed, and the importance of an heir and pride in the lineage are to the fore in some of the cradle songs from the medieval and early modern period that still survive. Such songs are almost solely the domain of the female poet: the child's mother, foster-mother, wet-nurse, or nursemaid are usually the authors. Some of these songs take the form of a *tàladh* or lullaby, praising the man that the child will be when he grows up. An example of this is 'Tàladh Choinnich Òig' ('Young Kenneth's Lullaby'), composed around 1670 and apparently addressed to Kenneth MacKenzie, Lord of Kintail:

O Mhic Choinnich fhuair thu 'n t-urram
Théid thu mach gu làidir ullamh
Dh' òladh leat fìon Baile Lunnainn
Mach go Loudie le d' chuid giullan.
...
Chan 'eil Coinneach ach 'na leanabh
Cha d' ràinig e aois a sheanair
Sealgair an fhèidh a' s na gleannaibh
Choilich dhuibh air bhàrr o mheangain

O MacKenzie you were honoured
You go out strongly armed
You would drink wine from London
Go out to Loudie with your followers.
...
Kenneth is but a child yet
He hasn't reached his grandfather's age
Hunter of the deer in the glens
And the black-cocks from the branch-tops[12]

The first stanza indicates a grown man, held in esteem by his contemporaries and old enough to drink wine and able to muster a force of men, while the second stanza given here reminds us that he is, in fact, still a child, with his grandfather being set as an example to emulate. This is in itself interesting, as it could be taken to imply that the composer considered the child's grandfather to be a better role model than his father. However, if the grandfather was still

12 John Macinnes, '*Tàladh Choinnich Òig*: Young Kenneth's Lullaby', *Scottish Studies* 7 (1963), 226.

alive and chief of the clan, the poetess is merely showing her diplomatic skills in praising him within her praise of the child.

Later on in the poem, there is exaggerated praise of young Kenneth, where his foster-mother describes his future power in terms of the number of men who would follow his call to arms:

'S lìonmhor duilleag th' air an draigheann
eadar Bealltainn agus Samhuinn.
's lìonmhor' na sin sgiath is claidheamh
'n gualainn Choinnich Òig am Brathainn.

Many are the thorns on the blackthorn
Between May and November
More plentiful than that are the shields and swords
[Standing] at the shoulder of young Kenneth of Brahan.[13]

In an age where the heir having reached maturity before the death of the chief was of great importance to the continuation and retention of clan power bases, it is perhaps not too surprising that 'Tàladh Choinnich Òig' also contains a charm put on the child in order to keep him safe from all harm:

Na dhean an gobhann an claidheamh,
Na dhean an ceàrd an ceann leathann,
'S na dhean an [fh]leisdear an t-saighead,
'Chuireas Coinneach òg 'na laidhe.

Let the smith not make the sword,
Let the craftsman not make the spearhead
And let the fletcher not make the arrow
Which will lay young Kenneth low.[14]

This (and some of the other imagery in 'Tàladh Choinnich Òig') echoes a much longer passage in the earlier 'Taladh Dhòmhnaill Ghuirm' (c.1610), which ends on a long incantatory run in which the foster-mother invokes the power of all the elements and the strength of the legendary heroes of her clan to protect her charge. Here, the bond between foster-mother and child is expressed quite clearly:

Gu 'm bheil mi dhuit   *mar tha do phiuthar,*
Mur 'eil mi 'm bàrr   *tha mi uidhir.*

I am to you as your sister
If I am not more I am equal.[15]

Changes in wider society are also reflected in Gaelic song, with a growing awareness than clan strength alone was not enough to secure territory and influence. This is evident in the song beginning 'B' fheàrr leam gun sgrìbhteadh dhuit

13 Macinnes, '*Tàladh Choinnich Òig*', 226.
14 William Mackenzie, 'Leaves from my Celtic Portfolio', *TGSI* 7 (1877–8), 118.
15 A. and A. MacDonald, *The Macdonald Collection of Gaelic Poetry* (Inverness, 1911), 35.

fearann' ('I wish that your lands would be written for you'), probably composed sometime before 1550. Although the child himself is not named in this song, there is enough evidence to identify him. The lands mentioned suggest that he is a Cameron of Locheil, and this is proved by the naming of his ancestors:

Ogha Eobhain 's iar-ogh' Ailean
'S iar-ogh' Dhonuill Duibh bho 'n darach.

Grandson of Ewan and great-grandson of Allan
And great-grandson of Black Donald from the galley.[16]

From this information Mackellar deduced that the child

> must have been 'Eobhan Beag Mac Dho'ill 'ic Eobhain', the grandson of the famous chief Ewan Allanson. Ewan 'Beag' was born around 1522. He was the son of Ewen Allanson's eldest son Donald who died in 1537, predeceasing his father by ten years. The great great grandfather, referred to in the lullaby, must have been 'Donald dubh', the chief who fought at Harlaw in 1411.[17]

As well as providing evidence for the identity of the child, the position, if not the name, of the bardess can be deduced, as much by what she leaves out as by what she includes:

> The lullaby must have been composed by the nurse, who was one [of] the clan. Had it been the mother that composed it, she would have made loving mention of the child's father, but the nurse would ignore him as he died without attaining to the honour of being chief, and she could only feel entitled to be proud of her nursling as the offspring of a line of chiefs.[18]

This poem perhaps gives us insight into the way in which children were regarded in this period. They were precious, not in their own right, but as representatives of a noble lineage and as security for the future of the clan. Therefore, the child of the chief was not only the heir of all the noble men who had preceded him, but his existence also (it was hoped) guaranteed that the line, and therefore the strength of the clan, would continue. This perhaps underlines why Màiri Nic Phàil gave the chief's son precedence over her own child in her lament for Eachann Òg, and why the authors of 'Tàladh Choinnnich Òig' and 'Tàladh Dhòmhnaill Ghuirm' invoked higher powers to protect the children in their care. It is significant that there is virtually no description of the child himself in the Cameron poem, although at the end his nurse makes it clear that the song was sung as a lullaby to an infant of whom she was very fond:

'S bòidheach d' aodann 's caoin leam d' anail,
Socrach ciùin a rùin do chadal.

16 Mary Mackellar, 'Unknown Lochaber Bards', *TGSI* 12 (1885–6), 212.
17 Mackellar, 'Lochaber Bards', 212.
18 MacKellar, 'Lochaber Bards', 212.

Your face is beautiful to me and your breath is delightful,
Sleep peacefully and quietly, my love.[19]

The foster-mother or nurse of the heir of the Sleat family would seem to be the composer of 'Mo cheist air altram mo ghlùine' ('I love the nursling on my knee'). This is a fragmentary song, all the elements of which it is impossible to reconcile as being addressed to one person.[20] That the composer was in a position of trust within the household, overseeing the care of the son and heir, seems evident from her assertion:

Na 'm bu bhean a dheanadh lochd mi
Cha bhiodh oighre air a' chnoc Slèibhteach.

If I was a woman to do harm
There would be no heir on the hill of Sleat.[21]

This gives insight into the position of absolute trust that nursemaids held in this period, and the power that they could have wielded, if they so wished, over the future of the clan. For this reason, they were usually of the clan themselves, but not close enough to the chief to benefit from abusing their position. The fact that the comment here is made in the context of the heir of the Macdonalds of Sleat is particularly interesting, given the legend connected with the Macdonalds quitting Duntulm Castle in the first half of the eighteenth century. According to this story, the heir was being dandled by a nursemaid, but fell from a window onto the rocks below, and died instantly.[22] The subject of at least part of this poem lived much earlier, however, being possibly Donald, son of Sir James MacDonald of Sleat, who was an only child in the mid-1630s. Following the pattern that we have seen in other songs, the author is concerned with the power and position that her young charge will enjoy in adulthood, and lists the friendly clans who would rise to support him if he were in need.

***Màthair* to *Leanabh*: Birth Mothers to Children**

So far this chapter has considered fosterage and the bond between foster-parent and foster-child. Turning now to songs composed by birth mothers to their children, one of these forms an interesting counterpoint to two of the songs

19 Mackellar, 'Lochaber Bards', 212.

20 Some Gaelic songs were collaborative compositions, mainly those used for waulking the tweed or other communal work, so they do not have a single author or a single subject. However, multiple authorship is not confined to work songs. Because most Gaelic songs have come down through the oral tradition, some have later accretions, with contemporary verses added to an older original, or two separate songs with the same tune are sung together. This patchwork effect causes problems when trying to identify the original subject and/or author of a poem.

21 D.S. Thomson, *The Macdiarmid MS Anthology* (Edinburgh, 1991), 79.

22 Terry Marsh, *The Isle of Skye* (Milnthorpe, 2009), 239.

previously discussed. The seventeenth-century 'Òran do Lachainn Mac-Gilleain' ('Song to Lachlan MacLean') composed by Nic Gilleathain is possibly addressed to the Chief of Duart, but opens with a lament for her daughter. This lament takes up over half of the poem, a strong indication that the poetess considers the death of her daughter to be a loss equal to, if not greater than, the death of her own siblings:

'S mise chaill na deagh bhràithrean,
Chuir mi uile gu tràigh iad;
'S i 'n aon nighean a chràidh mi 's an uair so.

It is I who have lost the good brothers,
I sent them all across the water [for burial];
It is the one daughter who grieves me at this time.[23]

Her maternal pride in her daughter's beauty and skills, describing them in the same way as one would describe and praise the appearance and aptitude of a chief, is evident. Her praise also gives insight into the lifestyle of a noble household of the time, with a refined young lady expected to be extremely beautiful, of a steadfast nature, and an excellent seamstress:

Sùil bu mhìogaiche sealladh
Fo chaoile na mala,
Mar gum biodh an t-òl leana air na cuachan.

Beul tana dearg daite
Mu 'n deud bu leòir ceartais,
Sùil chorrach ghorm ghlas gun bhith luaineach …

Chan fheil léine mhic tighearn',
Chuireadh òganach uime,
Nach deanadh mo nighean-sa fhuaigheal.

Eye of most sparkling aspect
Under the slender eyebrow,
Like drinking ale from cups.

Slender red-hued lips
Around even teeth,
Blue-grey passionate eyes which were not fickle …

There is no lord's son's shirt,
Which a youth might don,
That my daughter could not sew.[24]

This song echoes much of the praise found in 'Cairistìona', while serving as a neat counterpart to Màiri Nic Phàil's song: here, the mother acknowledges the

23 A. Maclean Sinclair, *Na Bàird Leathanach*, 2 vols (Charlottetown, 1900), ii, 167.
24 Sinclair, *Na Bàird*, ii, 176.

deaths of adult males, who would have been more important from the point of view of the clan, but her maternal perspective gives prominence to her daughter.

It was not only fosterage that was used as a means of extending the clan power and strengthening the internal cohesion of a clan; children born outside wedlock were also important. Far from being a challenge to the authority of the legitimate heir, in an age where strength in numbers counted, these children were seen as an important addition to the chief's family and in most cases proved themselves to be important allies of the heir. Gaelic noblemen were quick to acknowledge their illegitimate children, bringing them under their guardianship and, in many cases, into their homes. Although this was a relatively common occurrence, it is clear that the wives of these noblemen were not necessarily accepting of it. An example from the last quarter of the sixteenth century tells of the origin of the Mackenzies of Coull:

> It is said that Alexander [1st Mackenzie of Coull] when quite an infant was sent home to his father, Colin of Kintail, to Brahan Castle, who consulted with his lady, Barbara … as to what he should do with the little stranger. She was naturally incensed at her husband's infidelity and the proposed addition to the family circle, and indignantly replied – 'Cuir 'sa chùil e,' that is 'put him in the ash-hole or corner'. The Baron perceived the imprudence of further offending his lady; but being naturally of a humane disposition, and anxious to act honourably to his innocent offspring, he went out with the boy, and on his return informed his lady that he had acted upon her suggestion, and left him in the *Coul.* He secretly sent Alexander to the place … called 'A' Chùil', or Coul, to be nursed and brought up there by a respectable woman who then resided there, and thus carried out to the letter, if not the spirit, of his lady's request; and at the same time performed his duty towards his afterwards distinguished son.[25]

Perhaps playing on the unashamed expansionist policies of the Clan Campbell, there is also the story told about Duncan Campbell of Glenorchy, Donnchadh Dubh na Curraic (Black Duncan of the Cowl) who died in 1631:

> He had a great many illegitimate children, and he never denied any women that came to him with a child. – One came with a large bat rolled up in a flannel, a corner of which he lifted up to see the child, when he exclaimed, 'O! 's goirid a tha eadar a bhial 's a shròn, 's olc am biatach bhios ann; bidh gu math ris!' ('O! There isn't much between his mouth and his nose. He'll be a poor eater; be good to him').[26]

The mothers of these children seemed to accept that once the child's father was married – if that was not already the case – they would have to hand their child over to the care (or otherwise) of his wife. Beathag Mhòr's song to Màrtainn a' Bhealaich, composed around 1700, concerns the child that she bore him. She had evidently been the mistress of Martin Martin and he was the father of her son, but she must have been well below him on the social scale, and thus unable to marry

25 A. Mackenzie, *History of the Clan Mackenzie* (Inverness, 1879), 440.
26 NLS, Manuscript 2135, 304.

him. This Martin was probably the eldest son of Donald Martin of Beallach in Skye, who eventually married a daughter of Lachlan Maclean of Vallay in North Uist. If this identification is correct, he would have been a nephew of the more famous Martin Martin, author of *A Description of the Western Islands of Scotland*. Beathag seems to bear Martin no grudge for not marrying her, and she even gives him some advice on his choice of wife:

Ma théid thu dh' Uibhist an eòrna
Thoir té bhòidheach dhachaidh as.

Thoir dhachaidh té shocair chiallach
Riaraicheas na caipteanan.

If you go to Uist of the barley
Take a beautiful woman home.

Take home a gentle, sensible woman
Who will satisfy the captains.[27]

This may indicate that Martin's marriage had already been arranged when Beathag composed the song, with her implicitly praising the woman who would be in charge of her son's upbringing. It would certainly have been imprudent of her to be as scathing about MacLeod women as she is, if there was a chance that one of them would be looking after the child:

Ma bheir thu bean a Sìol Leòid
Gun iarr i mòran fhasanan.

Ma bheir thu bean a Sìol Tharmoid
Marbhaidh i le macnas thu.

If you take a wife from the Macleods
She will expect everything that is in fashion.

If you take a wife from the Macleods of Harris and Dunvegan
She will kill you with wantonness.[28]

It is not known why she had such a low opinion of Macleod women, although she may have been basing her comments on experience, given that she was a native of Skye, and that the Martins were related to the Macleod chiefs of Dunvegan.[29] Despite her love for Martin, the main theme of her song is her concern for the welfare of the child, who will soon be taken from her to be brought up by his father and his new wife. This is why she takes such an interest in Martin's choice of bride, wishing misfortune on any woman who would mistreat him, but blessing a stepmother who would show him love:

27 Beathag Mhòr, 'An Cùl Bachalach', *Gairm* 9 (1954), 47.
28 Beathag Mhòr, 'An Cùl Bachalach', 47.
29 Charles W.J. Withers, 'Introduction', in *A Description of the Western Isles of Scotland* (Edinburgh, 1999), 4.

Is ma bhuaileas i le feirg e
Guma meirg thug dhachaidh i.

Is ma bhuaileas i le fuath e
Guma luath 'n a' chlachan i.

Ach ma bhuaileas i le gràdh e
Guma blàth fo d' achlais i.

And if she should chastise him out of anger
A curse on the one who brought her home.

And if she chastises him out of hatred
Let her soon be in the grave.

But if she chastises him out of love
Let her be warm in your arms.[30]

One can only imagine the heartache suffered by Beathag Mhòr at the thought of giving up her son to the care of another, even though it might be in his own interests – at least in the sense of moving higher up the social scale. This song illustrates the acceptance of illegitimacy in earlier Gaelic society. The child was acknowledged by his father, to the extent that he was to be brought up by him, and the mother does not mention any hardship or shame that she has suffered from having a child out of wedlock. Indeed, we have other Gaelic songs from this period in which a mother expresses her pride in having borne a nobleman's child, indicating that Gaelic society at this time did not disapprove of such liaisons. Here, Beathag Mhòr regrets that she cannot marry Martin herself, but she accepts the situation, and the only thing which concerns her is that Martin should choose a bride who would be kind to her son.

It has to be noted, however, that the acceptance of relationships between the nobility and lower classes only went one way. The other side of this coin is seen in the story behind 'Biodh an deoch-s an làimh mo rùin' ('Let this drink be in the hand of my beloved'), said to have been composed by a daughter of MacDonald of Clanranald who was banished to Coll for having an illegitimate child by one of her father's servants. The song, dating from around 1661, is mainly one of praise to her brother, the new chief, on his paying a visit to Coll, but in some versions the bardess also expresses her desire to go to Uist, where her son was fostered, and her gratitude to the woman who brought him up:

Mo rùn air muime na' macaobh,
Bhiodh 'ga 'n altrum air a' glùin.

My regards to the foster-mother of the sons
Who would nurse them on her knee.[31]

30 Beathag Mhòr, 'An Cùl Bachalach', 47.
31 Macdonald, *The Macdonald Collection of Gaelic Poetry*, 341.

The song is one of joy at being reunited with her brother, and at the prospect of finding her child again. The great sorrow which the bardess must have suffered on being parted from her family for so long is transformed into happiness when she realises that she is now able to return. This song also highlights the different treatment of men and women: for a nobleman to have a child by a low-born woman was nothing unusual or for either party to be ashamed of, but for a woman of noble birth to have a child by a low-born man resulted in her disgrace and at least in this instance, the man's death for his 'crime': 'Bha pàisde aig nighean Mhic 'ic Ailein ris a' ghille aig a h-athair. Chaidh an gille a a shracadh as a chèile eadar dà each' ('ClanRanald's daughter had a child by her father's servant. The servant was ripped apart between two horses').[32] It is not known what status, if any, this child was given in his or her grandfather's household, although the fact that a foster-mother had been appointed would indicate that the child, unlike the mother, had not been disowned.

It is unclear how long some of these practices carried on in the Highlands: the increasing influence of the Presbyterian church made extra-marital relationships less socially acceptable, and the chief's status relied on landownership rather than martial power. We do know, however, that the tradition of fosterage continued into the early modern period, and was still to be found when Samuel Johnson undertook his tour of the Hebrides in 1773:

> There still remains in the Islands, though it is passing fast away, the custom of fosterage. A laird, a man of wealth and eminence, sends his child, either male or female, to a tacksman, or tenant, to be fostered. It is not always his own tenant, but some distant friend that obtains this honour; for an honour such a trust is reasonably thought. The terms of fosterage seem to vary in different islands ... Children continue with the fosterer perhaps six years, and cannot, where this is the practice, be considered as burdensome.[33]

The attitude to aristocratic children in Gaelic society changed with the decline of the clan system, but it could be argued that the decline of the clan system also began with these children. After 1609, children of the Gaelic nobility were used by the government as an integral part of their plan to Anglicize (and thereby pacify) the Highlands and Islands. The Statutes of Iona, which twelve of the leading figures in the Gaelic Highlands were forced to sign, introduced a number of measures designed to curb the 'barbaritie and incivilitie' of the Highlands. While the Statutes were not altogether undesirable, with some of the measures designed to restrict the activities of those taking advantage of the custom of Highland hospitality, and to reduce the burden on the common people of maintaining the chieftain's household, the sixth statute had the effect of distancing the clan leaders from their people by taking them away from their home districts when young, ostensibly for the purpose of education:

32 J.L. Campbell, *Songs Remembered in Exile* (Aberdeen, 1990), 161.
33 Samuel Johnson and James Boswell, *Journey to the Hebrides* (Edinburgh, 1998), 119.

> Every gentleman or yeoman in the Islands possessing 'thriescore kye,' and having children, to send at least his eldest son, or, failing sons, his eldest daughter, to some school in the Lowlands, there to be kept and brought up 'quhill they may be found able sufficientlie to speik, reid, and wryte Inglische.[34]

As Kenneth MacKinnon notes:

> This enaction was the first of a succession of measures taken by the Scottish government specifically directed towards the extirpation of the Gaelic language, the destruction of its traditional culture and the suppression of its bearers.[35]

Although the Statutes of Iona did not take effect immediately throughout the Highlands and Islands, the effect of the sixth statute was felt on two levels. Firstly, it removed the future leaders of the clans from their ancestral homeland during their formative years and, secondly, it distanced them from the language and culture of the people whom they were destined to lead.[36] It produced the kind of alien clan leader described in Roderick Morison's 'Òran do Mhac Leòid Dhùn Bheagain' ('Song to MacLeod of Dunvegan'), who saw his ancestral lands as a source of income and nothing more. The Statutes were ratified by an Act of the Privy Council in 1616, where the use of children as an Anglicizing force was even more explicit:

> Therefore that they (the chiftanes and principal clannit men of Ylles') shall sent their bairnes being past the age of nyne yeires to the schollis in the Lawlandis to the effect that they may be instructit and trayned to wryte and reid and to speake Inglische; and that nane of their bairnes sall be served air unti them nor acknawlegeit nor received as tennentis to his Majestie unless they can wryte, reid and speik Inglesche.[37]

This meant that children could not inherit their ancestral lands unless they had been educated away from their ancestral language and culture. Although the Gaelic clans were not destroyed by the Statutes of Iona or the Act of 1616 by themselves, the ancient ties between chief and clan were undoubtedly weakened by their imposition.

So what was it like to be a child in early modern Gaelic Scotland? It was to be aware of one's position in society, in terms of both class and gender, but also to be aware of an old world order slowly being forced to change. The clan system, Gaelic culture, and the Gaelic language were all being purposely eroded by a government that saw them as alien and subversive. Education was being used as

34 D. Masson (ed.), *Register of the Privy Council of Scotland, vol. IX A.D. 1610–1613* [*RPC*] (Edinburgh, 1889), 28–9.

35 K. Mackinnon, *Gaelic: A Past and Future Prospect* (Edinburgh, 1991), 46. For some recent reassessments of the Statutes of Iona, see Martin MacGregor, 'The Statutes of Iona: Text and Context', *Innes Review* 57:2 (2006), 111–81; Alison Cathcart, 'The Statutes of Iona: The Archipelagic Context', *Journal of British Studies* 49:1 (2010), 4–27.

36 For further discussion of the significance of future Highland leaders being educated in Gaelic, see Chapter 3 in this collection.

37 *RPC*, x, 773–6.

a tool to erode the link between the Gaelic nobility and their followers, although the old values of blood ties and pride in ancestry had not been completely extinguished. Despite the obligations and deprivations that the status entailed, it was perhaps simpler to be the child of a commoner than the offspring of a noble, for at least then the child was brought up in its own family, by its own parents, and within the framework of its own language and culture.

6

*Depictions of Childhood in David Allan's Family Group Portraiture of the 1780s**

Nel Whiting

In the early 1780s David Allan (1744–96) produced two informal family group portraits in which Scottish children feature prominently.[1] By exploring these portraits in depth and alongside archival letters, much can be learned about constructions of elite Scottish childhood during the Scottish Enlightenment and within the context of post-Union Britain. Contrariwise, this essay also demonstrates that by exploring past historical processes, concerns and issues through the lens of children and youth, we can further nuance our understanding of important historical events. More than merely reflecting contemporaneous ideas about childhood, such images were central to the presentation, representation, and re-presentation of childhood.[2] Described by Marcia Pointon as 'visual rhetoric', portraiture played a crucial role in constructing what she calls 'the ideology of childhood' in the eighteenth century.[3] Contemporary family portraiture depicted informality in the actions of its young subjects, as children were recognized as inhabiting a distinct stage of life, yet their importance in dynastic concerns remained an essential message in these portraits.

* The author would like to thank the following for their help with this essay: Sir Patrick Hunter Blair, Christine Ewing, Jane Anderson, Peter Burman, Kate Retford, Mary Modeen, Chris Whatley, Steve Kent, the anonymous readers, and Janay Nugent and Elizabeth Ewan.

1 Both portraits are oil on canvas. The Hunter Blair portrait is on display at the National Gallery of Scotland in Edinburgh and the Atholl portrait is at Blair Castle in Perthshire. For biographical information about David Allan see Thomas Crouther Gordon, *David Allan of Alloa 1744–1795: The Scottish Hogarth* (Alva, 1951); Basil Skinner, *The Indefatigable Mr Allan: The Perceptive and Varied Work of David Allan 1744–1796. Scotland's First Genre painter* (Edinburgh, 1973); Grier Robertson Gordon, 'Scottish Scenes and Scottish Stories: The Later Work of David Allan', unpublished Ph.D. thesis, University of Glasgow (1990); Kate Retford, '"The small Domestic & conversation style": David Allan and Scottish Portraiture in the Late Eighteenth Century', *Visual Culture in Britain* 15:1 (2014), 1–27; Nel Whiting, 'Gender and National Identity in David Allan's 'small, domestic and conversation' Paintings', *JSHS* 34:1 (2014), 20–39.

2 Maria Pointon, *Hanging the Head: Portraiture and Social Formation in Eighteenth-Century England* (New Haven and London, 1993), 190–2.

3 Pointon, 'Hanging the Head', 178. For an introduction to the notion of visual rhetoric see Sonja K. Foss, 'Framing the Study of Visual Rhetoric: Towards a Transformation of Rhetorical Theory', in Charles A. Hill and Marguerite Helmers (eds), *Defining Visual Rhetorics* (Oxford, 2004), 303–13.

A society's construction of childhood does not map easily onto the lived reality of individual children, any more than a portrait can be read as a straightforward reflection of a child's life experience. In part, this is because portraits of children necessarily involved adults as much as they did their young subjects. Painted by adults, they were also commissioned by adults and reflected adult attitudes about children. In other words, the painted child embodied adult concerns, worries, hopes, and expectations for the individual depicted and, equally significantly, adult attitudes about the state of being that is childhood.[4] A distinction needs to be made between children as real, sentient beings, and childhood as a cultural construct assembled in and through various discourses, including medical, legal, literary, painted and pedagogical.[5] In this light, this essay is better understood as a history of images of Scottish childhood rather than as a history of Scottish children per se.

Where children have always been important subjects in European art history, prior to the eighteenth century their most conspicuous incarnation was as the Holy Child rather than every-day, earthly creatures. The eighteenth century saw a change in this pattern and a flourishing of child portraiture in Britain, with children depicted at the centre of family life in affective relationships with their parents.[6] By the 1780s childhood was understood as a distinct phase in life, as is evidenced by the wealth of pedagogical literature, children's literature, toys and special clothes.[7]

[4] Pointon, 'Hanging the Head', 190–2. For additional discussion of the representation of children through adult voices, see Chapter 3 in this collection.

[5] Ludmilla Jordanova, 'Children in History: Concepts of Nature and Society', in Geoffrey Scarre (ed.), *Children, Parents and Politics* (Cambridge, 1989), 3–24.

[6] For an overview and different perspectives about that artistic flourishing, see: J.C. Steward, *The New Child: British Art and the Origins of Modern Childhood, 1730–1830* (Berkeley, 1996); Dorothy Johnson, 'Engaging Identity: Portraits of Children in Late Eighteenth-Century European Art', in Anja Muller (ed.), *Fashioning Childhood in the Eighteenth Century: Age and Identity* (Aldershot, 2006), 101–16; Desmond Shaw-Taylor, *The Georgians: Eighteenth-Century Portraiture and Society* (London, 1990); Sara Holdsworth and Joan Crossley (eds), *Innocence and Experience: Images of Children in British Art from 1600 to the Present* (Manchester, 1992); Kate Retford, *The Art of Domestic Life: Family Portraiture in Eighteenth-Century England* (New Haven, 2006); Pointon, *Hanging the Head*; Marcia Pointon, 'Charming Little Brats: Lawrence's Portraits of Children', in A.C. Albinson, Peter Funnell and Lucy Peltz (eds), *Thomas Lawrence: Regency, Power and Brilliance* (New Haven, 2011), 55–83; Mirjam Neumeister (ed.), *The Changing Face of Childhood: British Children's Portraits and their Influence in Europe* (Cologne, 2007); Shearer West, 'The Public Nature of Private Life: The Conversation Piece and the Fragmented Family', *Journal for Eighteenth-Century Studies* 8:2 (1995), 153–72; Philippe Ariès, *Centuries of Childhood: A Social History of Family Life* (London, 1962); Lawrence Stone, *The Family, Sex and Marriage in England 1500–1800* (Harmondsworth, 1990).

[7] J.H. Plumb, 'The New World of Children in Eighteenth-Century England', in Neil McKendrick, John Brewer and J.H. Plumb (eds), *The Birth of a Consumer Society: The Commercialization of Eighteenth-Century England* (London, 1982), 286–315; Aileen Reibero, *A Visual History of Costume: The Eighteenth Century* (London, 1983); Matthew Grenby, *Children's Literature* (Edinburgh, 2008). For earlier examples of these items in this collection, see: clothing, Chapters 1 and 3; toys, Chapters 1 and 4.

Paradigmatic of such thinking was Rousseau's influential semi-novelized educational tract *Emile*, which is based on the premise that 'childhood has its place in the sequence of human life; the man must be treated as man and the child as a child'.[8] In many ways exemplary of eighteenth-century philosophizing on gender roles as well as childrearing, *Emile* stressed the 'natural' differences between boys and girls, men and women. These differences resulted in their complementary contributions to society and justified differing education for boys and girls. Rousseau stressed the importance of 'nature', in the form of outdoor life, posited as a preferable method of instruction to book-learning. Appropriately paced experiential learning was cited as essential to develop a person capable of living within a corrupting society. Home-grown Enlightenment talents such as John Gregory, James Fordyce, Hugh Blair and Henry Mackenzie propagandized similar notions in sermons, periodicals, pamphlets and novels, highlighting the collective cultural imagination and circulation of ideas across Enlightenment Europe.[9] Beyond childhood, as John Dwyer has convincingly asserted, Scottish Enlightenment literati, in common with Rousseau, believed the stage of youth was a period of specific interest, the period when feelings of sociability and humanity were awakened.[10]

Described by Christina Hardyment as 'probably the most widely read child-rearing manual of its age', *Emile* was embraced by the elite as well as the literati.[11] One enthusiastic reader was the duchess of Atholl, who invited David Allan to Blair Atholl in the summer of 1781 to produce the portrait used as one of the case studies in this essay. Writing to her sister in 1785, she expressed her pleasure at reading the book and her desire to discuss it.

> I have gone through Emile with pleasure & now I believe I shall let myself be tempted to write a little out of it. I hope it will not be long before we can have an opportunity of talking over the Book together although the snow of yesterday & today is not quite so favourable to that.[12]

Influential in Scotland, within a year of its initial 1762 publication *Emile* had been translated into English and published in Edinburgh by Alexander Donaldson and John Reid, reprinted several times and reproduced in the *Scots Magazine*, an Edinburgh periodical and a mouthpiece of the Scottish Enlightenment literati.[13]

8 Jean-Jacques Rousseau, *Emile* (Middlesex, 2007), 42. First published in 1762.

9 See, for example, John Gregory, *A Father's Legacy to his Daughters By the Late Dr Gregory of Edinburgh. A New Edition* (London, 1781); James Fordyce, *Addresses to Young Men* (London, 1777); James Fordyce, *Sermons to Young Women: by James Fordyce, D.D. The eighth edition, corrected and greatly enlarged* (Dublin, 1796); Hugh Blair, *Sermons* (London, 1819); Hugh Blair, *Advice to Youth; containing a compendium of the duties of human life in youth and manhood* (London, 1808); Henry Mackenzie, *The Man of Feeling* (London, 1771).

10 John Dwyer, *Virtuous Discourse: Sensibility and Community in Late Eighteenth-Century Scotland* (Edinburgh, 2003), 72–91.

11 Christina Hardyment, *Dream Babies: Childcare from Locke to Spock* (London, 1983), 18.

12 NLS, MS 16004 (254), Duchess of Atholl to Hon. Mrs Graham, 30 January 1785.

13 Jo-Ann E. McEachern, 'The Diffusion of *Émile* in the Eighteenth Century', in Jean Terrasse (ed.), *Rousseau et l'éducation: études sur l'Émile* (Sherbrooke, 1984), 116–25; Dwyer, *Virtuous Discourse*, 15.

David Allan's portraiture reflects and propagandizes these Enlightenment ideals of childhood and youth.

Eighteenth-century portraits fulfilled many social functions. As Shearer West argues, portraits 'serve a multiplicity of aesthetic, political and social functions' and were usually created with the understanding that they would serve a public role, that they would be seen by a variety of people.[14] They were at one level a status symbol, exhibiting that the sitter had the money to pay for a portrait and the time to sit for it. They were also, as Stana Nenadic contends, 'luxury items displaying fine clothing and a fashionable presence'.[15] David Allan himself gave some insight into another role of portraiture when he described 'the small Domestic & conversation style' of portraits as 'the most useful as it is the means of everlastingly joining friends together on the canvace'.[16] Portraits could be used as a substitute for the person represented or to commemorate a relationship or event.[17] They were, in part, commissioned and painted with an eye to posterity. As a result, where family portraits may have presented an informal relationship between the subjects, the presence of young people demonstrated the importance of children for dynastic succession.

Where a portrait is produced shapes its content; the specific context of post-Union, eighteenth-century Scotland introduced particular themes and meanings to family portraiture. In the second half of the century North Britishness emerged as the dominant national identity of the urban elite; this had allegiance to the British state but was predicated on an identification with, and loyalty to, Scotland as a distinct country.[18] The British state was seen as a civilizing force; it stood for improvement in governance, economics, agriculture, manufacturing, town-planning, manners, and the practice of religion. As Stana Nenadic has demonstrated, this took on a distinctive flavour in the Highlands.[19] A fascination with ancient Gaeldom and looking back to a heroic past, sat alongside loyalty to

14 Shearer West, *Portraiture* (Oxford, 2004), 43.

15 Stana Nenadic, *Lairds and Luxury: The Highland Gentry in Eighteenth-Century Scotland* (Edinburgh, 2007), p. xii.

16 EUL, Laing Manuscripts, La IV fols 1–4, David Allan to the Earl of Buchan, 3 December 1780.

17 West, *Portraiture.* See also Pointon, *Hanging the Head*; Gill Perry, Kate Retford and Jordan Vibert (eds), *Placing Faces: The Portrait and the English Country House in the Long Eighteenth Century* (Manchester, 2013).

18 Colin Kidd, 'North Britishness and the Nature of Eighteenth-Century British Patriotisms', *The Historical Journal* 39:2 (1996), 361–82; T.C. Smout, 'Problems of Nationalism: Identity and Improvement in Later Eighteenth-Century Scotland', in T.M. Devine (ed.), *Improvement and Enlightenment* (Edinburgh, 1989), 1–21; R.J. Finlay, 'Caledonia or North Britain? Scottish Identity in the Eighteenth Century', in Dauvit Brown, R.J. Finlay and Michael Lynch (eds), *Image and Identity: The Making and Remaking of Scotland through the Ages* (Edinburgh, 1998), 143–56.

19 Nenadic, *Lairds and Luxury.* See also Robert Clyde, *From Rebel to Hero: The Image of the Highlander 1745–1830* (East Linton, 1995); Rosalind Carr, 'The Gentleman and the Soldier: Patriotic Masculinities in Eighteenth-Century Scotland', *JSHS* 28:2 (2008), 102–21.

the British state for both the Highland and the urban elite.[20] The Allan portraits of the 4th duke of Atholl's family and the Hunter Blair family discussed in this essay represent a geographical spread, with one depicting a Highland duke and his family and the other Lowland gentry. Both portraits utilize Enlightenment ideologies of childhood to assert dynastic interests within their specific historical context.

One element of this specific context was the emphasis Scottish Enlightenment thinkers placed on family life as a patriotic imperative which, in maturity, would enable the children to sustain a stable modern Scottish polity.[21] Education in a domestic setting with the active involvement of parents was seen as the best place for stimulating appropriate moral feelings.[22] Education here, as in many eighteenth-century texts, equates to 'upbringing' and was defined in Johnson's dictionary as the 'formation of manners in youth; the manner of breeding youth; nurture'.[23] James Fordyce described this task as 'the anxious yet delightful labour, of training your common offspring to virtue and society, to religion and immortality'.[24] With the family as a seat of learning, family harmony was both a necessary pre-condition and an exemplar for a child's development; it was a backdrop to and role model for their play and education. Harmony displayed in a family portrait was more than conventional gloss, but operated to convey social meaning.

Such domestic harmony exudes from Allan's portrait of the banker, landowner and Lord Provost of Edinburgh, James Hunter Blair and his family painted in 1785. The portrait, which shows James, his wife Jean and nine of their fourteen children taking a family walk at their Dunskey estate in Ayrshire, is teeming with life, movement and detail. There is a strong rhythmic dynamic, an amassing of undulating lines that creates a multi-layered and deep sense of concord. The wave that leads our roving eye from one character to another is echoed in the cadences of the landscape and, in a more muted way, in incidental detailing. Looking from left to right we are led from the eldest son, John, up through the eldest daughter, Ann, up again to Jean, reaching the crest of the wave with James. We then move back down to the girl, Clementina, who is holding a baby in a chariot, then back up to the boy whose arms are aloft and holding a whip, then over the two boys pulling the carriage, down to the two little children on the right of the picture. This arc is repeated in the line of bushes directly behind the family, in the hill on which sits the family house, and yet again in the distant hill. Incidental detail, such as the line of the boy's whip, James's tricorn hat and the ribbons fluttering on Ann's dress reinforce the rhythm of the picture and the sense of pictorial and familial harmony. Familial harmony is also delineated at

20 Carr, 'The Gentleman and the Soldier'; Viccy Coltman, 'Party-Coloured Plaid? Portraits of Eighteenth-Century Scots in Tartan', *Textile History* 41:2 (November 2010), 182–216.

21 Dwyer, *Virtuous Discourse*, 10–18.

22 Dwyer, *Virtuous Discourse*, 81.

23 Samuel Johnson, *A Dictionary of the English Language* (London, 1775).

24 James Fordyce, 'Sermon 1', in *Sermons to Young Women*, 16.

6.1 Painting, David Allan, *The Hunter Blair Family*, 1785, from the private collection of Alan and Carol Murray.

the point at which pictorial construction and narrative intersect. On the left Ann attempts to pull her brother away from his reading to join the rest of the family at play. Her gesture is repeated in that of her father and mirrored by the youngest children on the right. This sense of familial cohesion created by the rhythms in the construction is more than artistic organization; it reflects and reinforces contemporaneous discourse on family life. Familial harmony was vital to the development of children, and children represented the future of the family line and a sustainable modern Scotland. Familial harmony, dynasty and patriotism are thus intertwined

Turning to the picture's narrative content, the frolicsome group of younger children asserts that childhood was understood as a distinct life stage. The children are depicted very much at play; they are pulling a cart with a wooden handle and rope, being urged on by one brother who runs, arms aloft. The dog, running amongst them with ears back and tail up, appears to be yapping and adding to the noise, suggesting the excited exuberance of the children. The youngest child on the far right of the picture has fallen down in his exertions. Rousseau advocated just such exercise and outdoor life as an essential part of a child's education. A child should not be smothered or cosseted or kept indoors, rather let 'him run about, let him struggle and fall again and again'.[25] The two youngest children and baby are depicted here in dresses and that the baby is free to move its limbs is seen in the way it is sucking its hands. The three slightly older boys wear a type of 'skeleton suit', a pair of high-waisted trousers buttoned to a jacket, an outfit designed specifically for children and with the view to being comfortable for them.[26] The Hunter Blair children's clothing would have met with Rousseau's approval, as he states in *Emile*, 'The limbs of a growing child should be free to move easily in his clothing; nothing should cramp their growth or movement … The best plan is to keep children in frocks as long as possible and then to provide them with loose clothing'.[27] They are distinguished as children by their clothes and actions in play, but also physically through their chubbiness, their facial expressions and, in the case of the littlest two, the fluffiness of their hair. Hogarth's view that children 'have movements in the muscles of their face peculiar to their age, as an uninformed and unmeaning stare, and open mouth, and simple grin' seems perfectly captured on this canvas.[28] These little people then are portrayed not as miniature adults or even as future adults, but as children – loose-limbed, and free to move, get dirty and make noise. Childhood, the portrait asserts, is a distinct life-stage apart from adulthood. This represents a rhetorical shift away from the formality in the depiction of children as little adults evident in earlier portraits.[29] It is not a simple case of art following life, but signifies the way portraiture played

25 Rousseau, *Emile*, 41.
26 Ribeiro, *A Visual History of Costume*, 137.
27 Rousseau, *Emile*, 87.
28 William Hogarth, *The Analysis of Beauty* (New Haven and London, 1997), 98. First published in 1753.
29 West, *Portraiture*, 133.

a key role in the presentation, representation, and re-presentation of the notion of childhood, giving visual expression to the notion.

By indicating with seeming approval the rough and tumble of his younger children and their dog, James asserts pictorially his affiliation with the notion that childhood should be a time apart from adult life. Furthermore, given the association of the virtues of just such a domestic country upbringing as the Hunter Blair children are shown experiencing with the creation of a stable modern Scottish polity expounded by the Scottish Enlightenment moralists, the family's patriotic credentials are thus rendered in paint. That such progressive ideas should conveniently allow display of the family estate, thereby asserting a certain position in society, is opportune for landowning commissioners of paintings like James. As Leah Leneman and Rosalind Mitchison have shown, the distinction between nobility and gentry was less marked in Scotland than England; it was not the absence of a link with trade that made for respectability, but the reality of landowning.[30] A family portrait of this sort enabled a display of the family estate, significant because landowning was synonymous with power and status. Its function as a symbol of status is reflected in its size – at 98x48 inches, this is a canvas on a grand scale. In this way, this informal family portrait is hardly less a statement of power and prestige than if James had been depicted in chains of office. Here then the Hunter Blair family's claims to be respectable are asserted, as are their Enlightened and patriotic credentials as North Britons and proud Scots of the Union.

Within all the fraternal turmoil, Clementina's role in the game is to be pulled, ladylike in her carriage. Her quiet stillness as she stares out at us acts as a pause, a lull, on our eye's roving journey over the characters. She exhibits none of her brothers' exuberance and freedom of movement as she nurses her little sibling. She is shown learning the 'honourable station' of motherhood.[31] Fordyce argued that motherhood was 'a sphere of activity which you all hope to fill, and for which you ought to qualify yourselves as much as possible'.[32] At eight-years-old, Clementina is certainly depicted beginning her qualification early. In this she is not alone; it was a pictorial commonplace at this time to show portraits of girls nursing siblings, dolls or animals, therefore depicting play in imitation of the adult world.[33] According to Rousseau, in another of his self-fulfilling circular arguments, the 'doll is the girl's special plaything; this shows her instinctive bent towards her life's work' and such play should be encouraged.[34] Imitation, education and play were closely linked in the ideology of childhood; portraiture, a medium as prescriptive as it was descriptive, both promoted and reflected this notion.

30 Leah Leneman and Rosalind Mitchison, *Sexuality and Social Control: Scotland 1660–1780* (Oxford, 1989), 55.
31 Fordyce, 'Sermon VI', *Sermons*, 93.
32 Fordyce, 'Sermon VI', *Sermons*, 95.
33 Pointon, *Hanging the Head*, 194.
34 Rousseau, *Emile*, 311.

Without the opportunity for an official role in civic life, girls at this time were educated with a focus on accomplishment rather than deep learning.[35] Indeed John Gregory advised young women to keep any learning they have 'a profound secret, especially from men, who generally look with jealous and malignant eye on a woman of great parts'.[36] A curriculum could include singing, dancing, reading, writing, painting, French, Italian, history, geography and astronomy, these latter few to enable her to make polite conversation. She also needed to learn housekeeping and bookkeeping as she was to run a household. Girls at the time learnt from a broad curriculum, but with the specifically gendered purpose of becoming a wife and mother. As Katharine Glover has shown, the elite habit of educating their sons in London was increasingly being extended to daughters during the latter stages of the eighteenth century, and girls' education represented a substantial investment for some families.[37] Ann Hunter Blair was just such a girl, as letters from her father attest. Slotted in between information about business, gossip from friends and parliamentary matters are frequent references to the then twelve-year-old Ann's progress in her social education.

> I was at a ball last night at Mrs Herries's where Annie performed indeed mightily well. She also play'd on the harpsichord, the piano forte & sang; every Lady allowed she plays with great taste & a good ear & I believe she will have a good voice – all her masters say she is distinguished in the various branches of her education. I take her to see Mrs Siddons on Tuesday, the famous tragedian.[38]

Ann's education involved formal instruction with 'masters' and a round of visiting polite social places (balls, tea-drinking visits to friends such as the Herries, and the theatre) where she displayed her accomplishments. The word 'taste' is crucial here, linked as it is to the notion of politeness. Identified by Paul Langford as a 'key-word' to understanding the mentality of the time, politeness was more than simply good manners; it was a social process that promoted civility, sociability, rationality and improvement.[39] At an individual level, Lawrence Klein characterizes it as 'the art of pleasing, in company and conversation' related to

35 Deborah Simonton, 'Women and Education', in Hannah Barker and Elaine Chalus (eds), *Women's History: Britain 1700–1850 An Introduction* (London and New York, 2005), 33–56; Katharine Glover, '"Polite London Children": Educating the Daughters of the Scottish Elite in Mid-Eighteenth-Century London', in Stana Nenadic (ed.), *Scots in London in the Eighteenth Century* (Lewisberg, 2010), 253–70; Karen O'Brien, *Women and Enlightenment in Eighteenth-Century Britain* (Cambridge, 2009).

36 John Gregory, *A Father's Legacy to his Daughters. By the Late Dr Gregory of Edinburgh. A New Edition* (London,1781), 31–2. First published in 1774, the book was written after the death of his wife in 1761. The ideas contained within the book cohere with those of Rousseau and highlight the European-wide circulation and cross-fertilization of ideas amongst Enlightenment thinkers.

37 Glover, 'Polite London Children'.

38 Ayrshire Archives [AA], Hunter Blair Papers [HBP], Bundle 58/51, James Hunter Blair to Jean Hunter Blair, 18 March 1783.

39 Paul Langford, *A Polite and Commercial People: England 1727–1783* (Oxford, 1989); Lawrence Klein, 'Politeness and the Interpretation of the British Eighteenth Century', *The Historical Journal* 45:4 (2002), 869–98; Michèle Cohen, '"Manners" Makes the Man:

gendered expectations and conduct.[40] Ann's education was grooming in politeness. Fourteen at the time of the portrait and having shed the puppy fat still present on her siblings, she is slim and straight and wears an elegant, low-cut green dress which displays all her feminine potential. She encourages John to join the family at play, displaying the attributes of concern for others and polite sociability which would be key to her future success as a woman.

In contrast to Ann, lolling on a rock, book in hand, twelve-year-old John, or Jackie as he was known in the family, is elegantly dressed in a smart red coat, breeches, stockings and shiny shoes. He appears reluctant to join in the childish games of his younger siblings, as if aware of himself at a different life stage on the cusp of adulthood. His clothes, gestures and facial features distinguish him pictorially from the younger children. He is depicted as a 'man of feeling', a notion that passed from the pages of Henry Mackenzie's best-selling novel of that name and entered the pictorial lexicon with Joseph Wright's 1781 portrait of Sir Brooke Boothby whose pose John echoes.[41] The 'man of feeling' was of noble stock, benevolent, interested in improvement and overflowing with fine moral sentiments. There was a strong discursive link between patriotism, national identity and improvement in the works of the Scottish literati, and improvement could be construed as a patriotic act.[42] Although there is none of the paraphernalia we have come to associate with Scottishness, in many ways this portrait resonates with Scottish Enlightenment ideals. James himself was responsible for the building improvements in Edinburgh and Portpatrick, and for agricultural improvement on his estate; the pose of the son can be read as hope that he would continue his father's improving legacy once his youth was over and he passed into full manhood. In other words, this portrait is dynastic in its function and infused with Scottish Enlightenment sentiments.

Describing John in a letter to his wife the year after the portrait was painted, James stated,

> Jackie in truth pleases me very much; his manners are refined, his language good except speaking rather fast; his dispositions are excellent & please every lady he meets with; – in conversation he blends gentleness, spirit & good sense and I find his prejudices ware off as much as I wish them.[43]

In his father's eyes John was becoming the ideal young North British gentleman he is depicted as in the portrait. The prejudices that Hunter Blair referred to were

Politeness, Chivalry, and the Construction of Masculinity, 1750–1830', *Journal of British Studies* 44:2 (2005), 312–29.

40 Klein, 'Politeness and the Interpretation', 874.

41 Henry Mackenzie, *The Man of Feeling* (London, 1771). Joseph Wright's portrait of Sir Brooke Boothby is in the collection of the Tate Gallery. For information about the man of feeling in eighteenth-century portraiture see the chapter of that name in Shaw-Taylor, *The Georgians.*

42 Smout, *Problems of Nationalism*; Katharine Glover, *Elite Women and Polite Society in Eighteenth-Century Scotland* (Woodbridge, 2011); Dwyer, *Virtuous Discourse.*

43 AA, HBP, Bundle 51/100, James Hunter Blair to Jean Hunter Blair, 3 April 1786.

discussed in earlier letters from a man called Blane, a mentor whose role was to look out for John's interests and visit him in London in his father's absence.

> I am glad to find that he is still in the way of overcoming his aversion to the school – and I think I have some sway in reasoning him out of what you so properly call his local prejudices, and in making him comprehend the necessity of accommodating and assimilating himself in language & manners with the rest of the boys – and I have held out to him as further inducements to do so that you will be determined his progress in the English language, and in manliness of behaviour with regard to the time you may think it necessary to keep him at school.[44]

'Local prejudices' here means not speaking or behaving politely as a proper British gentleman. Alexander Murdoch and Richard Sher have persuasively argued that the emphasis, as here, on 'accommodating' and 'assimilating' should not be seen as evidence of rejecting Scottishness, but as pragmatic – speaking English 'properly' was a means to an end for the North British.[45] It certainly appears to have been a real focus of concern for John's father, who received regular reports on this aspect of his son's development: 'He is more reconciled to the school than I could have believed, and he even improves in his language, tho' but slowly.'[46] This concern for losing a Scottish accent and colloquial turn of phrase was shared by many of the Scottish nobles and literati of the time who wished to appear polite rather than provincial. It is perhaps not surprising then that poor John, bullied in Westminster school and at his boarding house for his speech, received scant sympathy from his father and Blane when he complained. Writing in response to his father, John says:

> Indeed, my Dear Papa, I have read your letter with great attention & will try to bear my afflictions as well as I can, though I am fully persuaded that this boarding house will never be agreeable to me, as all the boys join in plaguing and teasing me.[47]

The plaintive voice of a bullied youth collapses the intervening years and still has the capacity to move. Such melancholy is absent from the canvas; it is a performance that glosses over the fact that in the eyes of his peers, his father, and his mentor, John is yet to achieve full competence in the matter of politeness.[48]

Impoliteness needed to be guarded against at all costs, as other Hunter Blair correspondence suggests. Writing to Jean in 1783 when John was ten, James says, 'I forgot to tell you I approve of Jackie going to the dancing, but pray send

44 AA, HBP, Bundle 87/64, G. Blane to James Hunter Blair, 19 December 1785.

45 Alexander Murdoch and Richard Sher, 'Literary and Learned Culture', in T. Devine and R. Mitchison (eds), *People and Society in Scotland, Volume 1, 1760–1830* (Edinburgh, 1988), 127–42. For more on the political importance of language-training in children, see Chapters 3 and 4 in this collection.

46 AA, HBP, Bundle 75/26, G. Blane to James Hunter Blair, 14 March 1786.

47 AA, HBP, Bundle 87/50, John Hunter Blair to James Hunter Blair, 30 November 1785.

48 Peter Burke has argued that portraits depict 'not social reality so much as social illusions, not ordinary life but special performances': Peter Burke, *Eyewitnessing: The Uses of Images as Historical Evidence* (London, 2001), 28.

him where the best people are but this to yourself.'[49] Jean had identified local dance classes that appear to have met with James's disapprobation, as he stated in his next letter to her, 'If you all think well of Sealy's School be it so, but I rather feared there would be low County there.'[50] The idea that the Hunter Blair children should go to the right classes, with the 'best people', and not mix with 'low' types, is illuminating. Polite sociability was key to a child's learning, as bad habits could be picked up in the wrong circles; a society that 'dismissed the impolite as the provincial' appears capable of dismissing the provincial as impolite.[51] James's comment to not disclose this conversation to the children also strongly suggests a sense of propriety – that which is appropriate for children's ears and that which should be filtered out in the conveying of a message to a child. In other words, children should be protected from adult concerns, they should be allowed a childhood. This is a sentiment that also bounces boisterously out from the portrait in the form of rumbustious children playing.

The distinctness of childhood as a life stage is equally apparent in the visual rhetoric of the portrait Allan produced for the duke and duchess of Atholl in the summer of 1781. Allan described the portrait in a letter to Sir William Hamilton, uncle of the duchess and a long-term patron of the painter:

> I painted them on the green, with the Duke returning from the hunting in the Highland dress, his gun under his arm and in the other a heath cock which he holds out to the little marquis who is running to take it. The Duchess with the others sitting on a bank looking on, and in the distance Athole House with a view of the country, which please very well and figures about two feet high.[52]

As Allan states, the family are gathered outside, their estate displayed behind them. The young marquis of Tullibardine wears infant petticoats; with rosy cheeks and chubby arms outstretched, he is the very picture of Rousseauesque rude health. The portrait suggests that because of his life stage he has spent the afternoon with his sisters and mother, and is now tottering towards his father, who is returning from stalking. The child is obviously too young to walk any distance, and, common sense suggests, too young to take out shooting. But according to Rousseau it was more than common sense, it was 'natural' that such a young child should be with its mother: 'The earliest education is most important and it undoubtedly is woman's work. If the author of nature had meant to assign it to men he would have given them milk to feed the child.'[53] Using naturalizing arguments, Rousseau constructed women and men as 'naturally' different and made for different roles; their biology, temperaments and skills all conspired to make this so. Motherhood was, in this way, women's natural work and women should be children's earliest nurturers and teachers. This began with

[49] AA, HBP, Bundle 51/59, James Hunter Blair to Jean Hunter Blair, 18 March 1783.
[50] AA, HBP, Bundle 51/60, James Hunter Blair to Jean Hunter Blair, 21 March 1783.
[51] Glover, *Elite Women*, 6.
[52] Hopetoun House, Hopetoun archive, bundle 3482, David Allan to Sir William Hamilton, 6 November 1780.
[53] Rousseau, *Emile*, 6.

6.2 Painting, David Allan, *John, Fourth Duke of Atholl and his Family*, 1780, from the collection at Blair Castle, Perthshire.

breast feeding, 'the sweet task imposed … by nature', which became a popular ideal amongst the elite in the late eighteenth century.[54] This is coyly alluded to in the Atholl portrait with the alignment of the sleeping baby the duchess holds to her breast. Allan's composition is far from unique. While it would be 'impolite' to show a woman actually breastfeeding in such a portrait, reference to it by such a gesture became increasingly common in mother-and-child portraits at the time.[55]

The sense of the gender difference that children learned from an early age and that was central to Rousseau and also much Scottish Enlightenment debating and philosophizing is expressed very strongly in this portrait. Divided down the middle, a line, if actualized, runs through the marquis of Tullibardine in the centre of the picture. To the right is the female and feminine side of the picture. The duchess sits below a tree wearing a dusky pink dress and a shawl held in place by flowers, presumably collected by five-year-old Lady Charlotte, who wears some in her hair and has others gathered in her skirts. A little cart that she has been playing with also contains flowers. Flowers are associated with Flora, Roman goddess of flowers and spring and suggests Charlotte is in the spring of her life, blooming but not yet adult. She comports herself with controlled poise; all is pretty, sedate and constrained. According to John Gregory, one of 'the chief beauties in a female character, is that modest reserve, that retiring delicacy'.[56] Five-year-old Charlotte is seen to have these in abundance; with her neat gestures and pretty flower-collecting habit, she is displayed as if learning what it means to be respectably, politely feminine.

To the left of the picture is the masculine and male side: the gamekeeper Crerar, and the duke, tall and erect, replete with the accoutrements of stalking. Atholl is dressed in full traditional costume, with a bonnet with a red-and-white checked band and black feather (a symbol of his status as a chieftain), matching red-and-white hose, and a kilt with sporran.[57] This is reinforced by Crerar who is also dressed in Highland costume, and the very specifically Highland landscape with its massive mountains and bruised skies. Strictly speaking, the duke's outfit breaks the prohibition on the wearing of such costume introduced in 1746 and only repealed in 1782. This is not, however, the anti-government statement it might have been in the 1740s. As Viccy Coltman has shown, from its identification with Jacobitism, tartan evolved into fabric worn by loyal Highlanders, proud Scots within the Union.[58] Portraiture did not simply follow the trend here, it was a key way in which Scottish identity was recreated and expressed. This portrait is

54 Rousseau, *Emile*, 14.

55 Shaw-Taylor, *The Georgians*.

56 Gregory, *A Father's Legacy*, 26.

57 Ann Sutton and Richard Carr, *Tartans: Their Art and History* (London, 1984).

58 Coltman, 'Party-Coloured Plaid?'. See also Clyde, *From Rebel to Hero*; James Holloway, 'Images and Identity: The Cultural Context of Portraits', J.M. Fladmark (ed.), *Heritage and Museums* (Lower Coombe, 2000), 163–8; Robin Nicholson, 'From Ramsay's *Flora MacDonald* to Raeburn's *MacNab*: The Use of Tartan as a Symbol of Identity', *Textile History* 36:2 (2005), 146–67; Murray G.H. Pittock, 'Patriot Dress and Patriot Games: Tartan from

very much a statement of the duke's identification of himself as a loyal Highland clan chief. This Scottish identity, different from the Lowland Enlightenment North Britishness of the Hunter Blairs, is nonetheless of what Smout calls the 'concentric loyalty' type, which tended to reinforce British nationalism rather than contradict it'.[59] Play was a significant element in constructing this identity, with Highland games, dance, verse and song as a focus of interest for polite, Enlightenment, homosocial clubs (such as the Highland Society, of which the duke was a founder member).[60] Embedded thus within Scottish Enlightenment ideas, this loyal Highlander identity could be polite when performed by gentlemen such as Atholl. We see this when class intersects with gender in Crerar's pictorially ambiguous position. Here his sex enables him to share the male half of the picture with the duke, but his class means he falls outside the polite circle of the family, which is formed by the duke – his back to the gamekeeper – and visually completed by the family dog at the centre bottom of the picture. Even the dogs in both halves tell a deep gender tale: the eager alert hunting dogs sniffing at the recently killed stag contrast with the curled-up pet dog sleeping gently on the feminine and domestic side of the portrait.

The young marquis at the centre of the picture is literally and symbolically between the male and female worlds. He may still be in skirts and have spent the afternoon with his mother and sisters, but he is figuratively aligned with the other males as he stretches a pudgy hand towards the game bird his father holds out to him. He has his back turned to his mother and sisters and is running excitedly towards the men, literally and metaphorically leaving the world of women behind him. His place is as the next head of the Atholl dynasty, so it is not just the bird, or even manhood, that the child reaches for with his chubby little hands, but his inheritance, his birthright, the Murray dukedom of Atholl. His inheritance is emphasized by his central position directly below the house that is the ancient family seat. His importance is stressed not only through his pictorial placement, but also by the way that he is emotionally centre stage; our eyes are drawn to him through the eyes of his father, sister, mother and retainer, all of whom are focussed on him. So while this might be an informal portrait of a family at play, it remains in many senses a dynastic statement. The portrait also

the Jacobites to Queen Victoria', in Caroline McCracken-Flesher (ed.), *Culture, Nation and the New Parliament* (Lewisberg, 2007), 158–74.

59 Smout, 'The Problems of Nationalism'.

60 Sir John Sinclair of Ulbster, *An Account of the Highland Society of London, From its Establishment in May 1778 to the Commencement of the Year 1813* (London, 1813). The society was established as part of the drive to 'improve' the Highlands by supporting schools and agricultural innovations. The society was also concerned to preserve the culture of the Highlands, towards which end it published a Gaelic dictionary and arranged poetry competitions. It was also a place for men to meet and discuss issues of concern. For further information about the role of clubs and debating societies in Scottish Enlightenment culture, see David McElroy, *Scotland's Age of Improvement: A Survey of Eighteenth-Century Literary Clubs and Societies* (Pullman, 1969); Rosalind Carr, *Gender and Enlightenment Culture in Eighteenth-Century Scotland* (Edinburgh, 2014). For more discussion of the role of play, see Chapter 4 in this collection.

signifies the duke's aspirations to pass this loyal Highland identity to his son and heir. The power of portraiture means of course that visually, materially and indelibly, as far as posterity is concerned the duke has done so; for centuries countless people have observed this portrait and its message.

Families like the Hunter Blairs and Murrays, who lived between London and Scotland, were part of a trend of escalating assimilation of the Scottish elite into London social life in the late eighteenth century.[61] Stana Nenadic has argued that the Scots in London helped develop a notion of Britishness while simultaneously creating a Scottish one.[62] This duality of experience and identity meant that many children of the Scottish elite by this time often had 'a bi-cultural upbringing'; they were Anglicized but Scottish, both Scottish and British.[63] This essay has highlighted the differing ways that Scottish identity within the concentric-loyalty framework could be graphically displayed. It has revealed that the accoutrements of Scottishness, such as tartan and Highland sport, could be utilized, but that they do not need to be present for Scottishness to permeate the canvas. The notion of adults handing on this identity to their children shows that, despite the informality of the portraits, dynasty and primogeniture remained important concerns. The essay has considered what Allan's works imply about the gendered socio-cultural expectations, aspirations and behaviours of childhood and family in this historical context. It has highlighted the different expectations of boys and girls, and how these are played out pictorially. It has shown how portraiture, much more than reflecting pre-existing ideas, contributed to the construction of childhood as a distinct period in the life cycle, engaging with other discursive vehicles in a complex exchange of concepts. The decorative nature of these portraits, the way they seem to capture a private and spontaneous moment in time, belies their faculty to influence, to promote, construct and perpetuate ideas. Therein lies their power, agency and utility as message bearers.

61 Glover, *Elite Women.*

62 Stana Nenadic, 'Introduction', in Nenadic (ed.), *Scots in London*, 13.

63 Glover, *Elite Women*, 38.

7

Slave Children: Scotland's Children as Chattels at Home and Abroad in the Eighteenth Century

Dolly MacKinnon

In a portrait painted by Sir John Baptiste de Medina, James Drummond, 2nd titular duke of Perth (1673–1720), Jacobite, stands proudly looking straight into the eyes of the viewer (Plate 7.1). Immediately behind Drummond's right hand, which rests on his helmet, the light catches on a metal collar encircling a child's neck. A young black boy, a nameless chattel, stares up at this figure of Scottish nobility. The child is characterized by his dark skin, and what Joseph Leo Koerner might describe as 'his eccentric placement' oblique to the main focus on Drummond.[1] Within the frame, the boy is simultaneously 'more visible than others through his stand-out difference', but the dark background from which he emerges renders him 'less visible' to the gaze, which is drawn back to Dummond.[2] This visible and yet invisible presence acts as a metaphor for the place of slave children in Scottish history, for he is an object in the painting rather than the subject of the portrait.

At its most simplistic level, Drummond's portrait depicts the young slave boy in unambiguous terms, for his silver collar, while ornamental, is also the symbol of his slave status, as well as a preventative measure inhibiting escape. This painting of a domestic slave is, in David Bindman's conception, 'an exercise of rank'.[3] Within British art of this period, enslaved 'black grooms and pages were among the many signifiers of rank that could be invoked by painters to suggest that old values would survive, or had survived civil conflict'.[4] Painted at the turn of the eighteenth century, after Drummond's return to Scotland from the Continent, this nameless domestic slave child is both the property of his owner, and, as is typical of eighteenth-century portraiture in Scotland, also a symbol of rank, fashion and status. Furthermore, in an age of increasing social mobility caused

1 Joseph Leo Koerner, 'The Epiphany of the Black Magus Circa 1500', in David Bindman and Henry Louis Gates, Jr. (eds), *The Image of the Black in Western Art from the 'Age of Discovery' to the Age of Abolition: Artists of the Renaissance and Baroque*, III, Part 1 (Cambridge, MA, 2010), 7–92, especially 35; John Goldworth Alger and John Gibson, 'Drummond, James, styled fifth earl of Perth and Jacobite second duke of Perth (1674–1720)', *ODNB*.

2 Koerner, 'The Epiphany of the Black Magus', 35. For more on the significance of children's placement in portraiture, see Chapter 6 in this collection.

3 David Bindman, 'The Black Presence in British Art: Sixteenth and Seventeenth Centuries', in Bindman and Gates (eds), *The Image of the Black in Western Art*, 235–70, especially 259.

4 Bindman, 'The Black Presence in British Art', 270.

7.1 Painting, Sir John Baptiste de Medina, *James Drummond, 2nd titular Duke of Perth 1673–1720. Jacobite*, c.1700.

by the economic expansion into new-world markets in the American colonies and the Caribbean, old-order forms of rank could be mimicked and replaced by the inordinate wealth of the growing merchant class. In the Scotland of the eighteenth century, therefore, slaves were also traded and purchased by merchants, for whom these slave children and youths could reflect 'the exotic world beyond Europe, now open to trade and imperial adventures'.[5]

At their most complex, these types of images of the Scottish nobility and wealthy merchant class may also be depictions of a father and biological son or daughter. Slave children could be the biological product of slave women or adolescent girls subjected to sexual exploitation and forced sexual relations. However, it is only when those slave children were claimed by their white Scottish fathers through acts of manumission that this reality is demonstrable in limited public and private archives. This is why the topic has received scant attention. The slave women who gave birth to these children are also largely absent from histories of slavery, and the paternity and maternity of the majority of Scotland's slave

[5] Bindman, 'The Black Presence in British Art', 270.

children now lies beyond the written record, in the DNA of any of their descendants. Nevertheless, despite the scarcity of sources, it is a subject that needs to be pursued.

The lack of historical focus on the history of slave children and adolescents has rendered child slaves largely absent from existing historical debates about childhood.[6] Kate Chedgzoy notes that central to childhood studies are the interconnected questions concerning how childhood is to be defined, as well as how children were to be known, 'perceived and enabled to articulate their own kinds of knowledge'.[7] Slave childhoods offer an important new trajectory currently missing from existing studies of early modern childhood.[8] An analysis of child slaves enables us to revisit, test, and contest Lawrence Stone's conception of early modern families and their 'resigned acceptance of children'.[9] Stone's formulation did not include slave children, and therefore his uniform approach must be replaced instead with simultaneous gradations of childhood realities. It also allows us to extend Keith Brown's study of Scottish nobility to include those who were the biological progeny of owners involved in the sexual economy of slavery.[10] Slave children and adolescents do not fit into accepted conceptualizations of childhood work.[11] Key distinctions separated the experiences of children as servants from the experiences of children as slaves: children who were apprenticed or salaried had some right to self-determination over their lives, marital intentions, work and family prospects; slave children, unpaid and enslaved, held none of these rights of self-determination.

This essay focuses on thirty-two specific examples of slave children and youths within premodern Scotland, demonstrating a black presence and the recoverable aspects of slave children's paternity, maternity and manumission. Within this discussion there are also important implications for gender roles and patriarchy, for the majority of these slaves were male, and while girls and women were

[6] See Jerome Teelucksingh, 'The "Invisible Child" in British West Indian Slavery', *Slavery and Abolition: A Journal of Slave and Post-Slave Studies* 27:2 (2006), 237–8.

[7] Kate Chedgzoy, 'What, Are They Children?', in Kate Chedgzoy, Susanne Greenhalgh and Robert Shaughnessy (eds), *Shakespeare and Childhood* (Cambridge, 2007), 7.

[8] Naomi J. Miller and Naomi Yavneh (eds), *Gender and Early Modern Constructions of Childhood* (Farnham, 2011); Patricia Crawford, *Blood, Bodies and Families in Early Modern England* (Harlow, 2004); Stephanie Tarbin and Philippa Maddern (eds), *Material Worlds of Childhood in North-Western Europe c. 1350–1800* (Farnham, forthcoming). The history of children and slavery is just beginning to emerge. See Colleen Vasconcellos, *Slavery, Abolition, and Childhood in Jamaica, 1788–1838* (Athens, 2015); Colleen Vasconcellos, 'The Process: Finding Enslaved Children's Place, Voice and Agency within the Narrative', *a/b: Auto/Biography Studies* (forthcoming); Colleen Vasconcellos, '"'to so dark a destiny My lovely babe I've borne": Enslaved Girls in Jamaica, 1750–1838', in Miriam Foreman-Brunell (ed.), *'Mother's Little Helper' and More: Essays on Girls and Work* (Champaign, forthcoming); and Audra Diptee, 'African Children in the British Slave Trade During the Late Eighteenth Century', *Slavery and Abolition* 27:2 (2006), 183–96.

[9] Lawrence Stone, *The Family, Sex and Marriage in England 1500–1800* (New York, 1977).

[10] Keith Brown, *Noble Society in Scotland: Wealth, Family and Culture from the Reformation to the Revolution* (Edinburgh, 2000).

[11] Allison James, Chris Jenks and Alan Prout, *Theorizing Childhood* (New York, 1998).

present they are less prevalent and less visible in the archive. Using evidence from eighteenth-century newspaper advertisements, art, family papers and manumissions, this essay uncovers a new perspective on Scotland's fledgling history of childhood and youth.

As Robert Burns stated in another context, 'Facts are chiels that winna ding.'[12] In 2007 the Scottish Government acknowledged that at least seventy enslaved Africans lived on Scottish soil in the eighteenth century.[13] More recently, John W. Cairns, although observing that the exact number of women, men and children of African descent can never be known, has estimated that between 1702 and 1780 there were just under one hundred individuals, in addition to identifying one Native American and an 'Asiatic bond servant'.[14] Cairns calculates that of those one hundred, only one in ten were women. Although noting a perceptible increase in these numbers for each decade of the eighteenth century, he concludes that women and girls remain under represented.[15] Ongoing research will continue to reveal new evidence about Scotland's slaves. Tom Devine, in *Scotland's Empire*, observed the continuing controversy regarding the role of Scots in the slave trade and slave colonies.[16] Dependence upon institutional slavery was a central pillar of the creation of wealth, of new world economies, and of the process of colonization.[17] Devine's study demonstrates that while the involvements of Scottish merchants did not match the levels and scale of their counterparts in other countries, the links between Scotland's economy and slavery are irrefutable.[18] The ports of Leith and Glasgow carried into Scotland tobacco, sugar, spices and cotton for local markets fuelled by growing demand. Although the slave labour responsible for these consumables was not shipped in the volumes to be found for the English ports of London, Liverpool or Bristol, there were some slaves sent to Scotland, both for domestic service and to complete apprenticeships.[19] For example, Edward Burd, a merchant from Leith, paid for clothing and other items for his slave 'Cato', who was apprenticed to a wright.[20]

12 Robert Burns, 'A Dream', in James Currie (ed.), *The Works of Robert Burns in Prose and Verse* (New York, 1826), 23. 'Facts are chiels that winna ding' means that 'facts are fellows that cannot be overturned or disputed'.

13 Scottish Executive, *Scotland and the Slave Trade: 2007 Bicentenary of the Abolition of the Slave Trade Act* (Edinburgh, 2007), 20.

14 John W. Cairns, 'After Somerset: The Scottish Experience', *Journal of Legal History* 33:3 (2012), 302, 306.

15 Cairns, 'After Somerset', 303.

16 Thomas M. Devine, *Scotland's Empire 1600–1815* (London, 2005), 244; Stephen Mullen, *It Wisnae Us: The Truth about Glasgow and Slavery* (Edinburgh, 2009).

17 See Douglas Hamilton, 'Transatlantic Ties: Scottish Migration Networks in the Caribbean, 1750–1800', in Angela McCarthy (ed.), *A Global Clan: Scottish Migrant Networks and Identity since the Eighteenth Century* (London, 2006), 48–66.

18 Devine, *Scotland's Empire*, 244.

19 Madge Dresser, *Slavery Obscured: The Social History of the Slave Trade in Bristol* (Bristol, 2007); Madge Dresser and Peter Fleming, *Bristol: Ethnic Minorities and the City 1000–2001* (Chichester, 2009).

20 NRS, RH15/54, Edward Burd, Merchant in Leith, Accounts 1736.

As Neil Oliver has evocatively written, the substantial profits and family fortunes that shaped eighteenth- and nineteenth-century Scotland 'were shaved slice by slice from the naked backs of fellow human beings ... by buying and selling other mothers' sons and daughters'.[21] What is more, those profits could also be gained from the exploitation of one's own biological children.

Using evidence for elite aristocratic and merchant households as examples of Peter Laslett's 'houseful', a term coined to describe all the people living under one roof, ranging from nuclear and extended family members to servants (both resident and day servants), this essay focusses on qualitative case studies of slave children and youths.[22] Slaves within households held highly problematic positions. They conferred rank and status upon their masters and family, and yet they held precarious positions within the family and the law. Scottish households were spaces where the intersection between the biological family and all the others in the 'houseful' occurred. Slaves received board, keep and clothing, and in some cases occasional pocket money. What remains unknown is how many housefuls in eighteenth-century Scotland included biological slave children. A biological connection afforded the slave none of the automatic and hierarchical rights of their free siblings, parent or extended relations. A slave could be descended from a family member and resident within the household, yet occupy a liminal space that was neither familial nor free.

Scotland's slaves were largely domestic house slaves, and found within aristocratic and merchant households. As Iain Whyte concludes, while slaves appeared as brief descriptions in contemporary newspapers, frustratingly 'we know very little about their lives beyond' those scattered references.[23] For example, an advertisement selling 'a handsome black boy, about thirteen years of age, very well qualified for making a household servant, serving at table well', appeared in the *Edinburgh Advertiser* on 17 January 1769. He was a physically fit youth, for he is described as 'of a fine constitution, enured to the climate, and has had small pox'.[24] That he was 'enured' indicates that Scotland was not his native climate, but rather one he had grown accustomed to with time.

From the evidence in Scottish archives it is apparent that child slaves were either born into slavery, or were survivors of the gruelling Middle Passage crossings from West Africa.[25] George Dale was one such who had endured this

21 Neil Oliver, *A History of Scotland* (London, 2009), 283.

22 Peter Laslett (ed.), *Household and Family in Past Time*, second edn (London, 1972), 36; Dolly MacKinnon, '"I have now a book of songs of her writing": Scottish Families, Orality, Literacy, and the Transmission of Musical Culture c. 1500–c. 1800', in E. Ewan and J. Nugent (eds), *Finding the Family in Medieval and Early Modern Scotland* (Aldershot, 2008), 35–48.

23 Iain Whyte, *Scotland and the Abolition of Black Slavery, 1756–1838* (Edinburgh, 2006), 12; Professor J.W. Cairns, University of Edinburgh, is 'currently engaged in collecting information from diverse sources' about the African and Indian presence in Scotland during the eighteenth century, see 'After Somerset', 303, n. 77.

24 *Edinburgh Advertiser*, 17 January 1769, advertisement.

25 Teelucksingh, 'The Invisible Child', 237–50.

voyage. Writing his memoirs in 1790, Dale stated of his abduction in c.1775 that 'the practice of kidnapping [fragment missing] Children is ver Common in [the country] he came from', adding that his nation was known as 'Nago'.[26] Dale was not captured alone, for he was snatched along with his brothers and sister, and witnessed the callous murder of another young girl kidnapped with them: 'the little lassy becoming troublesome by screamings & crying (and perhaps thought less suited to their purpose being but young and a female) they struck off her head and left her there'. Dale described the 'passage towards the West Indies' in horrific detail, indicating that the slavers 'had a great number of slaves on board the ship' but that 'many died on the passage, and were thrown overboard'. The bodies, whether living or dead, 'were devoured, and swallowed by sharks' that 'always followed the ship'. Once on land in a Jamaican port, Dale was sold to Mr John William, who sent him to be an apprentice cook with Mr Howard of Kingston, 'who ... was very kind to him all the time he was with him'. On William's death, Dale was sold to Mr McColl, who, because of ill health, eventually returned to Greenock, taking Dale with him. Separation did not prevent Dale from attempting to find out the fate of his siblings. In 1790 he was able to recount that,

> with respect to his brothers and sister, they had been disposed of to a Mr Galley in King Street, Kingston, Jamaica, a Gentleman he thinks in the Law line, as he seemed always to have a great deal of business but knows nothing of them since, only he has heard that one of his brothers died since of the small pox.[27]

Child slaves were sometimes sent to Scotland 'as gifts or solicited from friends and relatives in the West Indies'.[28] William Colhoun, a ship's mate based in Sierra Leone, in a letter of 1775 outlined plans for his slave girl: 'I don't mean to sell her if my sister Betty will except of her, I will send her home [to Scotland] ... If Betty will not have her you may ex Janet [Colhoun's other sister] if she will be any serves to her and she shall have her.'[29] Colhoun stated she was 'a very fine girl about twelth years of age', and he indicated 'I have had her Eighteen mo[nths] with me.' Yet at no point in this letter is this child mentioned by name, and her simultaneous presence and absence is indicative of the history of slave children and adolescents. What this young girl thought of Colhoun is not recorded. Colhoun, however, wrote that 'She his very smart and will learn anything that his showing her. I have great regard for the Girl.' What is more, 'She can speak good English and I was the first white man [missing and torn] ever she saw.' Colhoun also considered an alternative course of action should neither of his sisters want her: 'If not, I know what to do with her as I never shall sell her she his been more serves to me than any white women that ever I know'd except Mother.' At this point in his life Colhoun was considering this girl as a potential

26 NRS, GD50/235/6, Transcription of the story of George Dale, Edinburgh 1790.
27 NRS, GD50/235/6.
28 Cairns, 'After Somerset', 304–5.
29 Glasgow City Archives [GCA], TD301/6/3/1.

lifelong slave companion, for 'if great god to spare me my life for two or three years till I come home, she will be more carefull over me in my old age than any white I can get'.[30] What her duties were remains unstated, and whether she was subjected to sexual abuse and exploitation is also unrecorded. In c.1775 she was twelve, but she had been purchased by Colhoun eighteen months earlier, indicating she must have been around the age of ten when she came into his possession.

As John Cairns points out, 'imported slaves aged ten to fourteen were considered particularly desirable purchases'.[31] Joseph Knight, who like George Dale had survived the Middle Passage and about whom we will read more below, also fitted this profile. So too did two eleven-year-old boys in advertisements from 1766, who were described respectively as 'Smart' and a recent arrival from 'North Carolina', and 'of healthy constitution' who 'can talk broken English'.[32] These slaves were old enough to be useful in a household, but once they reached adolescence their behaviour and compliance could change.

In addition to being brought to the West Indies through the Atlantic Slave trade, children were also born into slavery. A sexual economy in which slave children were fathered by free men ensured these children occupied an ambiguous space, not only between slaves and owners, but also within slave populations. The practical realities of this were set out by Patrick Stirling, the attorney at Hampden Estate in Jamaica, who in his will of 1776 stated:

> As every person resident in this country any time has children begot on the bodies of Africans or their descendants, and as you know I have some supposed or laid to my charge under the predicament, I request that you will procure that freedom of those not free in the first place and leave them entitled to all rights and privileges of Englishmen and one thousand pounds sterling to the male if his freedom can be procured, and another thousand pounds sterling to the daughter.[33]

Another example involves Dr James Clarke (d. 1819) from Aberdeen, who went to Dominica in 1770 where he owned Clarke Hall Estate. During a forty-year period he had 'an African-European woman who was known to everyone as Mary Clark, although Clarke never married her'.[34] They had four surviving children: Anna Eliza, Sarah, George and Edward. Of those children, Anna Eliza went to the British Isles and married the surgeon Mr Sims in London, while the sons remained in the Caribbean – George as a millright in Jamaica, and Edward as a clerk in Dominica.[35] In 1767, a slave woman called Betty was brought to Scotland by Peggy Hall, the natural daughter of the deceased Alexander Hall, hinting at the possible complexities of the houseful in early modern Scotland.

30 GCA, TD301/6/3/1.

31 Cairns, 'After Somerset', 295, n. 29.

32 *Edinburgh Evening Courant*, 27 September 1766, p. 3, and 6 December 1766, p. 3.

33 Jean Besson, *Martha Brae's Two Histories: European Expansion and Caribbean Culture-Building in Jamaica* (Chapel Hill and London, 2002), 65.

34 *A North East Story: Scotland, Africa and slavery in the Caribbean*, http://www.abdn.ac.uk/slavery/pdf/fortunehunters-caribbean.pdf (accessed 20 March 2013).

35 *A North East Story*.

Indeed, Betty arrived with a trunk of her possessions – suggesting a unique status – as slave masters often made only basic provisions of food and clothing for their plantation and house slaves.[36]

Whether free born, manumitted or enslaved, children fathered by white men met an unequal fate, one determined by and dependent upon both their race and the peculiarities of their circumstances. Men who travelled to the colonies soon availed themselves of male and female slaves to fulfil a number of functions. For example, Hugh Murray, who sailed to Jamaica in 1819 to manage a plantation, was quickly furnished by his employer with 'a decent apartment by myself, a Boy and a good horse to ride out and look after the Negros, when I please'. In addition, he reported that 'I have likewise got a very handsome Black girl for a House Keeper.'[37]

The letter sent to William and Allan Macpherson by their father, Lieutenant-Colonel Allan Macpherson (1740–1816), gives a rare glimpse into the practicalities of the sexual economy in the colonial world, and the circumstances surrounding the slave woman and biological children born into this unequal relationship: 'I by all means recommend to you to keep a decent Native woman of the Country where you may be as your constant concubine in preference to running after the loose & debauched Females.'[38] Macpherson, who had spent large tracts of his life in colonial postings such as India, sent this letter to his two sons shortly after their arrival in Guiana. William apparently took his father's advice and chose a slave girl called 'Countess', who was from James Fraser's Paradise Plantation where William was appointed a manager. William had initially intended to rename Countess as Harriet, after his sister, however after their first daughter was born in 1807 he called their slave child Harriet instead, after her biological aunt. In March 1807, shortly before William left to visit Scotland to see his parents, he purchased Countess from James Fraser for the sum of £120, leaving her and the infant under the supervision of his brother, an overseer at the plantation.[39] William asked Allan 'to act toward her and my child as you would wish me to do towards yours were you in my situation', and also 'to let me hear how she is by every letter which I expect once a month'.[40] Any biological offspring of white men and enslaved women was clearly a matter of contention, for he also added the request that 'any letter in which you mention Countess', please 'direct to me; my father and mother know nothing of the business, but I should like to see what you write about her before they see it'.[41] When William returned

36 NRS, GD206, Papers of the Hall Family of Dunglass, East Lothian, Letter, 26 August 1767.

37 Letter, Hugh Murray, Jamaica, to Thomas Balfour Esq, Stirling, 1 June 1819. Author's collection.

38 National Register of Archives for Scotland [NRAS], 2614, Private archives of the Macpherson family of Blairgowrie, still held in private hands, and listed in the NRAS, cited in Stephen Foster, *A Private Empire* (London, 2010), 141.

39 NRAS, 2614; Foster, *A Private Empire*, 141–2, 144.

40 NRAS, 2614; Foster, *A Private Empire*, 143.

41 NRAS, 2614; Foster, *A Private Empire*, 143.

to Guiana, he and Countess had two more slave children, Matilda (1809–?) and Allan (1810–96). As Stephen Foster has concluded, 'William chose Countess as his concubine and there is little likelihood that she had any choice in the matter.'[42] Although Countess (or Harriet, as William began to call her in later life) 'spoke English, or the local patois, which was part-English and part-Dutch, she was unable to read and write'. 'None of her words survive to tell us what she thought about her master or the situation in which she was kept', a situation that also removed her from enduring the back-breaking plantation fieldwork of her fellow slaves. It was only after the birth of Allan in 1810, William's third child but first son with Countess, that he decided to manumit not only both of his daughters and his son, but also their mother.[43] William then returned to Scotland taking the children, and leaving Countess behind. The male child, an heir by blood, proved to be the catalyst for the action of manumission, and one that demonstrated the gender divide in the slave experiences of women and girls, versus men and boys; hierarchical notions of male and female blood relatives could overturn other issues such as race.

The function of slave women as property is summed up by Robert Wedderburn, the son of a white planter father and slave mother, who recounted of his father's household in Jamaica that 'if any one proved with child – why, it was an acquisition which might one day fetch something at market like a horse or pig'.[44] Reflecting on his paternal connections, Wedderburn sets them out in unambiguous terms. 'My father ranged through the whole of his household for his own lewd purposes … my mother was forced to submit to him, being his slave.'[45] Wedderburn, like other children who were the progeny of a plantation-owner father, carried his father's name, but unlike his enslaved mother and sisters he was free, living out his childhood in Jamaica before coming to London in his adulthood, where he became a leading voice in the calls for abolition. The evidence suggests that the birth of a male slave child did appear to prick the conscience of some biological fathers – or at least awaken concerns of inheritance and dynasty – prompting them to free their male progeny.

In Scotland, slave owners exercised their ability to manumit slaves, but because the age of the slave is not given in these records it is impossible, in most cases, to determine the age at which they were freed. The case of Scipio Kennedy, however, is an exception, and also illuminating. Scipio was enslaved from Guinea on the West Coast of Africa, deprived of his own name from the age of six. Purchased by Captain Andrew Douglas, he was taken to Scotland. Douglas's daughter Jean married John Kennedy, and took Scipio with her to Culzean Castle, Ayrshire in 1710, where Scipio took on the last name Kennedy.

42 NRAS, 2614; Foster, *A Private Empire*, 389, 161.

43 NRAS, 2614; Foster, *A Private Empire*, 161, 162–7.

44 Martin Hoyles, *The Axe Laid to the Root: The Story of Robert Wedderburn* (London, 2004), 28; Robert Wedderburn, *The Horrors of Slavery and Other Writings*, ed. Iain McCalman (New York, 1991), 44–61.

45 Hoyles, *The Axe Laid to the Root*, 28; Wedderburn, *The Horrors of Slavery*, 44–61.

He was twenty-eight when he received his manumission, and chose to remain as a paid servant in the Kennedy household for the rest of his life.[46] In this case the relationship between manumitted slave and master proved strong after his manumission. Kennedy's right to self-determination, as well as his longevity and service were reflected in the willingness of the Kennedy family to build Scipio a residence on the grounds of Culzean Castle, where he and his wife Margaret Gray and his children would live until his death in 1774.[47]

Kennedy wrote in 1725 that 'I might have ... freedom by the law, on account of embracing the religion of the country.'[48] This belief also featured in the legal cases concerning three slaves: James Montgomery (1759), David Spens (1769) and Joseph Knight (1774–7). Each case was mounted by an owner attempting to prevent his slave from gaining freedom. While slave-holders assumed that a state of perpetual servitude existed on Scottish soil, this was not in fact the case in Scottish law. Both Scipio Kennedy and Joseph Knight were baptized in the Church of Scotland, public acts that brought them to the centre of their local communities.[49] Support from the Kirk was evident in the legal cases of Jamie Montgomery and David Spens.[50] Kennedy's freedom, once gained, saw him able to pursue relationships with women, which he clearly did. For example, his impropriety with Jean Fergusson for 'ye third time' was recorded in the Kirk Session Minutes dated 9 June 1728, reflecting his presence and recognition within this community.[51] He was repeatedly accused of sexual scandal and brought before the Kirk Sessions between 1727 and 1728 to answer the claims of the 'sin of fornication' made by Margaret Gray.[52] Perhaps Scipio's treatment at the Kirk Sessions – which shows him to have been an integrated member of the community liable to the same expectations as everyone else – reflects Scotland's experience of slavery. According to Whyte, this was markedly different from England, for:

> [a] comparatively small number of thinly distributed black slaves enabled them to be seen as individuals rather than as a group who might be a threat to white society. It was easier to see their plights as an unjust one and to appreciate the incongruity of slavery when slaves were encountered personally.[53]

Manumission records also provide valuable information on the maternity, if not the paternity, of slave children. For example, on 24 January 1786 William Stirling of Keir in the county of Perth, granted a boy called Charles his freedom

46 NRS, Ailsa Muniments, GD25/9/72/9, Manumission of Scipio Kennedy, 6 February 1725.

47 NRS, GD25/9/72/9. See also Jean Aitchison, *Servants in Ayrshire, 1750–1914* (Ayr, 2001), 15, 27.

48 Whyte, *Scotland and the Abolition*, 24.

49 For more on the baptism of slave children, see Chapter 1 in this collection.

50 Whyte, *Scotland and the Abolition*, 35.

51 NRS, CH2/562/1/381, Kirkoswald Kirk Session Minutes, 8 June 1728.

52 NRS, CH2/562/1/381, Kirkoswald Kirk Session Minutes, December 1727; February, March, May, June and December 1728.

53 Whyte, *Scotland and the Abolition*, 11.

from slavery, having received a payment of 10 shillings from John Stirling of Kippendavie. This single exchange 'hath manumised, Enfranchised and forever set free' this 'Mulatto boy'. Charles was the 'Son of a Negro slave named Cuba', and his manumission guaranteed that neither Stirling nor his heir could at anytime henceforth 'claim or challenge any right, title or interest whatsoever in or to the said Mulatto Boy named Charles or his future issue, offspring or increase'.[54] While we know the names of the boy Charles and his mother Cuba, what we do not know in this case is whether either of the men who manumitted this young boy was in fact freeing his own biological child, or that of a male relative. Manumission allowed the owner to feel a sense of generosity, but it could equally be motivated by self-interest. A slave owner who no longer had need of a particular slave could quickly cut his (or her) financial responsibility through manumission. Rather than attempting to sell the slave and incur both the costs of advertising and the inconvenience of finding a buyer, a slave could simply be set free. I have not found any examples yet of girls being manumitted in Scotland.

It is from newspaper advertisements for absconding slaves, or slaves for private sale or hire, that we can also gain a clearer understanding of the gendered nature of slave employments within the domestic household, as well as of the experience and agency of adolescent slaves. The thirty-eight advertisements published in the Scottish press listing 'runaways' or 'strays' were discussed by Iain Whyte. They were listed amongst advertisements for livestock, perpetuating the view that slaves were property that could be reclaimed.[55] The advertisements also claimed to have a foundation in law, so that 'any person apprehending the said negro slave, and lodging him … as every person knows the penalty … will be prosecuted'. The detailed descriptions of runaways sometimes included the slave's given name, an account of age, physical stature, and any distinguishing marks such as brands, as well as skin colour. Rewards were also intended to flush out the runaways, and ranged from two guineas to seven guineas.[56] For example in the *Glasgow Journal* of 30 December 1745, the following advertisement appeared: 'THAT on Friday last, a NEGROE BOY, about 15 Years of Age, deserted the Service of William Crawford, Junior, Merchant in Glasgow.'[57] The escape was possible because the slave, who is never identified by name, was at liberty and was 'supposed to have gone towards Stirling'. For those on the lookout for this youth he was identifiable: 'He Spoke very bad English, had on a Brown Freeze Coat, and Blue Waist Coat, and is much Innknee'd [knock-kneed].' Here his 'very bad English' suggests either an adolescent who had been enslaved late in his childhood, or possibly a rebellious adolescent who refused to speak the language of captivity. The advertisement's reference to 'Innknee'd' marked this slave out,

54 GCA, T-SK9/10.

55 Whyte, *Scotland and the Abolition*, 18; Cairns, 'After Somerset', 303, advertisements between 1701 and 1778.

56 Cairns, 'After Somerset', 306.

57 Advertisement in *Glasgow Journal*, 30 December 1745, facsimile reproduced in Mullen, *It Wasnae Us*, 11.

but may also have hinted at a lack of vitamin D in his diet as an infant and child. Rickets was a common disorder in child slave and non-slave populations. His return would prove profitable, for 'Whoever will bring back the said Boy to his Master, or give such Information of him, as that he may be apprehended, shall have a sufficient Reward.'[58] That there was apparently no need to give the slave's name suggests either that he was well known to some of the newspaper readership, or simply that his name was of no consequence.

Examples identifying a person simply by skin colour and gender are not uncommon in the archives, and include the 'Black Boy' listed as a servant of Mungo Smith Esquire Drongan from 1777 to 1779.[59] That 'Black boy' was called Jack Scott.[60] Murdoch Campbell of Rosend in Fife had a 'negro lad called CAESAR', aged eighteen, and 'a family of distinction' from the Canongate beside Edinburgh had an 'East-India Negro Lad' who was described as 'of the Mulatto colour', very well dressed and of sixteen to seventeen years of age.[61] The term 'boy' was also used pejoratively by owners to describe an adolescent or adult male slave, relegating them to perpetual child-like status. For example, an advertisement in the *Glasgow Courant* in 1758 listed the sale of 'A BLACK NEGROE BOY, about 5 foot 8 inches high and 17 years old.'[62]

What also emerges from these advertisements is the gender-specific duties of male and female slaves, with boys and men more likely to make a break for freedom because their duties took them outside the household unaccompanied. For women and girls the duties of washing, dressing and childcare were inherently domestic indoor activities, offering less likelihood of a solitary task that took them away from the confines of a watchful household setting. Trust once established, however, could provide slaves with the liberty to travel alone at the behest of their masters. 'As early as the 1740s, John Kincaird's "Negro Boy" Cato had the freedom to meet and get up to mischief in Edinburgh with Lady Stair's black pageboy.'[63]

In 1721 an eighteen-year-old black slave called Ann, with a 'brass collar about her neck' bearing the engraved words 'Gustavus Brown in Dalkeith, his negro', was advertised as missing.[64] Ann had taken an opportunity that had presented itself to abscond. Yet the collar, her skin colour, and her gender would have automatically marked her as out of place. Whyte suggests that collars may have

58 *Glasgow Journal*, 30 December 1745, facsimile reproduced in Mullen, *It Wasnae Us*, 11.

59 NRS, Servants Tax Returns 1777–1778, E326/5/1, cited in Jean Aitchison, *Servants in Ayrshire*, 15, 27. For additional discussion of children and youths being identified by their skin colour, see Chapter 1 in this collection.

60 'Black History Month', Ayrshire Archives, Exhibition.

61 *Edinburgh Evening Courant*, 15 March 1773, p. 3.

62 *Glasgow Courant*, 28 August 1758, Facsimile reproduction, Glasgow Story, Burrell Collection Photo Library, http://www.theglasgowstory.com/image.php?inum=TGSE00588 (accessed 20 March 2013).

63 NRS, GD150/3526/25, John Kincaird to James Watson, 28 August 1774, cited in John W. Cairns, 'After Somerset', 308.

64 *Edinburgh Evening Courant*, 7 March 1721, cited in Whyte, *Scotland and the Abolition*, 15.

been used in place of branding in Scotland, this being a 'more sophisticated and acceptable form of branding than the crude markings' burnt into the flesh of 'plantation slaves in the colonies'.[65] Scotland already had a tradition of collars in use for domestic livestock. There were cow collars and dog collars, as well as slave collars in use in the late seventeenth and eighteenth centuries. There may also have been a distinction between 'serfs' and slaves, given the evidence of one brass collar held in the National Museums of Scotland that contains the following inscription: 'Alexr. Steuart found guilty of death for theft at Perth the 5th of December 1701, & gifted by the Justiciars as a perpetual servant to Sir Jo. Areskin of Alva.'[66] Slave collars like the one in the duke of Drummond portrait 'could not be removed without a key and were usually inscribed with the owner's coat of arms or address'.[67] Gustavus Brown's social rank was evident in the collar secured to Ann's neck, marking this young woman as property to the illiterate, and specifically as Brown's property to the literate. What is not known is whether Ann was apprehended.

In addition to advertisements offering rewards for runaways, advertisements were also placed for those looking to purchase or hire slave labour. For example, an advertisement in the *Edinburgh Evening Courant* on 30 August 1766, offered for sale a nineteen-year-old woman and her infant child:

> To be disposed of
> A NEGRO WOMAN, named Peggy, about
> Nineteen years of age, born and brought
> up in Charlestoun, in the Province of South Caro-
> lina, speaks good English, and exceeding good
> House-wench, and washer and dresser, and is very
> tender and careful of children. She has a young
> Child, a Negro boy, about a year old, which will
> be disposed of with the mother. For particulars
> Inquire at the publisher of this paper.[68]

The advertisement describes Peggy in terms of her colonial provenance and unusually her childhood is mapped out for us, implying a long-term association between owner (either male or female) and slave. Peggy was 'born and brought up in Charlestown, in the Province of South Carolina'. Her childhood had provided her with saleable skills, for she 'Speaks good English', is an 'exceeding good House-wench, and washer and dresser, and is tender and careful of children'. Her ability with children was born out of personal experience, for to be 'disposed of with the mother' was Peggy's 'young child, a Negro boy, about a year old', who is given no name. Her infant son is categorized by gender, race and maternal descent only, and rendered fatherless. The grounds and circumstances

65 Whyte, *Scotland and the Abolition*, 15.

66 NMS, H.MR 3. See also E.F.L., 'Slavery in Scotland', *Notes & Queries* 5:115 (1852), 29; Whyte, *Scotland and the Abolition*, 15.

67 Bindman, 'The Black Presence in British Art', 259.

68 *Edinburgh Evening Courant*, 30 August 1766, p. 3.

regarding the need for this sale are not stated either. The reasons for selling a slave could include a change in economic circumstances, or an owner unwilling to cover the costs of a pregnant female slave, or slave mother and child. What are beyond the record are the emotions that arose when a man from within the household – perhaps a husband or son – fathered a slave child. In these instances his wife and/or other members of the family may have insisted that both the slave mother and slave child were removed from the house. Alternatively, sexual relations between slaves or between slaves and servants may also have resulted in female slave pregnancies.

The relationship between masters and the slaves they had purchased as children was a complex one, for as the child grew up there were certain levels of trust and expectations that came into play. Any deviation, or broken promise by the master or in turn the slave, could then result in increasing tensions and animosities that would only escalate as these enslaved children moved through their adolescence. A slave called Marshall, between fifteen and sixteen years of age, who was described as 'a good looking lad, tall and well made' who spoke with a 'broad Scotch' accent, absconded from Mr Naesmith in Stranraer when an opportunity presented itself in 1774.[69] Naesmith was keen to have the lad back, for he offered a reward of 'TWO GUINEAS (besides paying all the charges) … so he may be apprehended and brought back to services'.[70]

One eighteenth-century slave child who had sailed from the West Indies into a Scottish port was Joseph Knight. Knight was purchased at twelve or thirteen years of age in 1762 by the ex-patriot Scot John Wedderburn, a sugar planter from near Montego Bay, Jamaica.[71] When in 1769 Wedderburn decided to return home, he took his house-boy Knight with him. Wedderburn believed that a slave's enslaved status persisted on Scottish soil, however no Scots law of slavery existed, for while Scotland and England had united in 1707, their respective legal codes remained separate. 'No decision of any English court in Westminster Hall would have any direct effect in Scotland.'[72] Freedom for slaves hinged on an understanding of the right to choose, and the realization of service as comprising a voluntary contractual relationship with commensurate wages. Securing manumission also enabled these free men to marry, and to have and maintain a family. The right to familial self-determination was the breaking point for the slave Joseph Knight. When his fellow servant Annie Thomson was found to be pregnant, she was dismissed from the Wedderburn household, and Knight's request to allow them to live together was denied.[73] In Knight's case, Wedderburn had discussed the prospect of future manumission in an attempt to get him to submit to his current position. Yet nine years after Knight arrived in Scotland, the Court of Sessions in Edinburgh granted him his freedom in the

69 *Edinburgh Courant*, 14 February 1774, p. 3.
70 *Edinburgh Courant*, 14 February 1774, p. 3.
71 Cairns, 'After Somerset', 291.
72 Cairns, 'After Somerset', 298.
73 Whyte, *Scotland and the Abolition*, 17.

case of *Knight v Wedderburn* (1778). The *Caledonian Mercury*, on 17 January 1778, proclaimed to its readership that 'the rights of humanity were weighed in the scales of justice', and that 'it must give a very high satisfaction to the inhabitants of the United Kingdom, that the freedom of Negroes has obtained its first *general determination* in the Supreme Civil Court of Scotland'.[74]

A testament to the black presence in Scotland's urban and rural households is the eighteenth-century family portrait of John Glassford of Dougalston. In its recently restored state, the family portrait depicts the silhouette image of an unidentified black male servant as part of the houseful, standing in profile behind Glassford's chair.[75] Thanks to the restoration, this servant is once again visible to the viewer, having been painted out of the portrait at some point during the painting's history, reflecting the ambiguity, ambivalence, and at times absence of slavery from the Scottish historical narrative. The evidence for the existence of slaves is fleeting and can often comprise a single reference, as in the case of 'Colonel McDowell of Castle Semple', a Glasgow merchant and West Indian plantation owner, who 'had a "negro lad" named Cato' that 'ran away in 1748'.[76] Although the ability to assert agency is questionable, these young men and women were historical actors and could make their will known through their actions. This is evident in a case from Muirtown in Perthshire, when on 3 June 1768 'a stout lad' called 'London', aged seventeen, 'a negro slave' of 'Capt. Olyphant Kinloch', made a dash for his freedom.[77] Whether he would still answer 'to the name London' once free was a moot point.[78]

This essay has used the themes of a child slave presence, paternity, maternity and manumission to recover examples of slave children's lives, brief, scant and incomplete though they are. These examples shine shards of light on limited aspects of child and adolescent slave experiences. Slave children lived within the varied forms of household and plantation life. Some lived within the confines of the biological and extended family, while others existed as a member of a houseful – that is, all those children, women and men residing under the one roof, but on unequal terms. Historians have written about the presence of men and women as slaves in Scotland, and yet the childhood of those adults, and others like them, some of whom were born into slavery, is an area in need of further research. Most of the examples discussed here are male, and yet the slave women who gave birth to these children, like their daughters, are, at times, startlingly present. At its most complex, the relationship between slave and owner may

74 Whyte, *Scotland and the Abolition*, 18.

75 Glasgow Museums, 2887, oil on canvas painting by Archibald McLauchlan, *The Glassford Family*, 1767. For an English example of a similarly disembodied slave where only their hands appear on the periphery of a domestic scene, see William Hogarth's 'A Family Scene' (c.1735), in Amy Athey McDonald, '"A Bold Effort": Illuminating Images of Slavery in the British Empire', *Yale News*, 2 November 2014, http://news.yale.edu/2014/11/02/bold-effort-illuminating-images-slavery-british-empire (accessed 8 December 2014).

76 Cairns, 'After Somerset', 304–5.

77 *Caledonian Mercury*, 8 June 1768, p. 1, advertisements.

78 *Caledonian Mercury*, 8 June 1768, advertisements.

have been a biological connection. What has emerged throughout this chapter, however, is both the importance of, and yet disregard for, connections of kinship between owners and their slave children. Slave women functioned as property, offering two bonuses: their potential or demonstrated work abilities, and their reproductive capacity, both of which were calculated into their commercial sale value. The eighteenth-century family portrait of John Glassford of Dougalston, and his as yet unidentified black male servant, therefore makes visible once more an aspect of Scotland's history and the history of the Diaspora. The all-pervasive practice of child slavery in the twenty-first century should alert historians to look for its antecedents.[79]

[79] Jeremy Black, *A Brief History of Slavery: A New Global History* (London, 2011), 230–59.

8

Natural Affection, Children, and Family Inheritance Practices in the Long Eighteenth Century

Katie Barclay

> It has pleased God to bless me with Alexander, James, George, Euphan, Mary, Grace and Jean Chancelor, my children, procreat betwixt me and Mrs Jean Agneu, my spouse, daughter to Sir James Agneu of Lochnaw, Barronet, for whom, my natural love and affection, I am bound to provide (John Chancellor of Shiehill, 14 December 1720).[1]

The broad legal framework for Scottish inheritance practice had been in place for several centuries by the time John Chancellor wrote this bond of provision for his children in 1720. Within it, following both common custom amongst much of the Scottish landed classes and inheritance law, he arranged for part of his property to be placed in the hands of trustees to be sold for the benefit of his children. From the proceeds, he allocated 10,000 merks to each of his younger children and the remainder, if any, to his eldest son Alexander, who also inherited the family estate. As he noted within his bond, his choice to provide for his children was motivated by duty – he was 'bound to provide' – but a duty that originated in his 'natural love and affection' for his children.

The duty of love that parents owed children was a recurring motif across the early modern period, expounded as a 'natural' duty in sermons and conduct books, and placed alongside expectations that parents provide for, educate, and protect them.[2] During the seventeenth century, the growing popularity of natural law theories amongst lawyers and philosophers across Europe reinforced the importance of natural affection within the family. Most argued that this emotional bond between parent and child was a biological or innate response

[1] NRS, Papers of the Chancellor Family of Shieldhill, GD118/230, Bond by John Chancellor of Shiehill, 14 December 1720.

[2] Linda Pollock, 'Parent–Child Relations', in David Kertzer and Marzio Barbagli (eds), *The History of the European Family in Early Modern Times* (New Haven, 2001), 191–3; Gregory M. Colón Semenza, '"Second childishness" and the Shakespearean Vision of Ideal Parenting', in Naomi Miller and Naomi Yavneh (eds), *Gender and Early Modern Constructions of Childhood* (Aldershot, 2011), 223–6; Ilana Krausman Ben-Amos, 'Human Bonding: Parents and their Offspring in Early Modern England', *University of Oxford Discussion Papers in Economic and Social History* 17 (1997), 4–6; Joanna Bailey, *Parenting in England 1760–1830: Emotion, Identity and Generation* (Oxford, 2012).

designed to ensure the continuation of the population. As John Tillotson, a seventeenth-century archbishop of Canterbury whose works were reprinted in Scotland across the eighteenth century, noted with regard to the 'affection and tenderness' due to children: 'there cannot be a greater reproach to Creatures that are endued with Reason, than to neglect a duty to which Nature directs even Brute Creatures by a blind and unthinking Instinct'.[3]

Despite Tillotson's confidence, the origins of this instinct and the implications for the emotional relationship between parent and children were topics of considerable debate. A letter to the *Athenian Mercury* in the late seventeenth century encapsulated some of the problems raised by this understanding of affection. The letter-writer asked:

> Supposing a Parent, either Father or Mother, or both, were separated from their Child (being an Infant) for many years, and they shou'd meet unknown in some place unexpected to each other; whether there be such an Instinct in Nature, that these Persons shou'd have an Affection and Tenderness for each other on first Sight, and utterly unknown, which they never felt for any other Stranger? — If not, then what or where is natural affection?[4]

The editors of the *Mercury* responded that 'none can doubt' that natural affection existed, but whether it 'amounts to an Instinct' that would allow a mother to discover her child was 'not certain'. Despite this, they believed that it was 'sufficient, in ordinary cases to incline and fit any Rational Creature, for the Education of their own Off-spring'. This was a discussion that continued into and across the eighteenth century, where the Scottish philosopher Adam Smith's contribution was to argue that 'natural affection' arose from shared cohabitation, a 'habitual sympathy', not biology, and so did not extend to children who were separated from their parents in infancy.[5]

Far from simply being an abstract debate amongst philosophers about the nature of the relationship between parent and child, this discussion around the importance, role and implications of 'natural affection' between parent and child informed the ways people understood the nature of that relationship. Nowhere was this more evident than within Scotland's inheritance practices, where natural affection was a key principle and justification for their form, and yet what this meant in practice was in flux and debated in the Scottish courts during the inheritance disputes of the period. This essay explores the role that understandings of 'natural affection' played in shaping Scots inheritance practices, beginning with a discussion of the concept of natural affection within Scots inheritance law, before going on to explore how this idea was utilized within inheritance disputes.

[3] John Tillotson, *The Works of the Most Reverend Dr John Tillotson* (London, 1720), 524. Editions were printed in Scotland in 1748, 1759, 1760 and 1772.

[4] *The Athenian Oracle: being an entire collection of all the valuable questions and answers in the old Athenian mercuries*, 4 vols (London, 1703), ii, 388–9.

[5] Adam Smith, *The Theory of Moral Sentiments*, 2 vols (London and Edinburgh, 1792), ii, 69–74.

This essay speaks to a long running, if now slightly dated debate around the nature of affective relationships within the early modern family and whether parental love was the product of the modern, sentimental family or something more enduring.[6] It also contributes to a discussion around the nature of the eighteenth-century family, which increasingly emphasizes the importance of the unit of the household in creating the boundaries of the family and determining who was included under that heading.[7] In contrast, inheritance practices across most of Europe placed an emphasis on the biological family.[8] The concept of 'natural affection' was used to reinforce both the biological nature of the family and the ties created through shared space. This concept operated as a useful heuristic device to help eighteenth-century people, and in turn twenty-first-century historians, explore the nature of family relationships.

Natural Affection and Scottish Inheritance Law

Scots inheritance law primarily originated from feudal law, but was informed by both Roman and canon law, as wills and bequests were administered by the Commissary Courts (which drew on canon law).[9] It was consolidated, like the rest of Scots civil law, in 1681 (revised in 1693) by James Dalrymple, Lord Stair, in his opus magnum, *The Institutions of the Law of Scotland*. This was, as Lord Cooper put it, 'an original amalgam of Roman law, Feudal law, and native customary law, systemized by resort to the law of nature and the Bible'.[10] The importance of natural law to Lord Stair's construction of Scots law has been noted by a number of historians, informing and underpinning his interpretation and framing of legislation, legal precedence and customary practice that had often existed for centuries.[11] Not all of Lord Stair's interpretations of the law went unchallenged, but this text acted as the foundation of modern Scottish

6 Philippe Ariès, *Centuries of Childhood: A Social History of Family Life* (New York, 1962); Lawrence Stone, *The Family, Sex and Marriage in England 1500–1800* (New York, 1977); R.A. Houlbrooke, *The English Family, 1450–1700* (London, 1984); Linda Pollock, *Forgotten Children: Parent–child Relations from 1500 to 1900* (Cambridge, 1983); Keith Wrightson, *English Society, 1580–1680* (London, 1982); Alan Macfarlane, *Marriage and Love in England: Modes of Reproduction, 1300–1840* (Oxford, 1986).

7 Naomi Tadmor, *Family and Friends in Eighteenth-Century England: Household, Kinship and Patronage* (Cambridge, 2001); Naomi Tadmor, 'The Concept of the Household-Family in Eighteenth-Century England', *Past and Present* 151 (1996), 111–40.

8 Anne-Lise Head-König and Péter Pozsgai (eds), *Inheritance Practices, Marriage Strategies and Household Formation in European Rural Societies* (Turnhout, 2012); Lloyd Bonfield, 'Developments in European Family Law', in Kertzer and Barbagli (eds), *History of the European Family*, 87–124.

9 *An Introduction to Scottish Legal History* (Edinburgh, 1958), see chapters on heritable property, moveable property and succession.

10 Quoted in J. Irvine Smith, 'The Rise of Modern Scots Law, 1660–1707', *Introduction to Scottish Legal History*, 45.

11 Martin Hogg, 'Perspectives on Contract Theory from a Mixed Legal System', *Oxford Journal of Legal Studies* 29:4 (2009), 643–73.

law, the key legal authority that succeeding generations of lawyers, judges and legal writers would utilize and negotiate when creating new legal precedent. As a result, the principles of natural law, including the concept of natural affection, were central to the construction of inheritance law and practice across the long eighteenth century. Moreover, while not all families conformed to legal precepts, the law played a significant role in defining the nature of the family and acted as the final arbitrator of disputes when people disagreed over who was a part of it. Legal definitions were significant in shaping the social imaginary of 'the family', whilst also being informed by and reflecting social norms.[12]

For Stair, like many other natural law theorists, the family was a fundamental unit of society, and originated in the marriage relationship, as evidenced by the 'natural affection, which all sorts of men, in all places of the world … have unto a married state'.[13] The duties and obligations that arose between family members were also natural and God-given, arising 'from the Obedience Man oweth to his Maker, who hath written this Law in the Hearts of Parents and Children'.[14] Stair noted that parents' obligations to their children consisted of 'Natural Affection, Provision and Education', whilst children's were: 'Reverence, Obsequiousness and of Inter[t]ainment of Parents, not able to Intertain themselves'.[15] Later in the text, he affirmed that, once adults, children owed their parents 'tenderness'.[16] Relationships between siblings were also presumed to be affectionate and tied siblings into similar bonds of obligation as between parent and child:

> there naturally lyes greater Obligations upon them, each to other, than the common Obligations betwixt man and man, which are not only greater in the measure and degrees, as to love them, assist them, support them, and supply their necessities the more, by how nearer degree of Blood they are bound to them than to others, which is commonly acknowledged by all.[17]

For Stair then, natural affection was at the heart of the family relationship, both giving rise to, and motivating people to perform, their natural obligations to provide and care for each other.

While the nature of natural affection was the topic of some debate across the century, that it was the basis of the natural and legal relationship between family members was not significantly challenged. Interestingly, later Scottish jurists such as Lord Bankton (1685–1760) and John Erskine of Carnock (1695–1768) did not locate affection or love amongst the duties of parents and children (although both, like Stair, listed it as a duty of marriage), yet it was assumed to be the basis of the parental obligations of provision, protection, preservation and education,

12 J.A. Sharpe, 'The People and the Law', in Barry Reay (ed.), *Popular Culture in Seventeenth-Century England* (London, 1985), 248.

13 James Dalrymple, Viscount of Stair, *The Institutions of the Law of Scotland*, 2 vols (Edinburgh, 1693), i, 24.

14 Stair, *Institutions*, i, 37.

15 Stair, *Institutions*, i, 37.

16 Stair, *Institutions*, i, 40.

17 Stair, *Institutions*, i, 41.

and of children's responsibility to reverence, respect, and, in case of necessity, maintain parents.[18] Erskine argued that fathers were administrators-in-law to their children, as they were 'from the affection stamped by nature itself upon that relation, presumed to act to the best of their power for their children's interest', while Bankton argued that maintenance of children by parents 'is presumed to flow from natural affection'.[19] What had changed between Stair and Bankton and Erskine was that love had moved from a felt obligation – love as something that was performed and could be measured – to becoming an abstract impulse for action. This may suggest that later jurists were more pragmatic than Stair, listing obligations that were actually enforceable through a court of law, which was difficult in the case of a feeling. However, it may also reflect the wider shift in the meaning of love that occurred during the eighteenth century, where love became understood in more abstract terms as a feeling motivating action, rather than a felt duty marked by action.[20]

As affection was understood to arise naturally within the family, it followed that it could be used to define who was part of the family. The law's interest in classifying the family lay in three main areas: first, in controlling its formation through rules around marriage and divorce; second, as explored above, in asserting the legal obligations of members of the family towards each other; and third, in determining lines of succession for the purposes of inheritance.[21] In all three areas, the family was primarily understood as the 'nuclear family', that is husband and wife, parents and children, and siblings. Inheritance law was slightly more encompassing, listing the collateral relatives that would be entitled to inherit if the immediate family failed. This included aunts, uncles, nieces and nephews.[22] In law, the family was emphatically biological, with Stair arguing that 'by the common law, he is only heir who succeeds by right of blood'; for those who died intestate, once biological heirs were depleted, property returned to the crown.[23] Yet, as the rules of succession suggest, not all members of the biological family were equal, with some relationships prioritized before others.

The justification for this ranking across the family was explained in terms of natural affection, where particular familial bonds were more emotionally charged than others. The line of succession created by law was understood to be the 'will of the defunct' – in other words, what society presumed the deceased would have

[18] Andrew MacDowall, Lord Bankton, *An Institute of the Laws of Scotland in Civil Rights*, 2 vols (Edinburgh, 1751), i, 152–6; John Erskine of Carnock, *An Institute of the Laws of Scotland in Four Volumes*, 2 vols (Edinburgh, 1824), i, 153–63.

[19] Erskine, *An Institute*, i, 158; Bankton, *An Institute*, i, 232.

[20] Katie Barclay, *Love, Intimacy and Power: Marriage and Patriarchy in Scotland, 1650–1850* (Manchester, 2011). For a seventeenth-century example of a child's affection entailing a felt duty marked by action, see Chapter 3 in this collection.

[21] For a discussion of the law around the formation and duties of marriage, see Frederick Parker Walton, *A Handbook of Husband and Wife According to the Law of Scotland* (Edinburgh, 1893), and Barclay, *Love, Intimacy and Power*, Ch. 2.

[22] Stair, *Institutions*, i, 429–51; Bankton, *An Institute*, ii, 248–365.

[23] Stair, *Institutions*, i, 313.

wanted based on his or her expected natural affections. For this reason, the law of succession did not allow the 'Right of Representation' amongst collateral heirs – that is, for the heirs to a deceased collateral heir to inherit on the deceased's behalf – because 'the Propinquity of Blood, Natural Affection, and so the presumed Will of the Defunct is diminished'.[24] Yet, 'natural law' and traditional Scottish inheritance practices did not always line up so neatly. Stair argued that Scots law prioritized siblings over parents in the line of succession, as it was 'the continuance of that same Fatherly Affection ... because [siblings] stand in more need of Provision than the Father'.[25] Siblings inherited not because they had a higher claim to the natural affections of the deceased than did parents, but because of the affections of the parent towards the remaining siblings.

In contrast, relationships between non-family members were not expected to hold this natural affection, which had implications for the distribution of property. As Bankton noted, whereas 'a man' could give 'his wife, children, brother' his land out of 'natural love and affection', for the distribution of land to a stranger to be legally binding it 'must be for money, or other valuable consideration'.[26] The legal importance of 'affection' in the distribution of property can be seen in the standard use of phrases like 'as a token of my affection and attachment', 'out of regard, affection and esteem', 'for the love and affection', 'for love, favour and affection' that appeared in bonds and dispositions transferring property rights across the period, including in cases that did not involve immediate family members.[27] As well as likely reflecting the property owner's motivations for transferring property, affection became legal shorthand to justify and explain property transfers that circumvented normal lines of succession or the requirement for land to be exchanged for money to be lawful.

Within this context, the line of succession came to symbolize the appropriate depth of affectionate feeling that members of the family should hold towards each other, and, perhaps equally with that between husband and wife, the relationship between parent and legitimate child was understood as the most significant. Legitimate children were entitled in law to inherit from their parents, although the rules for succession were dependent upon whether property was heritable (land, buildings, and related items) or moveable (almost everything else). Unless otherwise determined by pre-existing entails or settlements, Scotland practised primogeniture, with the eldest son entitled to inherit his parent's heritable

24 Stair, *Institutions*, i, 432.

25 Stair, *Institutions*, i, 451.

26 Bankton, *An Institute*, ii, 245.

27 For example, NRS, Papers of the Munro Family of Foulis, GD93/343, David Bethune to Sir Robert Munro of Fowlis, 13 May 1734; Extract registered submission by Sir Harry Munro of Fowlis and John Munro of Culcairn, 3 August 1756; Papers of the Campbell Family of Duntroon, GD116/1/199, Extract registered disposition by James Campbell of Duntroon to Neil Campbell, his son, 3 April 1760; GD116/1/136, Disposition of Angus Campbell of Daltot, 1–6 October 1697; GD116/1/97, Disposition of Neil Campbell of Dountroon to Patrick Campbell, 1680; Papers of the Scott Family of Harden, GD157/3193, Codicil to the testament of Mary, countess of Breadalbane, 4 May 1660.

property; failing a male heir, the property was split equally between any daughters. Until 1868, heritable property could not be willed and so an heir or heiress could not be disinherited on their parent's death. However, land could be disposed of during the parent's lifetime through sale and settlements, effectively 'disinheriting' the heir, but also requiring the parent to give up their ownership of the same land. In practice, especially after 1685, the popularity of entailing estates took this decision out of the hands of individuals, leaving property to descend 'in trust' over generations.[28]

Primogeniture was not understood to arise from natural law, as this would contravene natural equity, where parents should love all children equally. Instead, it was an 'expedient' system that brought the public benefit of maintaining the estates of 'Great Families', necessary, for Stair, to defend the country from 'Sudden Invasions', and in the later eighteenth century, to ensure social order.[29] It also arose from the 'private' desire to preserve 'the Memory, and Dignity of Families, which by frequent Division of the Inheritance, would become despicable or forgotten'.[30] As Bankton rather romantically put it: 'The desire of immortality is so deeply rooted in the human frame, that it extends even to one's name and memory, after his death, that the same may be preserved in his representatives.'[31] In contrast, the division of moveable property was understood to arise from a 'Natural Obligation' for parents to provide for their children 'not only during Life, but after his Death'.[32]

The moveable property of a married couple was imagined into three parts, with a wife entitled to one third, a husband one third, and the children one third. In the event that one spouse was dead or there were no children, the remaining two parties halved the moveable property. Both husbands and wives were entitled to bequeath their own third freely by will, although a husband had a liferent interest in his wife's property if she predeceased him, so that bequests did not have to be fulfilled until his death. Children shared equally in their part of the moveables. If the eldest son succeeded to the family estate, he was excluded from this division, unless he was an only child. He received 'heritable moveables' that moved with the landed estate (such as particular furniture or the family jewels).[33] Legitimate children could not be disinherited from their rights to moveable property (unless they rendered themselves 'unworthy' by 'wicked and unnatural behaviour', such as parricide or treason), although, like heritable property, it could be disposed of

28 A.W.B. Simpson, *Legal Theory and Legal History: Essays on the Common Law* (London, 1987), 143–62.

29 Stair, *Institutions*, i, 437. For a discussion of the evolution of this feudal principle into a general concern with law and order, see Katie Barclay, David Lemmings and Claire Walker, *Governing the Emotions: The Family, the Law and the Press in the Long-Eighteenth Century* (forthcoming), Ch. 4.

30 Stair, *Institutions*, i, 437.

31 Bankton, *An Institute*, ii, 291.

32 Stair, *Institutions*, i, 434, 439.

33 Stair, *Institutions*, i, 439.

within the parent's lifetime.[34] If a parent left a heritable estate, but an insufficient moveable estate to provide acceptable portions for younger children, the heir to the heritable estate became obliged to support his siblings, although to what extent was a topic of legal debate finally resolved through legislation at the end of the eighteenth century.[35] Children could renounce their inheritance, or come to an equitable settlement with parents as an alternative to their legal share.

Illegitimate or 'natural' children were imagined as part of the family, in that they were entitled to care and provision from their parents, but their claim to property was weaker. In this, illegitimate children were situated just as in their status in law, on the outskirts of the family. Illegitimate children were those born outside of marriage, but they could subsequently be legitimized by the marriage of their parents (or, rarely, by letters of legitimation by the monarch). Scotland did not require a marriage ceremony for a legal marriage, leaving the legitimacy of children of irregular marriages open to dispute in court.[36] Illegitimate children were legally viewed as 'fatherless' and so could make no claim on their father's estates – either heritable or moveable. They could, however, inherit their mother's property and were entitled to a share of her moveables, alongside any legitimate half-siblings. This was because maternity, and its related affections, was not disputed, whereas, in law, the father of an illegitimate child was always 'uncertain'. Whether illegitimate children could inherit their mother's heritable property was a matter of legal debate during the century.[37] Natural children were entitled to receive any property willed to them by their parents, but could not bequeath their property on death unless they had their own legitimate offspring.[38]

After parent and child, the next most important family relationship was expected to be between siblings. Where siblings were each other's nearest kin, children who shared two parents excluded half-siblings from inheriting. In addition, the law prioritized patrilineal ties over matrilineal. In practice, this meant that half-siblings that shared a father were entitled to a share of each other's property (if the deceased had no 'full-blooded' siblings), but those that shared a mother had no claim on each other – even if the property in question had been inherited from the mother. So, if a son inherited his mother's estate and died without children, the estate would go to the son's nearest relative on his father's side, even if they had no biological tie with his mother and despite the fact the mother had other children (unless the entail decreed otherwise).[39] As a general rule, when looking for a nearest heir, relatives from the father's side had priority over the mother's family, in most cases excluding maternal kin entirely.

34 Bankton, *An Institute*, ii, 331.

35 Eileen Spring, *Law, Land and Family: Aristocratic Inheritance in England, 1300–1800* (London, 1993), 81–2.

36 Leah Leneman and Rosalind Mitchison, *Sexuality and Social Control: Scotland 1660–1780* (Oxford, 1989), 79–133.

37 Stair, *Institutions*, i, 429–51; Bankton, *An Institute*, ii, 308.

38 Stair, *Institutions*, i, 580.

39 Bankton, *An Institute*, ii, 308.

The result of this conceptualization of kin relationships within the law was to provide an ideal model for affective relations that shaped expectations for feeling between family members. Given the broader importance of both natural law theory and the law itself, these emotional expectations permeated eighteenth-century Scottish culture.[40] Adam Smith listed 'the Order in which Individuals are recommended by Nature to our care and attention', beginning with parent and child: a man's affections are 'more strongly directed towards his children than his parents', as 'the existence of the child … depends altogether on the care of the parent'. He next prioritized siblings, arguing that: 'The earliest friendships, the friendships which are naturally contracted when the heart is most susceptible of that feeling, are those amongst brothers and sisters … They are capable of giving more pleasure or pain to one another than to the greater part of other people.'[41] The author Jean Marishall similarly emphasized the importance of sibling ties, warning her school-aged nephew in her epistolary advice book (1789) to be careful that his friendships did not alienate his brothers, and that well-chosen friends would not try to 'insinuate themselves more into your favour than those who have a prior or natural right to your affection'.[42] She reminded him that 'a house divided against itself cannot stand; and that it is the neglect of those little attentions which gradually cools the affections much oftener than real injury'. She concluded by advising him that if one brother was more 'successful in life', it was his responsibility to aid the rest 'with advice, pecuniary assistance, interest, or whatever else is in his power, without injuring his nearer connections, a wife or children'.

Natural Affection and Inheritance Disputes

> [W]hen law-suits unluckily happen between very near relations, they are generally carried on with more keenness and acrimony, than any other questions which come before the court.[43]

The importance of this model of affective relationships within the family underpinned the debates that arose during inheritance disputes that came to the courts. Across the long eighteenth century, wills, bequests and cases where people died intestate that dealt with moveable property were generally tried in the regional Commissary Courts around Scotland, with the right of appeal to the central Edinburgh Commissary Court. It was rare for disputes over moveable property to be appealed to the high courts. Disputes that dealt with 'real' property, including heritable estates, were heard in the Court of Session and could ultimately be appealed to the House of Lords. In addition, the Edinburgh Commissary Court

40 For a discussion of the importance of these values in an English context, see Bailey, *Parenting in England*.

41 Smith, *The Theory of Moral Sentiments*, ii, 69–72.

42 Jean Marishall, *A Series of Letters*, 2 vols (Edinburgh, 1789), i, 65–7.

43 James Boswell, *The Petition of Miss Peggy Buchanan* (*s.l.*, 15 November 1770), 1.

was actively involved in determining the rights of succession, as it had jurisdiction over deciding the validity of marriages and the legitimacy of children from such marriages. As a number of inheritance disputes rested on such claims, some of these suits were effectively decided through the Commissary Court system.[44] In all these contexts, natural affection was used to explain and justify the behaviour of individuals and its absence used to criticize. More interestingly, what natural affection looked like and its implications for inheritance practices were disputed.

The importance of natural affection to succession law was reflected in a general assumption that a parent's loving treatment of their children was evidence of their biological relationship (or at least, in the case of fathers, the belief in that biological relationship). During the Blair bastardy suit in 1740, where the paternity, and so legitimacy, of the Blair sisters was contested by their cousins, the behaviour of their father towards them was considered to be central evidence of his acceptance that the children were his own. The father, Alexander Blair of Kinfauns, was variously described as a cruel or a loving father by different witnesses, who used his actions towards his daughters as evidence of his belief in their legitimacy. One witness for the pursuers argued that 'when the servants brought in the said child to the Room, he shutt his Eyes and keept them closs all the while the Child was in the Room and ordered her to put it away'; another noted that 'any Body that heard or observed Kinfawns Carriage and Expressions would think that he would be satisyed that the Child were dead'. In contrast, his daughters' witnesses argued that they 'had seen Kinfawns ... take the young Child in his Arms and walk over the Floor with it Which was ane Instance of Tenderness that the Deponent had seldom observed in Fathers'. Another argued that he always remembered the children's birthdays, and that the 'Child & her Maid sat by Kinfawns at table, and that Kinfawns cutt the Child's meat & fed her'. He was also described giving his children 'Suggar Candy' and taking delight in his toddler daughter running directly to him when being set down on the floor.[45]

Reflecting the belief that the duties of provision, education and care grew out of the natural affection that parents had towards their children, these physical markers of care were also central evidence of a familial relationship. Yet, as this was a duty to which both legitimate and illegitimate children were entitled, there was some debate over what the fulfilment of such duties evidenced. This discussion was heightened by a wider social belief that legitimate and illegitimate children were entitled to different types of provision and education, reflecting that illegitimate children held a lower social status.[46] In 1697, Nicholas Marjoribanks

[44] Leah Leneman, 'Legitimacy and Bastardy in Scotland, 1694–1830', *SHR* 80 (2001), 45–62.

[45] NRS, CC8/5/5/7, Anna Blair agt Jean Carnegie and Margaret and Anne Carnegie or Blair, 1740.

[46] Katie Barclay, 'Sex, Identity and Enlightenment in the Long Eighteenth Century', in Jodi Campbell, Elizabeth Ewan and Heather Parker (eds), *Shaping Scottish Identity: Family, Nation and the Worlds Beyond* (Guelph, 2011), 29–42.

claimed that her elder half-sister, from her father's first marriage, recognized her as a legitimate child because 'she did put her to Schooll, and gave her such education as she had herself when she was of her age, and particularly she was Instructed in the french language, and boarded her in a french woman's house, and frequently minded her on her death bed, with great kindnes & affection'.[47]

Whilst some trials seemed to reflect a straightforward understanding of the connection between affection and family identity, other cases reflected broader social anxieties over whether natural affection originated in a biological relationship or not. This was extensively explored in the Douglas legitimacy suit during the 1760s, where Lady Jane Douglas's affection towards her twin boys was used as evidence of their legitimacy and was a focus of discussion amongst the fifteen judges of the Court of Session. In this case, Lady Jane was accused of faking her pregnancy and claiming two French beggar children as her natural kin. The justice, Lord Barjarg, thought that: 'For this affection towards children not her own, it is indeed very difficult to account: But we must consider that Lady Jane was a lady of great humanity and charity, which might insensibly lead her to contract an affection for these children, whom she had deprived of their true parents.'[48] Lord Alemore agreed, arguing that Lady Jane's 'strong affection' was explicable as she was a woman of 'humanity', and, 'when she considered that the infants she had taken away from their real parents, must now be dependant upon her, the tenderness she was possessed of might naturally yearn upon such a thought'.[49]

Lords Auchinleck and Pitfour, who found the Douglas boys legitimate, saw this affection as evidence of the parent–child relationship, but particularly remarked on the fact that such affection was supported by a financial investment in the children. Auchinleck noted that 'with the warmest affection on the part of Lady Jane … what was very remarkable, though in great poverty, neither Sir John nor her were ever heard to grudge their giving these children a share of the very little they had'. Pitfour remarked that despite the parents' 'great [financial] distress and affliction', they 'upon every occasion express[ed] the most tender solicitude for the welfare of their children, whom they were then scarce able to maintain: all this behaviour speaks out strongly, that they were indeed their own children'.[50]

This debate was not just limited to the judiciary, but also formed a central part of the discussion surrounding this highly publicised case in the wider press. The writer of the anonymous pamphlet *Considerations on the Douglas Cause*, who

[47] NRS, CC8/5/1/2 & 3, Nicolas Marjoribanks agt John, James, & Edward Marjoribanks, 1697.

[48] Barrister at Law, *A Summary of the Speeches, Arguments and Determinations of the Right Honourable the Lords of Council and Session in Scotland upon that Important Cause wherein His Grace the Duke of Hamilton and others were Plaintiffs and Archibald Douglas of Douglas, esq, Defendant* (Edinburgh, 1768), 100.

[49] Barrister at Law, *Summary*, 112.

[50] Barrister at Law, *Summary*, 75–6, 134–5.

believed that the children were imposters, argued that affection for infants was not a product of biology as:

> Infants have a thousand nameless and irresistible ways of insinuating themselves into the hearts of those who have the care of them; and such people as are really surprised at Lady Jane's fondness for these two boys, must be fortified by the coldness of their own constitutions against the influence of one of the most powerful of the human feelings.[51]

Perhaps reflecting an anxiety over the strength of this argument, he also believed that Lady Jane and her husband did not show the requisite care for her children, leaving them with another when they were ill: 'Can any person of common sense and natural affection believe, that parents would intrust their sickly child with a man in this situation? It will never go down. This is too much iron even for the digestion of an ostrich.'[52] In contrast, the lawyer and diarist, James Boswell, in his pamphlet defending the Douglas children, argued that 'It is natural to suppose that people will not acknowledge and shew parental fondness for children which are not their own.'[53] He believed that this was a 'natural and unsuspicious principle' without which the foundation of all property would be insecure and people left in a 'wretched state'.[54] Unfortunately, he did not specify the origins of this 'natural' rule. Ultimately, the Cause was decided not on the basis of Lady Jane's affection, but on the larger concern alluded to by Boswell, the potential social instability that would be caused if the legitimacy of children acknowledged by their parents could be overturned without indisputable evidence. How the Douglas heir, Lady Jane's son, felt about this dispute over his legitimacy or his parents' affection is unknown.

This case first went to court shortly after the publication of Adam Smith's *Theory of Moral Sentiments* in 1759, where he argued that natural affection was a form of 'habitual sympathy'. In 1767, when the final appeal in a Scottish court was heard, both the *Theory of Moral Sentiments* and the *Speeches from the Douglas Trial* were advertised alongside each other in the *Caledonian Mercury*.[55] The 1760s were clearly a period where natural affection was a topic of interest and concern, yet, as the *Athenian Mercury* letters page suggests, similar questions had been raised in the seventeenth century and it was a debate that was to continue into the nineteenth century. Despite Philippe Ariès's argument that during the eighteenth century 'the sentiment of family is tied to the house, to the government of the house, to life in the house', the origins and nature of natural

51 *Considerations on the Douglas Cause* (London and Edinburgh, 1767), 33.

52 *Considerations*, 47. The belief that ostriches had amazing powers of digestion, and so were able to eat iron, originated in classical literature. It was a claim treated with scepticism in the eighteenth century.

53 [James Boswell], *The Essence of the Douglas Cause* (London, 1767), 4.

54 Boswell, *The Essence*, 7–8.

55 *Caledonian Mercury*, 16 November 1767.

affection were topics of considerable debate that would not be resolved during this period.[56]

Moreover, it was not just the nature of affective relationships between parents and children that were scrutinized in inheritance disputes. The obligations that arose from sibling relationships could be more contentious and just as emotionally tense.[57] In 1770, Peggy Buchanan came to court to protest her eldest brother's claim to their mother's estate. Peggy, now in her fifties, argued that the property had originally been her uncle's and that she had been his housekeeper with the expectation that the property would be settled on her. He died suddenly and it had been transferred to her mother, whom Peggy then lived with and cared for until the mother's death. She believed that her mother had intended the property to be given to her, but had been tricked into settling it on her brother. Peggy rested her claim to this property not only on her biological relationship with her uncle and mother (which her brother had equal claim to), but on her labour as their housekeeper and on the expectation that shared cohabitation over a number of years, including at the end of life, produced both an affective bond and a financial obligation.

From the outset, Peggy located this dispute in terms of her brother's unnatural behaviour towards her, arguing through her lawyer James Boswell, that 'She little expected any severe treatment from one, on whom, now that both her parents are dead, it was natural for her to depend for protection as a father: … instead of behaving to her with kindness and affection, he had dragged her into an expensive litigation'.[58] Peggy noted that, during his minority, her mother had acted as a factor for him without charge, believing that he would in turn care for his younger siblings after he came of age. In doing so, she described the extent to which he had benefited financially from the natural affection of his mother, and emphasized that affective family relationships should not put money (even that allowed by law) ahead of family.

Peggy believed that her brother's unnatural behaviour was a result of the system of primogeniture, engaging in a popular and long-lasting debate over the treatment of younger children that had been ongoing since at least the early seventeenth century.[59] She argued that

> It is well known that they who have much, always wish to have more, and in this country especially, the eldest son is for accumulating all he can get, without regard

[56] Quoted in Suzanne Pucci, 'Snapshots of Family Intimacy in the French Eighteenth Century: The Case of *Paul et Virginie*', *Eighteenth-Century Culture* 35 (2008), 93.

[57] For a broader discussion of sibling relationships in the eighteenth century, see Amy Harris, *Siblinghood and Social Relations in Georgian England* (Manchester, 2012) and C. Dallett Hemphill, *Siblings: Brothers and Sisters in American History* (Oxford, 2011).

[58] Boswell, *The Petition*, 1.

[59] Joan Thirsk, 'Younger Sons in the Seventeenth Century', *History* 54 (1969), 358–77; Helen Berry, *Gender, Society, and Print Culture in Late Stuart England: The Cultural World of the Athenian Mercury* (Aldershot, 2003), 93–4; Sarah McKenzie, 'Death, Inheritance and the Family: A Study of Literary Responses to Inheritance in Seventeenth-Century England', unpublished Ph.D. thesis, University of Warwick (2003).

> to the happiness and welfare of younger children, whom he is apt to have a strange disposition to look upon some how as a kind of inferior beings, though they are truly of the same blood with himself.[60]

Her brother, John Buchanan-Kincaid, immediately understood the implications of this portrait, emphatically replying through his counsel Alexander Lockhart, that 'she holds forth the respondent as a monster in nature, undutiful to his parent, and oppressing his poor *young* sister, grudging her the enjoyment of that pittance which her mother's bounty bestowed upon her, whilst he himself in most affluent circumstances'.[61] Recognizing the rhetorical and legal importance of natural affection, he attempted to distance himself from this presentation, arguing that his father's estate was heavily indebted and in poor condition. The inheritance of his mother's estate was necessary to shore up the family finances and, in particular, provide for his children. Interestingly, he pointed out that, despite her age, his sister had portrayed herself as a '*Miss in her Teens*' in order to gain greater sympathy from the court, when she was a woman in her fifties who received an annuity from him.[62] In doing so, he attempted to emphasize the greater claims of his young children to his natural affection, than a mature woman, who it was presumed could be expected to take some responsibility for herself. In this, he implied that the financial obligations arising from natural affection had its limits, especially with regard to the support of adults – a question that also arose in parent–child relationships. Dependence, whether as a helpless child or as an adult living on patronage, required the dependant to subjugate themselves to the will of the patron, often quite significantly. To be free from the will of the parent/patron required the ability to financially support oneself. Perhaps, ironically, childhood, where children had no legal will of their own, was also the period where their support was assured: the law acted to compensate children for their lack of independence and justified this by rooting it in natural affection. Once adults, this support was less necessary and so the obligation for both economic support and its requisite emotional ties was reduced.

A similar argument was made during the dispute over Agnes Farmer's will in 1760. Agnes had no children and her husband had predeceased her, so was free to will her property as she saw fit. She left her property to her two grand-nieces, Agnes Myles and Agnes Annan. Her brother and sister contested her will, arguing that she was not competent when the will was made, and that they should inherit as the next heirs under the line of succession. The lawyer Alex Lockhart used the affective basis of her bequests to argue on behalf of her grand-nieces that her choice was not from 'mere Whim or Caprice, but upon solid and substantial Reasons':[63]

60 Boswell, *The Petition*, 2.

61 Alexander Lockhart, *Answers for John Buchanan Kincaird* (*s.l.*, 20 November 1770), 2.

62 This was a reference to the popular 1747 farce of the same name by David Garrick.

63 Alexander Lockhart, *The Petition of Agnes Myles, Daughter of Andrew Myles, Baxter in Pitlessie, and Agnes Annan, Daughter of John Annan, Sometime Tenant in Kirktoun of Cults* (*s.l.*, 1760), 2–3.

> They were both her Name Daughters; one of them had been her Companion from her Birth, trained up in Family with her; her Brother and Sister were well advanced in Years, and abundantly capable to do for themselves; they had not lived in such Friendship with her as might have been expected from the Degree of Relation in which they stood.[64]

The petition noted that her property had gone to those 'who stood most in need of it'.[65] Like in the case of John Buchanan-Kincaid, Alexander Lockhart challenged the presumption of natural affection that should exist between siblings by pointing to another affective relationship. However, whereas Buchanan-Kincaid's natural affection for his children was commonly understood to be prior to that for a sibling, Agnes Farmer's choice differed from the line of succession and so needed greater explanation.

This was done by highlighting the breakdown in the sibling relationship – where her 'Brother in particular had persecuted her deceased Husband with uncommon Severity for a very trifling Debt' – and, conversely, highlighting the affective ties to her grand-nieces. Both shared her name, a connection that was popularly understood to create a bond of both affection and obligation, and usually reflected a more substantive relationship, such as that of godparent–godchild, or patron–client.[66] Moreover, one of Agnes's grand-nieces had lived with her from birth, creating a form of parent–child relationship that was expected to be marked by both affection and obligation, as can also be seen in the older Scottish tradition of fosterage that was designed with just this intention.[67] Finally, Agnes Farmer's will provided for younger family members who were more in need of support. In this, her affections reflected that most 'natural' of desires to help preserve the children of her family.

Agnes Farmer's grand-nieces drew on the rhetoric of natural affection to explain and justify their inheritance of their great-aunt's property. In doing so, they both reinforced the cultural and legal importance of the concept, whilst allowing for this emotional connection to be reinforced through the 'fictive' kin tie of a shared name and cohabitation. In this, all three women named Agnes challenged the primacy of biological connection. Ultimately, however, this challenge was allowed to arise because the law did not reinforce the sibling relationship to the same extent as that between parent and child. Agnes Farmer could not have disinherited her biological children, but there was no legal obligation upon her to follow the line of succession and pass her property on to her siblings.

64 Lockhart, *The Petition of Agnes Myles*, 2.

65 Lockhart, *The Petition of Agnes Myles*, 2.

66 Steven Murdoch, *Network North: Scottish Kin, Commercial and Covert Associations in Northern Europe, 1603–1746* (Leiden, 2006), 36–8.

67 Alison Cathcart, '"Inressyng of kyndnes, and renewing off thair blud": The Family, Kinship and Clan Policy in Sixteenth-Century Scottish Gaeldom', in Elizabeth Ewan and Janay Nugent (eds), *Finding the Family in Medieval and Early Modern Scotland* (Aldershot, 2008), 128–38. For more on fosterage, see Chapter 3 and Chapter 5 in this collection.

Conclusion

That members of the early modern family loved each other is no longer a topic of historical debate, but, as Joanna Bailey pointed out, the form and expression of love within the family can be historicized.[68] During the seventeenth century, natural law theories provided an explanation for the nature and origins of the affection between parents, children and siblings that had long been exhorted in sermons and conduct books. These influential theories permeated not only Scottish culture, but Scottish law, providing a model for affective relationships within the family that emphasized the nuclear and biological. Moreover, and partly because of the legal concern with property and provision, natural affection, financial obligation and inheritance practice became complexly intertwined. The economic behaviour of families, and individuals within families, was expected to reflect the affection they held for each other, and conversely, natural affection was marked through appropriate use and sharing of economic resources. This was a model that had particular implications for minor children. As natural affection was understood by many to be a mechanism designed to ensure the survival of the species, younger children were understood to have a greater claim to the family's economic resources and affection than older members, both reflecting and reinforcing the family's concern with reproducing itself over generations that can also be seen in the 'unnatural' practice of primogeniture.

Unsurprisingly, disputes over property distribution between family members were especially painful as they reflected a breakdown in the natural affection that should exist between its members. Such breakdowns arose in part because the strict line of succession did not always reflect the reality of affective behaviour within the population, where affection was also understood by some to arise from cohabitation, fictive kin connections, and friendship. Such challenges to the biological basis of natural affection reflect what Naomi Tadmor has identified as the importance of the 'household-family' to the early modern imagination, where 'the family' consisted of those who resided together, including servants and lodgers.[69] As the Buchanan and Farmer suits suggest, natural affection was understood by some to arise through cohabitation and form the same financial obligations that were associated with affection between biological kin. Having said this, even within these examples and enforced through the legal obligations placed upon parents, the nuclear and biological family always took precedence within Scotland, and whilst affective relationships could extend beyond it, such relationships were expected to be secondary to those within it. Children growing up in this environment, therefore, would have learned to prioritize their immediate family before other ties of affection, to connect affection with financial obligations, and, conversely, to understand acts of provision and education as acts of love.

68 Bailey, *Parenting in England*, 26.
69 Tadmor, 'The Household-Family'.

Part III

Constructing the Next Generation

9

*Preparing for Kingship: Prince Alexander of Scotland, 1264–84**

Cynthia J. Neville

Introduction

Towards the middle of the thirteenth century an unknown scribe used a blank space on one of the folios of the *Melrose Chronicle* manuscript to calculate the number of years that had passed between various historical events and his own day.[1] The jottings date to the period between March and June 1264, and the scribe was apparently moved to set his thoughts down on parchment following the birth at Jedburgh, on 21 January of that same year, of a son to King Alexander III.[2] The event was both joyous and, from the perspective of the Scottish political community, auspicious, for while the king had been married for more than a dozen years, to date his only child was a daughter. The birth of a son promised security in the future succession to the throne; certainly, this was how near-contemporary chroniclers viewed the event. One wrote that at news of the birth 'God's praises rang throughout all the ends of Scotland.'[3] The cleric's effusive language almost certainly expressed genuine enthusiasm rather than empty verbiage, for in the later thirteenth century direct succession to the throne from father to son was still something of a new phenomenon; until relatively recently, in fact, primogeniture in Scotland had been regarded neither as 'a fait accompli' nor 'inevitable'.[4] The birth of a son, then, pre-empted the likelihood

* The author wishes to acknowledge the support of the Social Sciences and Humanities Research Council of Canada in the research undertaken for this essay, as well as the helpful suggestions of the (anonymous) reviewer.

1 Alan Orr Anderson and Marjorie Ogilvie Anderson (eds), *The Chronicle of Melrose* (London, 1936) [*Chron. Melrose*], 26.

2 Dauvit Broun and Julian Harrison, *The Chronicle of Melrose Abbey: A Stratigraphic Edition. Vol. 1, Introduction and Facsimile Edition* (Edinburgh, 2007), 172; see also *Chron. Melrose*, xl, 26. Professor Duncan's suggestion of a birth date of mid-December 1263 is unconvincing: see A.A.M. Duncan, 'Sources and Uses of the Chronicle of Melrose, 1165–1297', in Simon Taylor (ed.), *Kings, Clerics and Chronicles in Scotland, 500–1297* (Dublin, 2000), 176, n. 109.

3 W.F. Skene (ed.), *Johannis de Fordun Chronica Gentis Scotorum. Historians of Scotland*, 2 vols (Edinburgh, 1871–2) [*Chron. Fordun*], i, 300 (Annal 56, for the year 1264).

4 Alasdair Ross, *The Kings of Alba, c. 1000–c. 1130* (Edinburgh, 2011), 112–13. See also Dauvit Broun, 'Contemporary Perspectives on Alexander II's Succession: The Evidence of King-Lists', in Richard D. Oram (ed.), *The Reign of Alexander II, 1214–49* (Leiden, 2005), 79–98; G.W.S. Barrow, *Scotland and its Neighbours in the Middle Ages* (London, 1992), 40.

of dynastic conflict at the close of Alexander III's reign, and the boy was baptized immediately by Bishop Gamelin of St Andrews with the same name as his father and grandfather.[5]

Historians have made extensive study of the many factors that went into the education and training of young men who were destined to rule the medieval kingdom of England.[6] In the last decade, moreover, a significant amount of historical and literary work has been devoted to the study of how changing notions of love, friendship and affinity in the later Middle Ages influenced the lives and upbringing of royal and aristocratic youths in England and western Europe more generally.[7] Collectively, this research has contributed to a new and much more nuanced understanding of the important place of childhood in framing and constructing fundamental ideas about gender, culture and community among the aristocracy. Considerably less research has been done in either area in the context of the Scottish experience in the premodern period,[8] and beyond the realm of royal biography little is known about the life cycles of royal children in the medieval kingdom.[9] This essay seeks to remedy that lacuna by examining the manner in which the elder of Alexander III's two sons, Alexander, was brought up to rule the kingdom of Scotland in succession to his father. The focus here is on the strategies that the king and members of the royal council adopted as they went about preparing the prince to 'come to kingship':[10] introducing him to the responsibilities associated with managing a household of his own; teaching him

[5] *Chron. Melrose*, 123.

[6] Katherine J. Lewis, *Kingship and Masculinity in Late Medieval England* (London, 2013), 67–83, 141–55; Ralph V. Turner, 'The Households of the Sons of Henry II', in Martin Aurell (ed.), *La Cour Plantagenêt (1154–1204)* (Poitiers, 2000), 17–52; Matthew Strickland, 'On the Instruction of a Prince: The Upbringing of Henry, the Young King', in Christopher Harper-Bill and Nicholas Vincent (eds), *Henry II: New Interpretations* (Woodbridge, 2007), 184–214; W. Mark Ormrod, 'The Royal Nursery: A Household for the Younger Children of Edward III', *English Historical Review* 120 (2005), 398–413; David Bates, 'The Conqueror's Adolescence', in John Gillingham (ed.), *Anglo-Norman Studies* 25 (Woodbridge, 2003), 1–18; W.M. Aird, 'Frustrated Masculinity: The Relationship between William the Conqueror and his Eldest Son', in D.M. Hadley (ed.), *Masculinity in Medieval Europe* (London, 1999), 39–55.

[7] The field is vast, but excellent starting points are the essays in John Haseldine (ed.), *Friendship in Medieval Europe* (Stroud, 1999). See also J. Meddings, 'Friendship Among the Aristocracy in Anglo-Norman England', in C. Harper-Bill (ed.), *Anglo-Norman Studies* 22 (Woodbridge, 2000), 187–204; Ralph V. Turner, 'Eleanor of Aquitaine and her Children: An Inquiry into Medieval Family Attachment', *Journal of Medieval History* 14 (1988), 321–35; Jean E. Jost, 'Loving Parents in Middle English Literature', in Albrecht Classen (ed.), *Childhood in the Middle Ages and the Renaissance* (Berlin, 2005), 307–28.

[8] Notable exceptions are the essays in Elizabeth Ewan and Janay Nugent (eds), *Finding the Family in Medieval and Early Modern Scotland* (Aldershot, 2008). See also David Sellar, 'The Family', in Edward J. Cowan and Lizanne Henderson (eds), *A History of Everyday Life in Medieval Scotland, 1000–1600* (Edinburgh, 2011), 89–108; David Ditchburn and Alastair Macdonald, 'Medieval Scotland, 1100–1500', in R.A. Houston and W.W.J. Knox (eds), *The New Penguin History of Scotland* (Harmondsworth, 2001), 127–32.

[9] For more on this topic, see Chapter 1 in this collection.

[10] The expression is borrowed from W.M. Ormrod, 'Coming to Kingship: Boy Kings and the Passage to Power in Fourteenth-Century England', in Nicola F. McDonald and W.M.

the skills required to negotiate the sophisticated web of power, privilege and intrigue inherent in the exercise of patronage; instructing him in the myriad ways in which a wealthy and powerful youth might project an authoritative presence in deed, word and image; and, not least, instilling in him an appreciation of the arts of manly rule. In all these matters, Prince Alexander's mentors had ready access to a series of useful exemplars, not least in the neighbouring realm of England. Recent studies of the early careers of Henry 'the Young King', Edward III, Richard II, Henry V and Henry VI all shed important light on the great variety of resources – human, material and fiscal – that shaped the childhood and teenage years of the youths who came to rule the medieval English throne.[11] Prince Alexander's Scottish tutors drew on a similarly rich array of resources.

In some respects the care and effort that King Alexander III and his counsellors expended during the childhood years of the prince were a reflection of contemporary social norms and expectations, which held that royal sons should receive broad exposure to the world of letters, the intricacies of diplomacy, and the arts of warfare. The prince's correspondence, discussed below, reveals a thorough grounding in the first two of these areas. In the later 1260s, however, there were more urgent reasons for the king of Scots and his council to ensure that the young man receive a carefully planned and well-executed education in the business of power politics. The memory of Alexander III's early years on the throne remained fresh in the minds of the king himself, his wife, and several senior members of the royal household, chief among them the chancellor, the high steward, the chamberlain and the senior justiciar.[12] At the death of Alexander II in 1249 the throne had passed to a boy aged seven. The ensuing years proved deeply unsettled, with noble factions competing for control of the person of the king and, from early 1252, heavy-handed interference in the day-to-day business of the Scottish court from the young ruler's father-in-law, Henry III of England. Occasionally, tensions had escalated into open conflict.[13] Alexander III's assumption of adult rule in (or soon after) 1258 brought to a close a turbulent period of minority rule, and it is not unreasonable to suggest that his experiences as a young king and the brevity of his own apprenticeship lay at the heart of many

Ormrod (eds), *Rites of Passage: Cultures of Transition in the Fourteenth Century* (Woodbridge, 2004), 31–49.

[11] Strickland, 'On the Instruction of a Prince', 184–211; Ormrod, 'Coming to Kingship', 31–49; Lewis, *Kingship and Masculinity*.

[12] William Wischard bishop of Glasgow served as the king's chancellor 1259–73; Alexander Stewart was high steward 1241–82; William earl of Mar acted as chamberlain for two periods, 1251–5 and 1260–7; Alexander Comyn earl of Buchan was justiciar of Scotia 1253–5, and from 1258 to the late 1280s. All appear frequently in their official capacities in the written acts of Alexander III; see Cynthia J. Neville and Grant G. Simpson (eds), *Regesta Regum Scottorum, Vol. IV, Pt. 1: The Acts of Alexander III King of Scots 1249–1286* (Edinburgh, 2012) [*RRS, IV, Pt 1*].

[13] D.E.R. Watt, 'The Minority of Alexander III of Scotland', *Transactions of the Royal Historical Society*, 5th ser. 21 (1971), 1–23; and a reassessment in Alan Young, 'Noble Families and Political Factions in the Reign of Alexander III', in Norman H. Reid (ed.), *Scotland in the Reign of Alexander III, 1249–1286* (Edinburgh, 1990), 1–31.

of the decisions that went into the shaping of his elder son's upbringing. When Prince Alexander died suddenly (if, perhaps, not entirely unexpectedly) in 1284, a great deal of hard work and careful thought on the part of Alexander III and his advisers came to naught. Brief though it was, the prince's career offers historians an unusually well-documented opportunity to examine the figure of the royal heir in high medieval Scotland and to study the ways in which the political community went about preparing a prince to become a king.

Political Apprenticeship

A passage in another near-contemporary Scottish chronicle that noted the birth of the prince claimed that the date of 21 January 1264 was doubly auspicious, for 'in one and the same day the king got news, by one messenger, of the death of the king of the Norwegians, who troubled the king and kingdom; and, by another, of the birth of his new son'.[14] While this author was guilty of creative licence in dating the two events to a single day he attached much solemnity to the prince's birth, at least in part because, writing from a vantage point of twenty-odd years, he knew that the kingdom which the boy was destined to rule was still at a formative stage as a cohesive national unit.[15] In 1264 King Alexander III's adult rule was less than a decade old, and the Scottish crown had not yet realized its ambition to assert effective control over the western portion of the realm and the neighbouring isles. The anonymous annalist, who completed his work in the first half of 1285,[16] will also, however, have known that victory for the Scots would come very soon when, in July 1266, King Magnus IV of Norway formally ceded to Alexander III title to the Hebrides and the Isle of Man.[17] Given the momentous changes that had occurred on the international scene, it was perhaps natural for the author to want to fashion for later readers a clear link between the birth of an heir to the dynasty descended from Malcolm III and St Margaret, and the death of an inveterate enemy of the same royal house.

14 *Chron. Fordun*, i, 300 (Annal 56), and D.E.R. Watt (ed.), *Scotichronicon by Walter Bower in Latin and English*, 9 vols (Aberdeen and Edinburgh, 1987–98) [*Scotichronicon*], v, 346–7; see also the notes at 465–6. The king was Haakon IV, who died in December 1263.

15 Richard Oram, *Domination and Lordship: Scotland 1070–1230* (Edinburgh, 2011), 362–9; G.W.S. Barrow, *Kingship and Unity: Scotland, 1000–1306*, 2nd edn (Edinburgh, 2003), 129–46; Keith Stringer, 'Scottish Foundations: Thirteenth-Century Perspectives', in Alexander Grant and Keith J. Stringer (eds), *Uniting the Kingdom? The Making of British History* (London, 1995), 86–8; Ditchburn and Macdonald, 'Medieval Scotland', 150–8, 165–75.

16 Dauvit Broun, 'A New Look at *Gesta Annalia* Attributed to John of Fordun', in Barbara E. Crawford (ed.), *Church, Chronicle and Learning in Medieval and Early Renaissance Scotland* (Edinburgh, 1999), 16–17, 20–1; Dauvit Broun, *Scottish Independence and the Idea of Britain* (Edinburgh, 2007), 216–28.

17 *RRS, IV, Pt 1*, no. 61; see also *APS*, i, 420–1; R.I. Lustig, 'The Treaty of Perth: A Re-examination', *SHR* 58 (1979), 35–57.

The scribe who authored the portion of the *Melrose Chronicle* covering the year 1264 noted that the newborn prince was given the name Alexander 'at his father's command'.[18] Studies of medieval naming patterns suggest that the choice of forenames for children reflected a wide range of interests, personal, dynastic, ethnic and aspirational.[19] King Alexander III's choice for his firstborn son no doubt gave expression to the same general sentiments as those of his noble subjects, but several other factors were at work, and the chronicler's comment may have been more than purely speculative. In the middle years of the thirteenth century the Scottish crown was making a determined effort to cultivate new links with the distant past. The canonization of Queen Margaret (d. 1093) in 1250 offered the family 'a way into the pre-Conquest English royal genealogy'.[20] The celebration of King David I (1124–53), the youngest son of the newly made saint, as the ideal Scottish king was another aspect of this agenda,[21] and it was surely no coincidence that Alexander III and his queen gave the name David to their second son and that of Margaret to their daughter.[22] The personal name Alexander, however, had the salutary effect of pushing even further back the dynasty's connection with the past, for it recalled another of the saint's sons, David's older brother King Alexander I (1107–24). In a realm still at a formative stage in its development, the king's choice of name for the new heir positioned the boy at the nexus of both the past and the future of the dynasty.

Prince Alexander's status as the only son of the king of Scots lasted for almost a decade, until the birth of David in 1273, but already by 1265 the chamberlain of Scotland had assigned the infant an income for the support of his household.[23] The funds surely represented the gift of a benevolent father, but they were also a manifestation of Alexander III's wish to 'keep up with the Plantagenets'.[24] The

18 *Chron. Melrose*, 123.

19 For a good introduction see the essays collected in G.T. Beech, M. Bourin and P. Chareille (eds), *Personal Name Studies of Medieval Europe* (Kalamazoo, 2002); for Gaelic personal names in medieval Ireland, Wales and Scotland, see Freya Verstraten, 'Naming Practices Among the Irish Secular Nobility in the High Middle Ages', *Journal of Medieval History* 32 (2006), 45–53; A.D. Carr, 'What's in a Name?: Naming Patterns in Medieval Wales', *Archaeologia Cambrensis* 158 (2010 for 2009), 1–18; Matthew Hammond, 'Ethnicity, Personal Names and the Nature of Scottish Europeanization', in Björn K.U. Weiler et al. (eds), *Thirteenth Century England* 11 (Woodbridge, 2007), esp. 86–90. For the introduction of the name Alexander to Scotland, see Stephen Marritt, 'Coincidences of Names, Anglo-Scottish Connections and Anglo-Saxon Society in the Late Eleventh-Century West Country', *SHR* 83 (2004), 154, 166–7.

20 A.A.M. Duncan, *Scotland: The Making of the Kingdom* (Edinburgh, 1975), 553–4; Broun, *Scottish Independence*, 228–46, 273–4; Dauvit Broun, 'The Birth of Scottish History', *SHR* 76 (1997), 11; Brown, *Wars of Scotland*, 89–90; Ross, *Kings of Alba*, 148–9; Barrow, *Kingship and Unity*, 177–9; A.A.M. Duncan, *The Kingship of the Scots, 842–1292* (Edinburgh, 2002), 54–5.

21 G.W.S. Barrow, *David I of Scotland 1124–1153: The Balance of Old and New* (Reading, 1985); Oram, *Domination and Lordship*, 109–11.

22 Margaret's name recalled the identity not only of her English mother, the daughter of Henry III, but, more importantly, that of the recently canonized St Margaret of Scotland.

23 J. Stuart et al. (eds), *Rotuli Scaccarii Regum Scotorum. The Exchequer Rolls of Scotland*, 23 vols (Edinburgh, 1878–1908), i, 23, 20.

24 Barrow, *Scotland and its Neighbours*, 35.

grant ensured that in future the prince would enjoy an income of his own and an endowment appropriate to the heir to a European power of middle rank. The absence of a continuous series of exchequer records for this period makes it impossible to reconstruct the prince's household in detail, but the fact that the sheriff of Stirling alone rendered account for it in 1266 suggests that, initially at least, it was both small in size and modest in its requirements.[25] Alexander III, however, subsequently made more generous provision for his son when Earl Colban of Fife died sometime between 1270 and 1272, leaving an eight-year-old boy as his heir.[26] Wardship of the minor and control over his possessions passed by custom and law into the king's hands; he, in turn, directed that the lands be assigned to the maintenance of the prince's household. In the closing years of the thirteenth century the annual income of the earldom of Fife was calculated at close to £500, ranking the earl's wealth second only to the king among secular barons.[27] The death of Colban and the youthfulness of his heir therefore meant that for a good decade and more Prince Alexander could expect to enjoy the status of the richest magnate in the realm. Still another endowment followed soon thereafter, if under different circumstances. As noted above, by the terms of the Treaty of Perth of 1266 the Norwegian crown formally ceded to Scotland title to the western isles and the kingdom of Man. For some years Alexander III was content to govern the latter through a series of capable bailies and justiciars,[28] but when in 1275 the Manxmen insolently chose a king of their own it became evident that a more conspicuous demonstration of Scottish rule was in order. The king accomplished this, first, by sending a fleet to punish the islesmen and to avert the spread of revolt, and second, by appointing his son Alexander lord of Man.[29] The eleven-year-old prince was still too young to govern personally, but the grant of the title positioned him firmly at the apex of the political community of the isle (no longer the kingdom).

The prince's appointment in Man reveals much about the ways in which the Scottish crown gave expression to its aspirations to firm and effective governance. While the child prince was not yet expected to exercise personal authority, the bestowal of the lordship as a permanent territorial endowment (an appanage) was of considerable significance. It raised the boy to the rank of *rex designatus*, and signalled in a very public way his position as heir to the throne. The practice of granting appanages was familiar to contemporaries both in England and France,[30] but it had particular resonance in Scotland, where twelfth-century

25 Duncan, *Making of the Kingdom*, 602.

26 *Scotichronicon*, v, 380–1.

27 Duncan, *Making of the Kingdom*, 426–7, 585.

28 *RRS, IV, Pt 1*, nos 171–3, 241–4, 246.

29 Joseph Stevenson (ed.), *Chronicon de Lanercost, 1201–1346* (Edinburgh, 1839) [*Chron. Lanercost*], 98; George Broderick and Brian Stowell (eds), *Chronicle of the Kings of Mann and the Isles* (Edinburgh, 1973), 46.

30 J.R. Studd, 'The Lord Edward and King Henry III', *Historical Research* 50 (1977), 4–19; for France, see C.T. Wood, *The French Apanages and the Capetian Monarchy, 1224–1328* (Cambridge, MA, 1966).

members of the ruling dynasty had made a point of demonstrating publicly the joint governance of king and designated heir.[31] As new lord of Man, Prince Alexander thus became a living embodiment of royal custom and a powerful vehicle through which to give tangible expression to its history. Elevation to the lordship, moreover, placed him in a strong position to represent his father's authority in the region, and promised to offer him future opportunities to gain the 'practical training in associative rule' that was so essential a feature of a princely education.[32] The appointment sent another, equally clear message, if to a different audience. A charter datable to the period 1275x1281 purports to record a fresh grant on the part of the prince to the prior and canons of Whithorn. The grant comprised the lands of Ballacgniba and Dalmarown, the church of St Ronan and the chapel of St Ninian at Ballacgniba, all on the isle of Man.[33] In reality, this was no new gift: three earlier kings of Man had successively bestowed the same lands and churches on the priory.[34] The issue of the charter and its subsequent royal confirmation made bold statements about the claims of Alexander III and his heir over territory that now lay formally and permanently within the realm of Scotland.

Alexander III, his father-in-law Henry III, and his brother-in-law Edward I, were all highly skilled in the game of high politics, and the ceremonies associated with Edward's coronation in August 1274 gave each of them a different opportunity to project his own view of power and authority. The coronation was, predictably, a magnificent affair, the richness and splendour of which were carefully designed to impress all who attended, perhaps especially the king's Scottish neighbours.[35] Edward no doubt intended that the event serve as a timely reminder to Alexander III (if any were required) of the historic claim of the English crown to the fealty and homage of successive kings of Scotland, a claim that the young king had nevertheless skilfully refused to consider in 1251, at the time of his marriage to Edward's sister Margaret.[36] The drama of the coronation must also have driven home the point that Edward's enthronement included the ritual

31 Duncan, *Kingship of the Scots*, 52, 55–6, 59, 61 briefly discusses earlier royal appanages.

32 Strickland, 'On the Instruction of a Prince', 188, 199.

33 San Marino, CA, Huntington Library, Ellesmere Manuscripts, MS EL 993, a transumpt of 1504, which reproduces several extracts from the (now lost) register of the priory of Whithorn. The transumpt includes King Alexander III's confirmation of the grant, printed in *RRS, IV, Pt 1*, no. 170.

34 These are also recorded in the transumpt.

35 Michael Prestwich, *Edward I* (Berkeley, 1988), 89; H.R. Luard (ed.), *Flores Historiarum*, 3 vols (London, 1890), ii, 44–5. One chronicler claimed that the king of Scots, together with his wife and children, was 'specially invited to be at the coronation' by Edward I. *Scotichronicon*, v, 400–1.

36 The chronicler Nicholas Trivet wrongly claimed that Alexander performed homage in 1274. Thomas Hog (ed.), *F. Nicholai Triveti … Annales sex regum Angliae, qui a comitibus Andegavensibus originem traxerunt* (London, 1845), 291–2, 299; E.L.G. Stones (ed.), *Anglo-Scottish Relations, 1174–1328* (Oxford, 1970), no. 9; Duncan, *Kingship of the Scots*, 151–2, 159–60.

of unction, a privilege that the Scottish kings had yet to win for themselves.[37] Alexander II, for his part, made equally shrewd use of the coronation ceremonies for purposes of his own. When the author of the chronicle known as the *Gesta Annalia I* noted that Queen Margaret 'and her children' were there,[38] he may have had in mind not only Prince Alexander and his older sister, Margaret, but also the prince's younger brother David, born just a few months earlier. In the charged atmosphere of Anglo-Scottish relations, Alexander III's public display of an 'heir and a spare' served as a potent counterweight to Edward I's ambitions to claim lordship over the smaller realm.

The closing years of the 1270s marked the end of the first phase of Prince Alexander's education. He was, nominally at least, the head of a household of his own, the beneficiary of a substantial annual income, and a magnate of the highest rank. Although in his mid-teens he was still at law a minor, he was certainly old enough to assume a more active role on the political stage. It was for this reason that, in the opening months of 1279, Alexander III appointed a guardian for the prince in the person of Sir William Sinclair of Roslin.[39] Sinclair was a senior member of the royal council closely in touch with the political community, a baron with landed interests that extended throughout south-eastern Scotland and across the Anglo-Scottish border into the liberty of Tynedale in Northumberland, and the custodian of Edinburgh Castle and its treasury.[40] He is believed to have enjoyed a position of trust and friendship 'closer to Alexander III than any other Scot'.[41] The king's choice of this man as the prince's personal adviser therefore affords historians a rare glimpse of the comingling of affection and pragmatism that governed political life in the thirteenth-century Scottish court. Sir William Sinclair's position must have been much coveted, offering as it did direct access to the persons of the prince and the king and, through them, an avenue to the near-unchecked exercise of power. In medieval Scotland, as indeed elsewhere, patronage was in effect a currency, control of which placed Sir William and the prince at the centre of a complicated network of social and political relationships. The king and his advisers were well aware of this, but aware also of the prince's youth. While they were willing to give the royal heir the ability to dispense some patronage and to exercise limited political power, they were not prepared to give him free rein by entrusting him with his own seal, possession of which was a mark of political and social personhood and use of which was legally binding.[42] Prince Alexander did not, in fact, acquire a seal of his own until 1281,[43] when he had passed the age of fourteen, long recognized

37 *RRS, IV, Pt 1*, no. 181; Duncan, *Making of the Kingdom*, 554–8.

38 *Chron. Fordun*, i, 305 (Annal 61).

39 London, The National Archives [TNA]: Public Record Office [PRO], SC1/20/170; Duncan, *Making of the Kingdom*, 588.

40 M.L. Holford and K.J. Stringer, *Border Liberties and Loyalties: North-East England, c. 1200 to c. 1400* (Edinburgh, 2010), 253–4, 256–8.

41 Duncan, *Making of the Kingdom*, 588.

42 Cynthia J. Neville, *Land, Law and People in Medieval Scotland* (Edinburgh, 2010), 83–4.

43 *RRS, IV, Pt 1*, 14, 25–6, nos 135, 140.

in medieval culture as the age when a young man achieved adolescence.[44] Until then, he authenticated his acts with the seal of his father or that of Sir William Sinclair.[45]

As studies of Scottish noblewomen's legal capacity have shown, however, lack of a seal was no impediment to the exercise of real and meaningful patronage.[46] In March 1279, in a gesture designed simultaneously to make a public announcement of his status as heir and to inaugurate a new role as princely patron, Alexander wrote a letter to his uncle Edward I to request favour on behalf of a Scottish supplicant (discussed below). The letter resonates with the literary conventions that characterize all medieval petitions,[47] but while it is replete with the flowery words that embellished the written communications of royal authors the length and breadth of Western Europe, it is also quite remarkable for its blend of deference and self-confidence.[48] Sir William Sinclair's thoughtful guidance in the matter of the prince's relationship with Edward I is evident in another letter, probably written in June 1281, when arrangements were first being made for Alexander's marriage. Here, the prince enquires politely after his uncle's health.[49] Each of the letters in its own way sends a series of subtle messages about Alexander's sense of self, not least in being drafted in elegant Latin rather than the more casual French.[50] In the first, the prince writes as Edward's 'own nephew' to his 'most hearty uncle'; in the second, Alexander identifies himself more formally as the English ruler's *consanguineus*. In a third letter, discussed below, he has confidently become 'firstborn of Alexander, illustrious king of Scots'. There is something in all three letters of the civility owed by a teenager to an older man, but also a keen awareness that ties of kinship

44 For more on the significance of the age of fourteen in medieval culture, see Introduction and Chapters 1 and 10 in this collection.

45 *RRS, IV, Pt 1*, no. 171; TNA: PRO SC1/20/169, printed in *Chron. Lanercost*, i, 272; TNA: PRO SC1/ 20/170, printed in *Chron. Lanercost*, i, 474–5; and T. Rymer (ed.), *Fœdera, Conventiones, Litteræ etc.*, 4 vols in 7 parts (London, 1816–69) [*Foedera*], i, 611. Princess Margaret borrowed a seal when she wrote to her uncle Edward I, see TNA: PRO SC1/20/171; J. Bain (ed.), *Calendar of Documents Relating to Scotland* [*CDS*], 4 vols (Edinburgh, 1881–88), ii, no. 185.

46 Cynthia J. Neville, 'Women, Charters and Land Ownership in Scotland, 1150–1350', *Journal of Legal History* 26 (2005), 21–2, 25–6, 31, 37, 44–5; Matthew Hammond, 'Women and the Adoption of Charters in Scotland North of Forth, c. 1150–1286', *Innes Review* 62 (2011), 31.

47 Paul Brand, 'Petitions and Parliament in the Reign of Edward I', in Linda Clark (ed.), *Parchment and People* (Edinburgh, 2004), 27–30; Helen Lacey, *The Royal Pardon: Access to Mercy in Fourteenth-Century England* (York, 2009), 26–38, 44–9.

48 TNA: PRO SC1/20/169, printed in *Chron. Lanercost*, 473–4. For an English summary, see *CDS*, ii, no. 156.

49 TNA: PRO SC1/20/170; Innes (ed.), *National Manuscripts of Scotland*, i, Plate 65. An English summary appears in *CDS*, ii, no. 204.

50 W. Gillies, 'The Lion's Tongues: Languages in Scotland to 1314', in Ian Brown (gen. ed.), *The Edinburgh History of Scottish Literature*, 3 vols (Edinburgh, 2007), i, 52–62. Intriguingly, when Prince Alexander's sister, Margaret, wrote to her uncle in 1281, her letter was in French. PRO: TNA SC9/20/171, calendared in *CDS*, ii, no. 185.

endowed the prince with a status commensurate with that of his correspondent. The assertive tone of the prince's letters, moreover, contrasts quite sharply with the (substantial) body of correspondence that survives between King Alexander III and his English in-laws; much of this is markedly less cordial.[51] Despite the marriage ties that linked them, the two kings were frequently in dispute over the question of homage and fealty, or with respect to Alexander's rights as lord of the liberty of Tynedale.[52] Prince Alexander, it would seem, was mindful of the need to cultivate a good working relationship with Edward, but took care also to avoid language that might undermine his status as heir to a fully independent realm. The dates of the letters, coincident with, then quickly following, the prince's elevation to the public stage, reveal that Alexander was an astute student of Anglo-Scottish political relations – and a fast learner.

Sir William Sinclair's sure hand in implementing the Scottish royal council's designs in the matter of the prince's schooling as heir to the throne is apparent in other ways, chief among them the advice that he imparted about choosing political friends and the circumstances under which the prince should exercise his considerable patronage. Sir Ingram de Umfraville, on whose behalf the prince first petitioned Edward I in the letter of 1279 noted above, was one of the prince's close companions. He came from a powerful cross-border family, one of whose branches controlled the earldom of Angus and, through its connections with the Comyn and Balliol kindred, enjoyed close contact with the Scottish king and his council.[53] Sir Ingram's efforts to recover his father's English lands made a link with the prince's household particularly attractive to all the parties concerned – wealthy supplicant, ambitious tutor, and would-be patron. In the short term, friendship with the prince proved beneficial, for Alexander and his father successfully secured from Edward I a promise to restore the lands into Sir Ingram's possession.[54] Of greater significance in the longer-term context, the establishment of a patron–client friendship laid the foundations for a formal relationship between the Umfraville kindred and the young man who would one day be king of Scots.

Of greater potential significance were the links that Sinclair helped to forge between the prince and the men of the Vieuxpont family. They, too, were wealthy cross-border landholders: lords of Alston in Cumberland, supporters of

51 *RRS, IV, Pt 1*, nos 90, 92, 94–6, 99, 106–7, 109–10, 112–14, 116–18, 121, 123, 125, 136–8, 144–7, 150–1, 155, 160–1, 170.

52 The king's presence in the liberty is examined in Holford and Stringer, *Border Liberties*, 231–96.

53 Amanda Beam, 'The Umfravilles: Political Leadership on the Rise, 1100–1307: part 1', *History Scotland* 9:2 (2009), 27–31; Amanda Beam, '"At the Apex of Chivalry": Sir Ingram de Umfraville and the Anglo-Scottish wars, 1296–1321', in Andy King and David Simpkin (eds), *England and Scotland at War, c. 1296–c. 1513* (Leiden, 2012), 54–6; Holford and Stringer, *Border Liberties*, 375–6.

54 *RRS, IV, Pt 1*, no. 118; Joseph Stevenson (ed.), *Documents Illustrative of Scottish History*, 2 vols (Edinburgh, 1870), i, 45, 62; Keith M. Brown et al. (eds.), *The Records of the Parliaments of Scotland to 1707* (St Andrews, 2007–14), http://www.rps.ac.uk/1293/2/15 (accessed February 2015).

the Comyn kindred both in England and Scotland, and tenants-in-chief of, and bailiffs for, King Alexander III in Tynedale.[55] Sir Nicholas de Vieuxpont was also a friend, neighbour and political ally of Sir William Sinclair.[56] Like Sir Ingram de Umfraville, Sir Nicholas knew that no nobleman could survive the vagaries of court society without good political friends and ready access to the persons of the king and the prince. In the years between 1279 and 1282 Nicholas was locked in dispute with King Edward I over title to the Cumberland-based estate of Alston. He managed, in the end, to win firm title to the lands and their rich silver mines, but only after Prince Alexander had personally intervened on his behalf with King Edward I.[57] The prince interposed with his uncle again in 1282, this time seeking to assist Sir Geoffrey de Mowbray's designs to avoid paying a heavy penalty for respite of knighthood in England.[58] Sir Ingram, Sir Nicholas and Sir Geoffrey were not the only beneficiaries of these kinds of acts. Patronage was meaningful only if it represented a genuine partnership, useful only if it had lasting and profitable consequences for both lord and client. The gains that all three noblemen enjoyed in their interaction with the prince were obvious. Less tangibly, but surely as important, Lord Alexander's acts of patronage served to augment his own affinity by adding to his entourage men who would have personal and professional reasons to remain loyal to him in the future. The exercise of patronage that redounded to the benefit of the most prestigious aristocratic families of the land, moreover, increased the prince's visibility on the Scottish and English political stages. Finally, and perhaps most pragmatically, it helped to familiarize the young man with the business of governing.

After 1281, other members of the Scottish nobility came to appreciate that the prince's political weight in matters of consequence was more than merely nominal. In the opening years of this same decade members of the Comyn and Stewart kindred were deeply divided over control of the earldom of Menteith. In October 1282, William Comyn of Kirkintilloch, son of Sir John Comyn lord of Badenoch, wrote to the English king, asking him to use his influence to persuade both the king of Scots 'and his son' to rule in favour of the Comyn claim. Edward responded favourably and duly commanded that separate letters

55 Holford and Stringer, *Border Liberties and Loyalties*, 238–40, 254–6, 270–1; F.W. Ragg, 'Mauld's Meaburn, the Alston Mines, and a Branch of the Veteriponts', *Transactions of the Cumberland and Westmorland Antiquarian and Archaeological Society*, new ser. 11 (1911), 259–320, which includes a detailed genealogical chart of the family's widespread connections.

56 Vieuxpont was a witness to an act of April 1280 by which King Alexander III granted the lands of Inverleith (Midlothian) to Sinclair; *RRS, IV, Pt 1*, no. 130. Nicholas held the estate of Swanston, near Roslin, by marriage.

57 NRS, RH5/7, a draft of letters patent by Edward I commanding restoration of the manor of Alston to Nicholas de Vieuxpont; *Calendar of the Patent Rolls Preserved in the Public Record Office, Edward I* [*CPR*] (London, 1893–1901), *1281–92*, 29. Edward's grant is described here as having been made 'at the instance of the king's nephew Alexander son of Alexander'.

58 Sir Geoffrey was a member of an immensely wealthy cross-border family and was married to a daughter of Sir John Comyn I of Badenoch. G.W.S. Barrow, *The Anglo-Norman Era in Scottish History* (Oxford, 1980), 151, 185–6. The hoped-for respite was duly granted, again 'at the instance of the king of Scotland's son'. *CDS*, ii, no. 210.

be dispatched to Alexander III and his son.[59] In this matter at least, the Lord Alexander's opinion now also counted with his own father, and several months later the king of Scots awarded half the Menteith lands to Comyn.[60] Patronage of a less business-like sort, intended to garner spiritual rather than earthly returns, was yet another part of the learning process through which Sir William Sinclair guided his charge. The grant of lands and churches to the priory of Whithorn, noted above, and the drafting of a petition to the English crown seeking a pardon for a convicted felon, taught the prince valuable lessons about the ways in which members of the royal houses of contemporary Europe gave expression to the kingly qualities of piety and mercy.[61]

The Prince's Marriage

In the relatively brief period of his youth, Lord Alexander learned hard lessons about grief and the momentous consequences that might attend accident and illness. His mother, Margaret, died in the early months of 1275, while he was still a child;[62] in June 1281, 'amid the deep wailing of all the Scots, and the still deeper wailing of the king', he lost his eight-year-old brother David.[63] The death of the younger prince marked another important stage in the Lord Alexander's upbringing. It almost certainly precipitated final arrangements for his marriage, as it did also for the marriage of his sister, Margaret. Plans for both weddings were finalized within six months of David's burial in Dunfermline Abbey: a written agreement for Princess Margaret to marry King Eric II of Norway drawn up and sealed on 25 July 1281, and a series of documents concerning the marriage of Prince Alexander and Marguerite of Flanders finalized on 4 December of the same year.[64] The rapidity with which the two wedding ceremonies followed each other,[65] and, more tellingly, the elaborate provisions included in each of the agreements in the event that the Scottish bride or groom died without offspring,[66] reveal King Alexander III's determination to have his children produce

59 *CDS*, iv, no. 1763 and App. i, no. 5.

60 *Chron. Fordun*, i, 297–9 (Annals 52, 53); *Scotichronicon*, v, 380–1.

61 *CPR, 1272–1281*, 439, dated May 1282.

62 She died on 26 February 1275; Alan Orr Anderson (ed.), *Early Sources of Scottish History, A.D. 500 to 1286*, 2 vols (Edinburgh, 1922), ii, 671–2.

63 *Chron. Fordun*, i, 307 (Annal 63); *Scotichronicon*, v, 408–9; F.J. Amours (ed.), *The Original Chronicle of Andrew of Wyntoun*, 6 vols (Edinburgh, 1903–14), v, 128–9. The authors of these accounts note that the prince died at Stirling; a later chronicle claimed that 'he broke his neck at Roxburgh'; 'La Vraie Chronicque d'Escoce', in Dan Embree, Edward Donald Kennedy and Kathleen Daly (eds), *Short Scottish Prose Chronicles* (Woodbridge, 2012), 989.

64 *RRS, IV, Pt 1*, nos 132–5.

65 Margaret sailed to Norway in August and within a month of the sealing of her marriage agreement at Roxburgh had married Eric II. Knut Helle, 'Norwegian Foreign Policy and the Maid of Norway', *SHR* 69 (1990), 142–56.

66 The provisions made in Margaret's agreement are discussed in Duncan, *Kingship of the Scots*, 165–6.

a new generation of royal heirs. In 1281–82 he was still a widower and had as yet made no firm plans to remarry.

Edward I may well have had a hand in agreeing to a marriage between the Scottish prince and the daughter of the count of Flanders (a region that was the chief market for English wool),[67] but he had no say in the drafting of the contents of three separate documents that set out its terms.[68] High on the list of matters requiring detailed consideration in two of the documents were the tocher that Guy de Dampierre count of Flanders would offer together with the person of his daughter (£11,000), as well as the dower that King Alexander promised to provide should the bride outlive her husband (1,500 merks annually). More extraordinarily, a separate deed announced that in preparation for the prince's forthcoming marriage, Alexander III and his council had decided to review 'the ancient customs and practices of the kingdom of Scotland in use since time immemorial and now still in use for the succession to the throne'. The deed set out in intricate detail the lines through which title to the Scottish throne was to devolve, first, if Prince Alexander and Marguerite died before the king himself, or, second, should they fail to have children.[69]

Scholars have understandably devoted close attention to the agreements relating to the marriage of Alexander and Marguerite, not only owing to the circumstances that generated them, but more particularly from the perspective of the dynastic crises that followed the death of Prince Alexander in 1284, his sister Margaret of Norway just a few days later, and the king's own (wholly unexpected) demise in March 1286. The documents, however, are also valuable for what they reveal about the final stages of the political education of the heir to the Scottish throne, and about how the prince used the medium of these public documents to make a series of clear statements about his transition from youth into adulthood. None of the three deeds sealed in December 1281, nor a fourth, dated in November 1282, was produced in the Scottish chancery. They were, rather, the work of scribes associated with the writing office of Marguerite's father, Guy de Dampierre count of Flanders.[70] The structure of the documents is unusual, as is the Picard French in which they were written. Collectively, these and other diplomatic aspects of the deeds make it apparent that when Scottish envoys set off for Flanders late in 1281, they travelled with specific instructions to finalize the marriage plans. More important from the point of view of Prince Alexander, however, the dispatch of the embassy marked the occasion for the design of a seal of his own, the first of two that were fashioned for him in the following months.

The prince and his advisers clearly interpreted the impending marriage as turning points in both Alexander's personal life cycle and his public role in Scottish politics. Possession of a seal of his own marked an important stage in his

67 Duncan, *Making of the Kingdom*, 592.

68 *RRS, IV, Pt 1*, nos 133–5, 140.

69 *RRS, IV, Pt 1*, no. 133.

70 See detailed discussion in *RRS, IV, Pt 1*, 5, 12, 14, 25–6.

status as *rex designatus*, and for this reason, Alexander, his father and members of the royal council devoted much time and care to the design of the device. At just over three centimetres in diameter, the seal attached to one of the documents of December 1281 was only about a quarter of the size of the great seal of state with which the chancellor of Scotland regularly authenticated Alexander III's acts (a matrix of which travelled to Flanders with the envoys, together with that of the prince). It depicts, on a heater-shaped shield within a rounded trefoil, a lion rampant within a double tressure, and a label of five points. The legend reads +SECRETV' . ALEX . FILII . REGIS . SCOCIE . (privy seal of Alexander son of the king of Scotland).[71] There were complex layers of meaning in each and every one of these details; all were designed to convey coded messages to all who saw the seal. The lion rampant had been in use since the time of King Alexander II; the double tressure, first adopted by his father, recalled the ties of kinship between the prince and the royal house of France through the person of Marie de Coucy, queen of Alexander II.[72] The very size and design of Lord Alexander's seal, moreover, deliberately evoked the small seal that his father had used during his minority.[73] Thus was the prince's identity within the royal families of Scotland, England and France proclaimed on a waxen surface barely three centimetres across. The prince appended another, similar seal to a document dated in November 1282, after his ill health delayed the marriage to Marguerite by several months and diplomatic convention required that he affirm his earlier undertaking to her father. Here again, legend, design and imagery combined to project a carefully crafted representation of regal status. Attached to the deed (as the first had been) by means of an intricately braided crimson silk cord and, like the first, impressed in green wax and measuring just over three centimetres in diameter, it repeats on its surface the shield, lion and double tressure. On this second seal, however, the trefoil has become a sixfoil and to the background the prince has added fanciful rose branches. The legend, too, has changed, to the bolder and more mature S' ALEX . ILLUSTRIS REG' SCOTORUM PRIMOGE'NITI . (seal of Alexander firstborn of the illustrious king of Scots).[74] In the final clauses of both documents, more unusually still, the prince's authorial voice joins that of his father, first in making a formal confirmation of the tocher and dower arrangements, then in a declaration of his intention to authenticate his promises

[71] The deed is Archives de l'état à Namur, Chartes de Namur, no. 147. An image of the seal appears in Baron de Reiffenberg (ed.), *Monuments pour servir à l'histoire des provinces de Namur, de Hainault, et de Luxembourg*, 8 vols (Brussels, 1844–54), i, Plate 16, nos 127–8. There is a cast in NRS, RH 1/17, Drawer 56.

[72] John H. Stevenson and Marguerite Wood, *Scottish Heraldic Seals*, 3 vols (Glasgow, 1940), i, 4; L. Larchey, *Ancien armorial équestre de la toison d'or et de l'Europe au 15e siècle* (Paris, 1890), 256.

[73] Grant G. Simpson, 'Kingship in Miniature: A Seal of Minority of Alexander III, 1249–1257', in Alexander Grant and Keith J. Stringer (eds), *Medieval Scotland: Crown, Lordship and Community* (Edinburgh, 1993), 131–9.

[74] The original is Archives de l'état à Namur, Chartes de Namur, no. 157; with an image in Reiffenberg (ed.), *Monuments*, i, Plate 17, nos 137–8.

by means of his own seal. Evident here is Lord Alexander's pride in claiming ownership over a device all his own and in appending it to parchment documents that openly proclaimed his move into adulthood.[75]

The death of Prince David, the impending marriage to Marguerite de Dampierre and, it would appear, his own poor health, in July 1282 drove the prince to once again write to his uncle, Edward I. His request this time was simple: he asked the king to allow one Master Adam de Kirkcudbright to absent himself from his English estates for an extended period.[76] Master Adam, he wrote, had once been physician to Robert de Bruce earl of Carrick, but was now resident at the Prince's own court. When other physicians had all but given him up for dead, he wrote, Master Adam 'has restored me to health from the gates of death'. The prince noted that he remained yet under the physician's care, and that without his continued ministrations he feared that he might perish. Whatever the nature of the illness that afflicted him, Alexander was wise to fear it, for it delayed his marriage by several months. Eventually, however, in mid-November, the nuptial ceremonies were held at Roxburgh. The festivities were very much a public affair, attended, noted the author of the *Gesta Annalia I*, by 'a great many Scottish bishops, abbots, earls, barons, knights and other nobles', as well as by the cream of the Flemish nobility; altogether, they lasted some fifteen days.[77] In the very next sentence, however, the same chronicler reported in shocked tones the death, at Lindores on 28 January 1284, barely fourteen months after his marriage, of the 'distinguished youth' Prince Alexander, and he recounted the grief that swept across the kingdom at the news of the young man's passing.[78] 'Amid the incalculable sorrow of the whole people, the tears and groans of all the clergy, and the tears and sobs of the clergy, the king himself and the magnates', the twenty-year old heir was buried at Dunfermline abbey, beside his brother David.[79]

75 The document of December 1281 concludes: 'and I, Alexander, eldest son and heir of the king, who intend to take as my wife and loyal spouse the aforesaid Marguerite give her these [lands] in tocher, in the presence of my dear father the king … And in avowal of my intent firmly to observe [all the above] I have appended my seal to these letters, together with the seal of my lord and dear father, the king.' The deed of November 1282 reads: 'and in order to ensure that the above matters are held firm and lawful and that no prejudice shall befall my dear wife, the damsel Marguerite, I have appended my seal to the present letters together with the seal of my dear lord and father, the king of Scots, in confirmation of all the above'.

76 *Foedera*, i, 611. For Master Adam de Kirkcudbright, see D.E.R. Watt, *A Biographical Dictionary of Scottish Graduates to A.D. 1410* (Oxford, 1977), 306–8.

77 *Chron. Fordun*, i, 306–7 (Annal 63) and *Scotichronicon*, v, 410–11, which is based heavily on *Gesta Annalia I*, date the marriage to 15 November; the *Chronicle of Melrose* dates it to 8 November. Broun and Harrison, *Chronicle of Melrose Abbey*, 167–70. Marguerite was issued letters of safe conduct to travel through England in August. *CDS*, ii, nos 220, 221.

78 The precise date of Alexander's death and its causes are a source of some confusion among early chroniclers. The author of the *Gesta Annalia I* places the date late in 1283, but the author of *Scotichronicon*, v, 410–11, 502 has 28 January 1284. The author of *Chron. Lanercost*, 111, places the death on 21 January 1284, the prince's birthday. In any case, it can be stated with a degree of certainty that Alexander died either shortly before, or just after, he reached the age of twenty.

79 *Chron. Fordun*, i, 307 (Annal 63); *Scotichronicon*, v, 410–11.

The constitutional crisis that Prince Alexander's death precipitated has long dominated the scholarly study of Scottish politics in the closing years of the thirteenth century.[80] The influences on the near contemporary authors of the chronicles known as the *Gesta Annalia I and II,* the principle chronicle accounts of the period, have been especially closely examined. Not surprisingly, the annalists responsible for the portions of the Scottish chronicle covering the years 1284 to 1296 drew direct links between, on the one hand, the death of Prince Alexander in January and that of his sister Margaret in April of that same year, and, on the other, the 'days of lamentation and tears' that befell the kingdom after the death of the king himself in March 1286. These authors had good reason to do so: as one scholar remarked, by the end of this calamitous period the kingdom of Scotland 'was in danger of being rubbed out of history altogether'.[81]

The prince's death was also, however, described at some length by a contemporary English Franciscan who had lived and travelled in Scotland during the reign of Alexander III.[82] His work, later incorporated into the *Chronicle of Lanercost*, stated that at Cupar in Fife, on the evening before he died, the prince prophesied his own death.[83] This comment must, of course, be treated with some scepticism: the friar himself admitted that on occasion he allowed his imagination to overtake his dedication to a truthful narrative of events.[84] Yet, his account of Scottish affairs in the later thirteenth century includes a number of details that are not found in other chronicles, including a personal meeting between Prince Alexander and his uncle, Edward, in 1266, when the latter travelled to Haddington to visit his sister, Margaret queen of Scots.[85] Considerably less suspicious than the prophecy story is the author's statement that he obtained his information about the prince's last hours from people 'who were with him when he died, one a knight and his tutor, the other a rector of the parish church and his priest'.[86] The friar was an avid recounter of eyewitness testimony: he knew, for example, about the death by drowning of one of Queen Margaret's esquires, because her confessor had told him the story.[87] The chronicler also claimed that the prince had suffered from a lingering and debilitating illness; indeed, he was of the opinion that it caused the young man mental as well as physical distress. The allusion to Lord Alexander's passing at Cupar is probably inaccurate; here, the author may have made a mistake for nearby Lindores, which the well-informed author of the *Gesta Annalia I* claimed was the site of the prince's death. In any event, both estates lay within Fife, where the prince's chief landed possessions were located, and there seems little reason to doubt that it was here that he died.

80 Duncan, *Kingship of the Scots*, 169–219.
81 Broun, 'The Birth of Scottish History', 14.
82 A.G. Little, 'The Authorship of the Chronicle of Lanercost', *English Historical Review* 31 (1916), 270–9. This portion of the chronicle was written between 1280 and 1297.
83 *Chron. Lanercost*, 111.
84 Antonia Gransden, *Historical Writing in England, c. 550–c. 1307* (London, 1996), 499.
85 *Chron. Lanercost*, 81.
86 *Chron. Lanercost*, 111.
87 *Chron. Lanercost*, 95.

More intriguing still are the Franciscan chronicler's references to a knightly tutor or guardian, and a priest or chaplain. They suggest that Sir William Sinclair and Master Adam de Kirkcudbright remained in close attendance on Alexander in the several months after his marriage. Somehow, the thought of two friends close by the ailing prince's deathbed seems comforting.[88]

Conclusion

After his death Alexander fades quickly from extant records and is mentioned only in passing in the doleful business of settling accounts with his widow's father, which occupied the months immediately following his burial.[89] The process of his upbringing as prince and heir to the throne of Scotland and the efforts of his father and guardian to fashion a public role for him have left clear traces in extant source materials, but other aspects of his education, notably his spiritual life, are more difficult to reconstruct. Prayer and devotion must have been integral aspects of his education as a Christian prince, but the only basis for assessing the importance of such matters to Alexander is the partial text of a charter recording a gift of land and other property to the priory of Whithorn, discussed above. The language of the deed of conveyance is typical of contemporary grants in alms, and historians have long doubted that the formulaic terminology of texts like these express genuine pious sentiment. On the other hand, from the perspective of a young man who had struggled with illness for a good part of his life and had recently lost his mother, conventional expressions of piety may have had profound resonance and have been heartfelt.

Other important aspects of the prince's formation are equally ill documented. A lack of exchequer accounts from the 1270s and 1280s precludes a thorough assessment of the size of the prince's household or of the day-to-day business that occupied its officials. In the course of his childhood and early teenage years, moreover, Alexander must surely have received an education in literature and history appropriate to his wealth and gender, but here, too, extant evidence makes it impossible to offer detailed observations. The letters to Edward I reveal a sound knowledge of, and considerable dexterity in, the practice of diplomatic correspondence. They suggest, if obliquely, that the prince had access to the broad range of literary and learned treatises that circulated at the Scottish court, among them grammars, books of romance and history, and verse written in Latin, Scots, French and Gaelic.[90] As an elder son and a prince of the royal blood, moreover, Alexander must have received training in the arts of warfare

88 Perhaps especially in light of the fact that his uncle and aunt, the king and queen of England, spent a mere 3s 5d on prayers for the prince's soul. A.J. Taylor, 'Royal Alms and Oblations in the Later Thirteenth Century', in Frederick George Emmison and Roy Stephens (eds), *Tribute to an Antiquary* (London, 1976), 114.

89 *CDS*, ii, no. 247; Stevenson, *Documents*, i, 5–11, 12–17, 30–2, 41–4, 97–103, 118–19.

90 The varieties of oral and written literature circulating before the fourteenth centuries are explored in several essays in Brown (ed.), *Edinburgh History of Scottish Literature. Volume One.*

that were essential to the forging of elite masculine identity in the thirteenth century; so, too, must he have been introduced to the tourneying grounds that were such important avenues to social and political advancement for the aristocratic youths of his day. These aspects of the prince's life have left no mark in the sources, and his formal initiation into the ranks of knighthood – if it ever occurred – is nowhere celebrated. Equally surprising, given Alexander's active role in the governance of the former kingdom of Man and the prominent place that this position accorded him at the heart of the royal council, is the absence of the prince's name from the testing clauses of the several hundred royal charters and other deeds that issued forth from King Alexander III's writing office. In marked contrast to twelfth-century Scottish chancery practice in particular, the prince nowhere appears among the attestors to his father's acts.[91] The decision on the part of thirteenth-century scribes to omit mention of the prince's presence among the noble witnesses to the royal acts of lordship can only be a consequence of something other than scribal whim or archival accident. It may well represent a hitherto unnoticed feature of a carefully crafted programme designed to elevate the heir to the Scottish throne to a position distinctly above, and apart from, members of the secular and ecclesiastical aristocracy.

The uneven survival of documentary material relating to the early career of Prince Alexander may be problematic, yet readily discernible in extant sources are the several rites of passage that were essential to the making of any king in the later Middle Ages: the celebration of significant life events, widely advertised 'career firsts', and manifest assertions of the capacity to govern.[92] Alexander's betrothal and marriage, the crafting of a unique seal for his use, and royal appointment as lord of Man gave public expression to each of these stages. Collectively, they attest the existence of a well-conceived process by which the political community of late thirteenth-century Scotland sought to ensure the smooth passage to power of the heir to the throne. Just what manner of ruler a youth so thoughtfully prepared to govern the kingdom might have made as King Alexander IV, sadly, will never be known.

See also 'Introduction', in Thomas Owen Clancy (ed.), *The Triumph Tree: Scotland's Earliest Poetry, 550–1350* (Edinburgh, 1998), 6–11, 29–43.

[91] In the twelfth century, notably, Henry earl of Northumberland frequently witnessed the acts of his father, David I; on some occasions, moreover, he was accorded the status of co-donor with the king. G.W.S. Barrow (ed.), *The Charters of King David I* (Woodbridge, 1999), 5–8.

[92] Ormrod, 'Coming to Power', 32–48.

10

'At thair perfect age': Elite Child Betrothal and Parental Control, 1430–1560

Heather Parker

In 1557 a marriage contract was signed by James Ogilvy of Balnagerro and John Ogilvy of Innerquhairty for the betrothal of their respective children, Christian Ogilvy and Walter Ogilvy.[1] This contract stipulated that if the groom died before the wedding he was to be replaced by his brother James, and if James died, by their third brother, Andrew. The under-age couple was not expected to marry immediately but instead were to wed 'at thair perfect age'. This example was not out of the ordinary, as childhood betrothal was an important familial strategy for Scotland's nobles and lairds in the centuries preceding the Reformation. The nature of these betrothals was such that parents frequently disregarded the wishes of their children and the teachings of the Church in order to arrange the ideal match. Parents in lairdly and noble families in late medieval Scotland cared about their children, but they were also concerned with the management of their estates and status – fluid measures of social worth – that could be strengthened through marriage. Parents maintained control over the marriages of their children by retaining control over the lands and monies that were necessary to contribute to dowries, dowers and jointly held property. As a result, children were critical social capital and were often at the centre of family strategies to advance the legacy of their lineage, yet some of these betrothed youth did manage to assert agency in determining their own futures.

Historians have disagreed considerably about the emotional value medieval children had for their parents. In the mid-twentieth century, Philippe Ariès speculated about whether medieval parents, facing a high child mortality rate, invested emotionally in their children.[2] There is now a broad consensus among medieval historians that children were held with affection in their families.[3] Although largely debunked, Ariès's thesis did spur historians to examine the value children held in society. Beyond their emotional connections to their families,

[1] NRS, GD205/18/60, LX, no. 1.

[2] Philippe Ariès, *Centuries of Childhood: A Social History of Family Life* (New York, 1962).

[3] See Edward Shorter, *The Making of the Modern Family* (New York, 1975); Alan MacFarlane, 'Review: The Family, Sex and Marriage in England 1500–1800 by Lawrence Stone', *History and Theory* 18:1 (1979), 103–26; Shulamith Shahar, *Childhood in the Middle Ages* (London, 1989); Julie Hardwick, *The Practice of Patriarchy: Gender and the Politics of Household Authority in Early Modern France* (University Park, 1998); Nicholas Orme, *Medieval Children* (New Haven, 2001).

noble and lairdly children were pivotal in a culture obsessed with lineage and legacy. Not only did children ensure the continuation of a family's nobility and honour, but a judicious marriage also had the potential to advance a kin group. For some lairds and nobles, their strategy to ensure a good outcome for their children on the marriage market was to initiate marriage plans while the children were young. This could bring the nobility into conflict with the Church courts.

Childhood betrothal was subject to restrictions established by Rome, but families did not universally adhere to them. The Church had legal jurisdiction over marriage, and it put in place laws to protect the young and the unwilling from being coerced into marriage. Parents could commit their child to a formal betrothal once they reached the age of seven.[4] Officially, a marriage *per verba de presenti* – one with vows taken in the present tense – was not allowed until a girl was twelve and a boy was fourteen.[5] Additionally, betrothed children were not supposed to consummate their relationship until both parties had reached puberty.[6] A betrothed couple that had sex was considered to be legally married, even without a wedding ceremony, making it important for the Church to regulate betrothals as well as marriages.

These rules, however, were not universally followed and complainants took their cases of under-age marriage to the courts of the bishops' officials, the men who were assigned to deal with episcopal legal responsibilities. In August 1523, the Court of the Official of St Andrews annulled a marriage because a ten-year-old girl, Elizabeth Leith, who was married to Andrew Elphinston of Selmys, revoked her consent.[7] Elizabeth's case demonstrates that families occasionally ignored rules about a minimum age of consent of twelve for girls, but that when one of these cases did reach the courts, canon law was ultimately upheld. Regulated ages of consent were minimums, and they existed to protect the very young from forced marriage, not to ensure that all children were married early in their adolescence.

In special cases, the Church could provide dispensation for an under-age couple to marry. This occurred when eleven-year-old Princess Margaret and the thirteen-year-old French Dauphin, Louis, were married in 1436. It is likely that young couples such as this were spared the duty of consummation until a more appropriate age. Although impotence could be grounds for an annulment, sex was not actually required to complete a regular union.[8] As she was a princess, the benefits of Margaret's marriage alliance extended far beyond her family; the entire realm was affected. As such, the Church may have provided dispensations to betroth under-age royal children (especially if they were near the age of majority as Margaret and Louis had been), but this exception to the rule had no

4 John C. Barry (ed.), *William Hay's Lectures on Marriage* (Edinburgh, 1967), 5–15.

5 Orme, *Medieval Children*, 329.

6 Charles Donahue, *Law, Marriage, and Society in the Later Middle Ages* (Cambridge, 2007), 20.

7 *Liber Officialis Sancti Andree* (Edinburgh, 1845), no. 41.

8 James A. Brundage, *Law, Sex, and Christian Society in Medieval Europe* (Chicago, 1987), 188, 202.

parallels amongst the nobility whose marriage alliances were for the benefit of their family's legacy.[9]

Although canon marriage laws afforded children some protection from exploitation, pursuing court cases was onerous and many child betrothals escaped the Church's oversight, especially if the marriages themselves were not carried out until adolescence or adulthood. Nearly all of the contracts of betrothals for children younger than seven – the Church's minimum age limit for betrothals – escaped the notice of the Church courts. For instance, Annas Campbell and John Campbell of Ardkinglas were betrothed in 1571, when John was, at most, five years old. However, the marriage itself was not carried out until both the bride and the groom were of age, and as a result did not appear before the courts.[10] Ecclesiastical rules held limited weight when they conflicted with secular marriage customs that stemmed from real concerns. Parents had many competing priorities, including expanding their family's influence, maintaining connections with neighbouring lairds and nobles, and ensuring stable marriages for their children, and these could lead them to bend Church rules when practicable.

Although judicious marriages resulted in economic gain for some lairds and nobles, there were other factors for parents to consider when planning betrothals. A tradition of parental advice literature appeared in the fifteenth century that addressed the decisions that both parents and youth had to make in choosing appropriate marriage partners. These advice poems were part of a tradition of European advice literature that counselled parents on how to raise their offspring.[11] Among these pieces in Scotland were the fifteenth-century *Thewis of Gudwomen* and *Ratis Raving*.[12]

The Thewis of Gudwomen includes advice to young women about how to act honourably and honestly to have a successful marriage. In this poem, young betrothal and marriage do not simply stem from a desire to put firm plans in place between families. The poet argues that fathers should marry their children off while they are young to keep them from temptation and vice. If they do not, only the parents are to blame when something goes awry:

> For mony lordis ar nocht larg,
> Thinkand thai have our-gret charge,
> To mary thar barnis to thar estat;
> And oft thar lang baid cummys to lait. [often their long wait comes too late][13]

9 NRS, SP7/12.

10 *CL*, 30.

11 Kathryn Saldanha, '*The Thewis of Gudwomen*: Middle Scots Moral Advice with European Connections?', in Graham D. Caie (ed.), *The European Sun: Proceedings of the Seventh International Conference on Medieval and Renaissance Scottish Language and Literature, University of Strathclyde, 1993* (East Linton, 2001), 292.

12 Saldanha, 'The Thewis of Gudwomen'; *The Thewis of Gudwomen* and *Ratis Raving*, both in R. Girvan (ed.), *Ratis Raving and Other Early Scots Poems on Morals* (Edinburgh, 1939).

13 *Thewis*, lines 265–8. See also discussion in Chapters 1 and 11 of this collection.

This poem suggests that parents actually faced social pressures to engage in marriage arrangements when their children were young, but that the child's best interests were, instead, best met with early betrothals.

Appearing in the same manuscript as *The Thewis*, *Ratis Raving* records a father's guidance for his son and provides similar justification for betrothing boys at a young age. When it comes to marriage, the father advises that the qualities one normally looks for in a spouse, such as strength, good kin, wealth and skilfulness, can turn out contrary to expectation.[14] Instead, sons should choose 'lyklynes atour the laif / of contynans and of persone, / Of gud lynag and gud renown'.[15] The father thus discounts the typical worldly motivations for choosing a spouse and instead suggests alternative qualities that ought to result in a happier union. He adds that a woman who has a good mother should also be a good wife:

> For comonly thai folow kynd
> and gretly to the modiris strind [nature].
> sen thar is bot the lyklyest
> hald ay gud mother dochtir best.[16]

This literature held that it was critical that children enter into successful, lifelong unions. Doing so answered concerns about their long-term security and happiness, while also safeguarding any familial benefits that were gained through child betrothal. This advice held true for parents who were seeking to arrange a betrothal for their child, and, as *The Thewis* suggested, it was easier for a parent to control the selection of a partner when a child was young enough to unquestioningly follow the parental lead.

As mentioned above, Scottish advice literature was part of a genre of similar guidance that appeared throughout Europe addressing the decisions noble parents and their children made leading up to a betrothal. It was universally considered important to have a well-mannered partner with noble parentage. Maternal and paternal blood ties were equally important, because both contributed to the physical and emotional make-up of children.[17] It was also important to provide them with the correct type of education that would teach them the skills they needed in their family life. In her 1405 treatise, *The Book of the City of Ladies*, Christine de Pisan recommended teaching women land laws and budgeting skills so they could run their estates while husbands were away, and effectively manage their dowers during marriage and widowhood.[18] Scottish lords were well aware of this European literature, as portions of Christine de Pisan's writing were actually copied into the same composite manuscript that contained the Scottish

14 *Ratis Raving*, lines 927–34.
15 *Ratis Raving*, lines 936–8.
16 *Ratis Raving*, lines 939–42.
17 Shahar, *Childhood in the Middle Ages*, 163.
18 Shahar, *Childhood in the Middle Ages*, 221.

poem *Ratis Raving*.[19] These literary works were all clear that childhood was a time to spend considering marriage prospects.

Educational literature gained prominence in England in the early sixteenth century and taught that while boys and girls must both receive a proper humanist education and follow their parents' advice, young girls alone must be 'trained in respect of mariage, obedience to her head, & the qualities which looke that way'.[20] Girls were trained in housewifely offices such as housekeeping and child-rearing.[21] These English daughters were expected to obey their parents' wishes, with the understanding that their parents were ultimately looking out for the best interests of their children and families.[22] The existence of this type of literature, as well as curricula for the education of young girls that centred entirely on preparation for marriage, demonstrates that parents were preoccupied with concerns for their children's marriages during childhood itself, and that they spent considerable time discussing and preparing young children for their imminent nuptials.

However, marriage preparation during childhood was not always borne out in actual child marriages. Despite the copious evidence indicating that child betrothal was common, it is difficult to quantify it or to determine an exact age for first marriage in late medieval Scotland because there were no comprehensive records of marriages. As well, the minimum age for consent was not considered a universal age of majority. Instead, there were many different ages at which adolescents and young adults reached maturity for a variety of legal reasons.

Even when marriages were documented, it is often impossible to know the exact ages of the bride and groom for pre-Reformation marriages because there were no comprehensive birth records. Fortunately, this kind of demographic data is available for the late sixteenth century and the early modern period in general. Between 1560 and 1600, an average nobleman first married at the age of twenty-two, whereas noblewomen entered their first marriages at an average age of eighteen.[23] Noble families generally married earlier than the wider population because there were fewer financial concerns preventing the marriage, although raising a dowry could be a struggle. Rab Houston's examination of all ranks of society shows that the median age for women at their first marriage was

19 R. Girvan, 'Introduction', in *Ratis Raving*, p. viii.

20 Richard Mulcaster, *Positions Vvherin Those Primitiue ...* (London, 1581), 74, 151–2. See discussion of these works in Sara Mendelson, '"Obey and Be Attentive": Gender and Household Instruction in Shakespeare's The Tempest', in Naomi Miller and Naomi Yavneh (eds), *Gender and Early Modern Constructions of Childhood* (Farnham, 2011), 130.

21 Mendelson, 'Obey and Be Attentive', 130.

22 Anu Lahtinen, 'The Marriage Process in the Light of Family Corresondence: a Comparative Perspective on the Swedish Evidence', in Mia Korpiola (ed.), *Regional Variation in Matrimonial Law and Custom in Europe, 1150–1600* (Leiden, 2011), 256.

23 Keith Brown, *Noble Society in Scotland: Wealth, Family, and Culture from the Reformation to the Revolution* (Edinburgh, 2000), 115.

between twenty-six and twenty-seven years of age.[24] One in four women never married.[25]

It would be inappropriate to see these numbers as applicable to the whole later medieval period. They do show, however, that marriage age in post-Reformation Scotland was very much in line with European norms. English ducal families experienced a slowly rising average age at first marriage, increasing from 22.4 years for men and 17.1 for women between 1330 and 1479, to 24.3 years for men and 19.5 for women between 1480 and 1679.[26] Between 1550 and 1574, male and female children of the wider category of English peers had an average age respectively of 25.3 and 20.3 years for the first marriage.[27] These average ages show quite clearly that despite the prevalence of betrothals during childhood and adolescence, most weddings took place in adulthood.

Anecdotal evidence does exist from earlier periods in Scotland addressing the question of age at marriage, and the contents of ante-nuptial contracts provides especially interesting information on the attitudes towards the concept of maturity. Generally, marriage contracts between adolescents or adults were intended to be carried out as soon as practicable, and they included phrases such as 'in all gudly haste' to make this explicit.[28] Other agreements were clear that the betrothal was intended to last longer and sometimes included clauses requiring the bride and groom to reach a minimum age before they marry. This was sometimes driven by the legal minimum age limit for marriage. The 1469 contract of Margaret Preston and John Edmonston required that they marry 'as soon as they are of lawfull age'.[29] In a similar vein, the 1545 contract of Margaret Hamilton, daughter of the earl of Arran, and James Montgomery, master of Eglinton, stated that if the marriage did not occur within a year of James's fourteenth birthday, then the contract should be considered null.[30]

In 1557, when Christian Ogilvy of Balnagerro and Walter Ogilvy of Innerquhairty were contracted to marry, their contract used the phrase 'at thair perfect age'.[31] While the writers may have been referring to the legal minimum, other contracts in the following twenty years used this kind of language to refer to older children. A 1569 contract of Sir William Scott of Balweiry and Christian Douglas of Lochleven stated that they should marry when Christian 'beis of

24 R.A. Houston, *The Population History of Britain and Ireland 1500–1750* (London, 1992), 25.

25 Houston, *The Population History of Britain and Ireland*, 25.

26 T.H. Hollingsworth, 'A Demographic Study of the British Ducal Families', in D.V. Glass and E.C. Eversley (eds), *Population in History: Essays in Historical Demography* (Cambridge, 1965), 365.

27 T.H. Hollingsworth, *The Demography of the British Peerage* (London, 1964), 25.

28 For example, William Fraser, *The Scotts of Buccleuch*, 2 vols (Edinburgh, 1878), ii, 398; see further discussion in Heather Parker, '"In All Gudly Haste": The Formation of Marriage in Scotland, c. 1350–1600', unpublished Ph.D. thesis, University of Guelph (2012), 207.

29 NRS, AD1/64.

30 NRS, GD3/2/4/6.

31 NRS, GD205/18/60, LX, no. 1.

fourteine yeirs of age'.[32] If either of them were to die before this time, he or she was to be replaced by any other siblings yet to be born. Grizel Hay and Robert Hume were entered into a marriage contract by their parents in 1576 that specified they should not be married until they reached the age of eighteen.[33] A later contract defines 'compleit age' as fifteen.[34] These documents indicate that even those parents who chose to enter their children into early betrothals were not always eager for their children to marry as young as legally possible. Instead, they had a wider range of opinions on what age was considered appropriate. Further still, contracts that specified an age at which the families should proceed with the marriage were not representative of average ages of first marriages, but rather, they indicated minimum ages that parents considered acceptable for marriage. These documents also make clear that betrothal in childhood was relatively common among elites.

Some of the best evidence of the nature of childhood betrothal is found in the legal documentation created during the formation of marriage. Although betrothal and marriage contracts can often seem formulaic, the particulars of the marital arrangements are, in fact, quite revealing. While children and their marriages were critical social capital for families, the long-term wishes and individual preferences of the children were often addressed in the ante-nuptial contracts. When parents negotiated the contents of these agreements, they included clauses to maximize the chance that the arranged union would be agreeable for the couple. Many contracts explicitly addressed the question of the choice of marriage partner, albeit for the groom and not the bride. An indenture between Robert Arbuthnot and David Rate of Drumnagar referred to a marriage between David's son William and 'ane of the douchteris of the forsaid Robert'.[35] The parents agreed that the groom could have his choice of brides from a group of sisters. The choice provided to William could reflect a power difference between the two families involved in the marriage contract. There are, however, many contracts that offer this choice to boys, but none that offer a choice of husbands to a bride, and so it likely reflects the greater agency of men in general. Nevertheless, it does show that parents were considerate of some of their children's wishes as long as they were able to ensure that the two families were united through marriage. It also hints at the age of the children involved, implying that the potential spouses were too young for a choice to be determined before the contract was created.

Other contracts openly acknowledged the possibility of a disagreement. In the 1498 ante-nuptial contract of John Montgomery and Besse Edmonston, the parents of the bride and groom committed alternative children to the same marriage contract if circumstances were to require it:

> Gyf that it falying be dysches [death] or dessasend [dissent] of any of the forsaid persounis of Jhon or Besse the said lord bynds his secund sounn. Sa falyeand of

[32] NRS, GD150/451.
[33] NRS, GD110/169.
[34] NRS, GD112/25/108.
[35] Aberdeen University Archives, MS 3021/31.

> the secund, the thred. Sa falyeand of that thred, the ford, and inlikwys, falyeand of the said Besse, Kateren, so falyeand of Katren, Margaret, or falyeand of Margaret, Ellenn, for the quhilk mareagh beand completit.[36]

Even these more generous contracts still operated under the assumption that at least one of the children of the family would consent to the marriage, but they fail to address what will happen to the lands and moneys exchanged if none of the children assent to the union.

Ante-nuptial contracts also explicitly demonstrated that the parties involved wanted the betrothals and marriages to last. They included clauses ensuring the legality of a marriage, thus protecting it from a challenge. Beginning in the late fifteenth century, many contracts began to spell out the requirement for family members to seek a papal dispensation for any impediments to marriage, including spiritual affinity, marital affinity and consanguinity.[37] If any of these impediments were discovered or made public after the marriage occurred, the couple faced a possible annulment, which would result in illegitimacy of their children and an uncertain future for their mutual property. They could apply for a dispensation at any point in the marriage, and many couples were successful in gaining dispensations for issues that they claimed had only arisen after the union had taken place and after their children had been born. This was in line with the Church's official policy on granting dispensations.[38]

Other contracts stipulated that the parties involved would face fines if they withdrew from the agreement. These clauses were supported by legal treatises, which used fines as a method of ensuring that both parties followed through with their promises.[39] The 1509 contract of Archibald Douglas and Margaret Hepburn required both fathers to pay a 500–merk fine to the archbishop of St Andrews and the king if the contract was breached.[40] The inclusion of these elements in prenuptial agreements shows that lifelong marriage was important to these families, not just to preserve the financial arrangements that they put into place but also for the benefit of all the people involved in the marriage process.

It is important to remember that these types of arrangements had limited reach, for not all unions were covered by ante-nuptial contracts. They did not, for example, deal with elopements. By the late medieval period, the Church insisted that couples marry in public, with banns read in a couple's home parishes on three Sundays preceding the union to allow for objections to be raised.[41] Nevertheless, canon law did still recognize 'irregular' and 'clandestine' marriages as technically valid, and so many couples married in this way, regardless of the

36 NRS, GD3/2/1/16.

37 See, for example, the 1485 contract of Elizabeth, daughter of George Leslie, 1st earl of Rothes and William Hay, 3rd earl of Erroll, NRS, RH1/6/117. The teacher, William Hay discusses impediments to marriage in Barry (ed.), *William Hay's Lectures on Marriage*, 185.

38 James A. Brundage, *Sex, Law and Marriage in the Middle Ages* (Aldershot, 1993), 200.

39 James Balfour, *Practicks: or, a system of the more ancient law of Scotland* (Edinburgh, 1754), 97.

40 Fraser, *The Scotts of Buccleuch*, ii, 117–9.

41 R.H. Helmholz, *Marriage Litigation in Medieval England* (London, 1974), 27.

Church's displeasure. Most of the historical sources that discuss marriage negotiations deal specifically with regular marriage. Indeed, increasingly throughout the sixteenth century, contracts were explicit that marriage must happen *in facie ecclesiae*, or 'in the face of the holy Kirk', but this constituted only a portion of marriages among the nobility.[42] It is possible, too, that unwritten, informal marriage agreements existed between families, especially when the children were too young to consent, but the lack of documentation means that the proportion of informal arrangements cannot be accurately estimated.

When formal betrothal contracts were drawn up for children, a wide range of advisers took part in the process. Kin, clerics and lawyers were routinely involved in marriage negotiations, and offered advice on how to structure marriage contracts, and their appearance as witnesses to contracts make these connections clear. While both mothers and fathers engaged in negotiations, the fathers' names more commonly appear in the legal documents. In ante-nuptial contracts created between 1380 and 1600, mothers of the bride appear in six per cent of contracts and mothers of the groom in eighteen per cent, and this trend is consistent in documents relating to children.[43] One reason for mothers to sign marriage contracts was that the property arrangements included lands, such as dowers, for which these women had claims. Wealthy relatives also sometimes contributed to these contracts, either by gifting parcels of land to a couple or by lending their names and credibility to the contract itself as witnesses.[44]

Many lairdly and noble families engaged in the negotiations of child betrothals via correspondence across large distances. Unfortunately, very little Scottish evidence concerning these negotiations in the fifteenth and early sixteenth centuries has survived, and of the documents that do, most only concern marriages of members of the royal family. These include letters between Henry VIII and the Scottish court regarding the marriage of Prince Edward to Princess Mary during the 'rough wooing', and later correspondence concerning Mary's betrothal to the Dauphin.[45] There are also a handful of royal letters discussing marriages among lairds and their families. For instance, in 1541 James V wrote to the laird of Raith to discuss his son's marriage to the sister of the laird of Lochleven. Raith would not proceed with the marriage until he knew the king's opinion, and the king sent his approval.[46] The royal evidence from this period, and the ample noble correspondence from the 1560s onward, suggests that similar negotiations were occurring among the lairds and nobility in person and by messenger throughout the sixteenth century.

[42] For example, the contract of Lady Margaret Lyon of Guthrie and David Inverquharty in 1518: NRS, GD205/12/33.

[43] Parker, 'In All Gudly Haste', 221–2.

[44] For example, Robert Douglas of Lochleven arranged a marriage for his sister, Marion Douglas, to John Lindsay in 1530: NRS, GD150/283.

[45] NRS, SP13/37; SP13/47; SP13/79–83.

[46] William Fraser, *The Melvilles, Earls of Melville, and the Leslies, Earls of Leven*, 3 vols (Edinburgh, 1890), ii, 2.

The years following the Reformation provide more fruitful and extensive epistolary evidence for the involvement of noble families in negotiating child betrothals. Surviving letters of Katherine Ruthven and Colin Campbell, laird of Glenorchy, discuss matters pertaining to their family and their estates. They include two letters specifically addressing the marriages of their children.[47] These letters speak to pressing concerns, such as the attempt to negotiate a marriage union to lessen the ill will between the Campbells of Glenorchy and the neighbouring earl of Atholl.[48] They also discuss questions of the personal suitability of a candidate, the benefits of using friends and relatives as intermediaries, and the need to conduct more formal arrangements.[49] The proposed union with Atholl included the investigation by a friend's relatives that the bride was 'of good behavings'. The negotiations with the earl of Argyll for a second child betrothal promoted the union because it would contribute to the 'honorable service of our house and amite and luif betuix the twa houses of Glenurquhay and Ardkinglass by way of allyly'.[50] As a result of these discussions, Katherine and Colin's daughter Annas was betrothed in 1571, while still quite young.[51] Her contract was confirmed four years later, after the death of her father, indicating that she was no longer a minor.[52] It was reconfirmed in 1586 just before her wedding.[53] Her groom, John Campbell of Ardkinglas, could have been no older than five when the negotiations began.[54]

Katherine Ruthven's role in networking and fact-finding was not unique for a woman of her status and education. This type of networking was crucial to the proper functioning of these families, and women who had a good education and the skills to negotiate were seen as good mediators. This same letter collection includes one from Anabella Murray to Colin, Katherine's husband, asking him to serve as curator to her daughter.[55] Correspondence also exists from 1543 between Mary of Guise and Elizabeth Campbell, countess of Moray, with Mary pleading with Elizabeth to act as intercessor with her husband, who had failed to answer Mary's requests.[56] Correspondence of this sort indicates that even if women were not travelling in person, they could use letters to friends and family to spearhead negotiations for the betrothals of their children.[57]

Children were expected to submit to their parents' wishes, and this included when choosing a marriage partner, partly because childhood was closely

47 *CL*.
48 *CL*, 132.
49 *CL*, 29 and no. 110.
50 *CL*, no. 170.
51 NRS, GD112/25/31.
52 NRS, GD112/25/41.
53 NRS, GD112/25/45.
54 *CL*, 30.
55 *CL*, no. 189.
56 James Maidment, *Analecta Scotica: Collections Illustrative of the Civil, Ecclesiastical, and Literary History of Scotland*, 2 vols (Edinburgh, 1834–7), i, 345.
57 See Chapter 3 in this collection for more on mothers using correspondence to negotiate on behalf of their children.

embedded in the adult world.[58] Some parents went to great lengths to ensure that marriage plans were successful, and although violent coercion was rarely reported, subtler types of coercion were commonplace. Most children lived in their parents' homes, although boys more commonly than girls might be reared and educated in the art of manliness in a more prominent household.[59] Girls left home less frequently, but there are prominent examples of daughters sent to the families of their betrothed to be raised in a foreign court. Mary, Queen of Scots, left Scotland at the age of five after her betrothal to the Dauphin was finalized.[60] She then spent ten years in a foreign court before her marriage at the age of fifteen.[61] Despite this pattern among royalty and magnates, it was not typically seen among the lairds and lesser nobles. Instead, girls were raised and educated in their parents' household.

Although Mary's living arrangements were not typical of the Scottish nobility, it was, as we have seen, common for parents to enter their children into marriage contracts at a young age. The agency of children in the process varied considerably. While there is plenty of evidence, especially in advice literature, of children being given some choice in their marriage partner, other betrothals were drafted exclusively by parents. A small number even specified marriages between a bride and groom yet to be conceived.[62] It is clear that once these children arrived, they were expected to comply with their parents' wishes concerning their marriage. Many of the contracts included provisions in the case of a child's death, but very few addressed the possibility that a child would refuse to enter into a marriage.[63] This demonstrates a strong societal pressure to conform to parental plans.

This pressure to proceed with a marriage could also come from outside the family. Sometimes courts ordered couples to go forward with a betrothal to complete their contracts, such as when, in 1500, the Lords of Council ordered Andrew Kinnaird to marry Jonet Crichton before Whitsunday 'til get payment of the soumes awing til him efter the tenore of thair endentouris made betuex thame'.[64] Such practice was supported by legal scholars, such as the sixteenth-century lawyer James Balfour, who wrote that a marriage contract was an oath, and it legally must be followed through: 'the day contenit in the said contract beand bypast, gif ather of the parties refusis or delayis the completing of the said mariage, he may be callit befoir the Judge ordinar, and chargit to solempnizat [*sic*] the said matrimonie within ane certaine day'.[65] For those betrothed at a

58 Shahar, *Childhood in the Middle Ages*, 2.

59 Shahar, *Childhood in the Middle Ages*, 220.

60 Jenny Wormald, *Mary, Queen of Scots: Politics, Passion and a Kingdom Lost* (London, 2001), 62.

61 Wormald, *Mary, Queen of Scots*, 87.

62 NRS, GD150/136.

63 For instance, see the contract of John Lindsay of Collanetoune and Margaret Scott: NRS, GD100/282.

64 George Neilson and Henry Paton (eds), *Acts of the Lords of Council in Civil Causes. Vol. II. 1496–1501* (Edinburgh, 1918), 2, 385.

65 Balfour, *Practicks*, 97.

young age, the economic aspects of the contractual arrangements along with the social pressure to obey their parents left them with few opportunities to actively participate in the process.

In theory, Catholic doctrine protected the agency of betrothed individuals by imposing regulations requiring personal consent to marriage. By the late medieval era, the legitimacy of Scottish marriages was determined exclusively by the canon law of Rome. Theorists generally agreed that the single defining factor determining the validity of a marriage was the personal consent of the bride and groom.[66] As long as no other impediments to the marriage existed, a couple could exchange vows that bore the full weight of the law. Different realms applied marital law in their own way. For instance, although they recognized the Church's requirement for personal consent, Swedish secular courts also required parental consent to validate the marriage, thus limiting the ecclesiastical definition and excluding certain types of clandestine marriage that the Church would otherwise have considered valid.[67] In contrast, the Scottish Church tried to ensure that marital vows were taken in public, but as private vows were equally valid this caused no end to the legal confusion surrounding irregular marriages.[68] Consent had to be obtained freely, and 'force and fear' during the formation of a marriage could result in a challenge at court.[69] In clear-cut cases, such as that of Elizabeth Leith in 1526, a forced child marriage was immediately annulled.[70] However, generally the Church was cautious in granting annulments to individuals who claimed to have been forced into marriage through child betrothal or any other means.[71]

Similarly, supplications to the pope for annulments based on force and fear did not receive universally positive results. One such occurred in 1425, when Jonet Jardin claimed that a gang of men kidnapped her and forced her to marry James de Arnot. According to her plea, James imprisoned her for four and a half years, during which time the couple had a child.[72] Jonet's supplication for an annulment was successful, but she did not endear herself to the authorities during the process and was eventually excommunicated for her refusal to comply with their wishes.[73] Children were particularly vulnerable to these types of forced marriages. The Church's rules concerning forced unions were sufficient to address egregious violations of the principle of free personal consent, but the

66 Michael Sheehan, 'Choice of Marriage Partner in the Middle Ages: Development and Mode of Application of a Theory of Marriage', in Carol Neel (ed.), *Medieval Families: Perspectives on Marriage, Household, and Children* (Toronto, 2004), 162–3.

67 Lahtinen, 'The Marriage Process in the Light of Family Corresondence', 252.

68 For an index to impeded and confused marriages, see the table of contents in *Liber Officialis Sancti Andree.*

69 David M. Walker, *A Legal History of Scotland: The Beginnings to A.D. 1286* (Edinburgh, 1988), 611.

70 *Liber Officialis Sancti Andree*, no. 41.

71 Donahue, *Law, Marriage, and Society in the Later Middle Ages*, 21–2.

72 E.R. Lindsay and Annie I. Dunlop (eds), *Calendar of Scottish Supplications to Rome, 1423–1428* (Edinburgh, 1956), 114.

73 Lindsay and Dunlop (eds), *Calendar of Scottish Supplications to Rome*, 114.

proof required to obtain annulments did not allow for more subtle types of coercion relying on power differentials within a household.

The decision to negotiate a betrothal depended on mothers and fathers, but uncles, grandparents and siblings took on responsibility if they were contributing land or money to a marriage, or if they had a significant stake in the marital bonds created between the families. Relatives often helped with marriage arrangements for individuals of any age after the death of a parent, such as when Elizabeth Keith's brother arranged her marriage to the earl of Huntly in 1530 after their father's death at Flodden.[74] Children, however, were especially vulnerable, and their control could fall to people outside the family through wardship.

The culture of wardship was similar in Scotland and England. Felicity Riddy has analysed Hans Holbein's sketch of the family of Sir Thomas More to bring particular attention to the experiences of English wards in the households of their guardians.[75] While the portrait shows a family with obedient daughters who had difficulty breaking free of their father's paternal oversight, it also includes More's ward, Anne Cresacre, in the background. In the image, she is included in the household but marginalized from the family. Thomas More was Anne's third guardian, following two earlier experiences that were disastrous. After her father's death, Anne inherited a significant patrimony, and as a result she was kidnapped and betrothed to a neighbour's illegitimate son. When she refused to complete the marriage at the age of twelve, another dubious character took her in as his ward and betrothed her to his own son, while forcing the two children to consummate the union in an effort to diminish her ability to flee the abusive family. Both of these abductors were eventually condemned by the courts for their attempts to force Anne into marriage. She was then placed with Thomas More, a gentleman well known for his generosity towards his own daughters. Anne married More's son, John, a union to which she offered her public consent.[76]

Anne's case demonstrates the extent to which young heirs and heiresses were vulnerable to their guardians, who took liberties well outside the bounds of canon law. The court records for this type of 'force and fear' highlight only the cases that were brought to justice. Although Anne's situation shows a judicial intolerance of coercion, it also demonstrates the prevalence of coercion in society, and it suggests that there may have been other similar cases that did not appear before the courts. Her series of wardships also shows the limits a ward faced in exercising free choice concerning his or her marriage partner. While Anne was vocal in her dissent during her first two betrothals, her eventual marriage was consensual, albeit still to the son of her guardian. The vulnerable position of wards was similar in Scotland, where wardships were regularly gifted and sold to

[74] *Miscellany of the Spalding Club* 4 (Aberdeen, 1849), 138–42.

[75] Felicity Riddy, 'Fathers and Daughters in Holbein's Sketch of Thomas More's Family', in Rosalynn Voaden and Diane Wolfthal (eds), *Framing the Family: Narrative and Representation in the Medieval and Early Modern Periods* (Tempe, 2005), 19–38.

[76] Riddy, 'Framing the Family', 34, 37.

political favourites.[77] For instance, in 1458 – a year before he travelled to England as an ambassador for the king – William Borthwick was awarded the title Lord Borthwick and the wardship and marriage of heiress Mariota of Hoppringill.[78] The two were soon wed.

The experience of wards highlights the pressure they faced to marry according to their guardians' wishes. Children could also face this kind of pressure from their parents. Margaret Ruthven was betrothed to John Oliphant as a child, but in 1494 steps were taken to nullify the contract because of her persistent refusal to consent to the marriage.[79] Although her father eventually relented, this case also shows the extent to which parents would try to elicit nominal consent from their children, however reluctant they appeared at first. The account of Margaret's rejection shows her father's unwillingness to accept her refusal: 'And the lord Ruthven asked why she would not complete the said marriage. And she Margaret again answered and said because she had no carnal affection nor favour for him John, and that she declared this to her said father and mother a year ago and more'.[80] Margaret Ruthven's betrothal to John Oliphant would have meant wealth and stability for Margaret, because John was in line to inherit his grandfather's estates and title. It also would have been a reaffirmation of the links between her father Lord Ruthven, and John's grandfather Lord Oliphant. Yet, her success in avoiding betrothal demonstrates her ability to take control over her own marital future.

When parents planned betrothals for their children, they had a large number of factors to consider. Economic and political ties were important for the wider family and kin group, but they needed to be balanced with social factors that contributed to a successful union. Parents themselves were raised in a culture of arranged marriages, and they used the opportunity of their children's betrothals to reinforce their own ideals concerning social status. After betrothal, children did have ways to escape from these arranged marriages, especially when weddings were delayed until adulthood, but the rarity with which this appears in the records suggests that they rarely challenged the arrangements made by their parents. The extent to which children were allowed to make their own decisions depended greatly on the personalities of their parents, and their status. The eldest children of magnates, for example, typically had less freedom than the children of lairds. The care that parents took to arrange betrothals for their offspring and to protect them in marriage shows that generally children were valued family members. Children of Scottish lairds and nobles in turn understood their expected roles, and were usually willing participants in plans that were beneficial to the family as a whole.

77 Athol L. Murray (ed.), *Sinclair's Practicks* (Edinburgh, forthcoming), no. 537, p. 108; David M. Walker, *A Legal History of Scotland: The Later Middle Ages* (Edinburgh, 1988), 581–3.

78 *RMS*, ii, no. 650; Alexander Nisbet, *A System of Heraldry, Speculative and Practical*, 2 vols (Edinburgh, 1816), ii, appendix, 105.

79 J. Maitland Thomson, *The Public Records of Scotland* (Glasgow, 1922), 92–3.

80 Thomson, *The Public Records of Scotland*, 93.

11

Sons and Daughters, 'young wyfis' and 'barnis': Lyric, Gender, and the Imagining of Youth in the Maitland Manuscripts

Sarah M. Dunnigan

The manuscript miscellanies associated with Sir Richard Maitland of Lethington (1496–1586) are well known as a precious resource for an understanding of the circulation, transmission, and creation of late medieval and Renaissance Scottish poetry. The two collections (Folio and Quarto) belong to what Alasdair A. MacDonald has termed 'the great century for Scottish literary manuscripts',[1] raising questions about literary preservation, survival and popularity in early modern Scotland. Both volumes hold a mirror to the aesthetic, moral and political interests of a specific gentry household in an estate in East Lothian. Together they encompass a diverse and eclectic range of subjects that historically span several Stewart monarchies, and reflect religious and political sympathies allied to reformed thought.[2] Social, political and spiritual identities and affiliations under-

[1] 'Early Modern Scottish Literature and the Parameters of Culture', in Sally Mapstone (ed.), *The Rose and the Thistle: Essays on the Culture of Late Medieval and Renaissance Scotland* (East Linton, 1998), 92. In addition, MacDonald refers to the Asloan MS, the Arundel MS 285 and the Bannatyne MS, drawing attention to the relationship between manuscript and print, and the literary, social and religious impulses of the period that conceivably shaped their compilation (92ff).

[2] The Maitland Quarto manuscript is held in Cambridge, Magdalene College, Pepys Library, MS 1408, and the Folio in Cambridge, Magdalene College, Pepys Library, MS 2553. The manuscripts were edited in 1919 by W.A. Craigie, with introductory material, notes and glossary: *The Maitland Folio Manuscript*, 2 vols (Edinburgh and London), and *The Maitland Quarto Manuscript* (Edinburgh). All quotations in this essay are based on these editions. A new edition, Joanna Martin (ed.), *The Maitland Quarto*, published by the Scottish Text Society, appeared in 2015 just after the completion of this essay. The abbreviations MF and MQ are given parenthetically in the text, followed by the Roman number each poem has been assigned and a line reference. For a variety of textual and contextual accounts of the Maitland manuscripts, see: Joanna Martin, 'The Maitland Quarto Manuscript and the Literary Culture of the Reign of James VI', in David Parkinson (ed.), *James VI and I. Literature and Scotland: Tides of Change 1567–2013* (Leuven, 2013), 65–81; Joanna Martin, 'The Presentation of the Family in Maitland Writings', in Janet Hadley Williams and Derrick McClure (eds), *Fresche Fontanis: Studies in the Culture of Medieval and Early Modern Scotland* (Newcastle upon Tyne, 2013), 319–30; Priscilla Bawcutt, 'The Earliest Texts of Dunbar', in Felicity Riddy (ed.), *Regionalism in Late Medieval Manuscripts and Texts* (Cambridge, 1991), 183–98; and Priscilla Bawcutt, 'Manuscript Miscellanies in Scotland from the Fifteenth to the Seventeenth Century', in Sally

pin both collections, often with immediate and topical urgency, but the notion of identity also has particular roots, for these are manuscripts intimately bound up with one particular family. In terms of provenance, associations and thematic interests, familial identity, as Joanna Martin has recently demonstrated, is vital.[3] The wealth of poems ascribed to Sir Richard Maitland himself – described as a 'valyeant warrior wicht [strong brave warrior] / … With the pen the Poetis pairt weill playit' – means that Folio and Quarto are a composite celebratory testament to his creative and moral vision.[4] Poetic inscription ensures the perpetuity of the Maitland 'lyne and linage' (MQ, I, line 6), described in a commendatory poem by Robert Hudson as an 'ancient raice' (MF, CLXXXII, line 1). In the case of the Quarto, this notion of literary legacy or poetic survival becomes more poignant, given that its apparent date of compilation is the year of Maitland's death. In a very literal way, then, the manuscript is a memorial witness to Maitland and his family – '[h]is childaris childring' – for in its concluding section are funerary and elegiac poems.[5]

But the idea of family lies at the heart of these collections in other ways. This essay explores how a small but significant vein of poems imaginatively embody the relationships between parents and 'children'. It also looks at concomitant ideas of 'young' feminine and masculine conduct.[6] In many lyrics, the familial

Mapstone (ed.), *Older Scots Literature* (Edinburgh, 2005), 189–210. On the broader context of early modern Scottish manuscript culture, see Sebastiaan J. Verweij, '"The inlegebill scribbling of my impromptu pen": The Production and Circulation of Literary Miscellany Manuscripts in Jacobean Scotland, c. 1580–c. 1630', unpublished Ph.D. thesis, University of Glasgow (2008); Bawcutt, 'Manuscript Miscellanies'; and Denton Fox, 'Manuscripts and Prints of Scots Poetry in the Sixteenth Century', in A.J. Aitken et al. (eds), *Bards and Makars: Scottish Language and Literature, Medieval and Renaissance* (Glasgow, 1977), 156–71.

3 Martin, 'Presentation of the Family'. As Bawcutt, 'Manuscript Miscellanies', 196, notes in relation to Folio and Quarto, and another manuscript that contains copies of Maitland's poems, '[a]ll three collections originated in family piety'.

4 Quotation from MQ, p. xix, 'Ane Sonet to the Authour In comendatioun of his buik', lines 11–12. On Maitland's own poetry, see A.A. MacDonald, 'The Poetry of Sir Richard Maitland of Lethington', *Transactions of the East Lothian Antiquarian and Field Naturalists' Society* 13 (1972), 17–19; A.A. MacDonald, 'Sir Richard Maitland and William Dunbar: Textual Symbiosis and Poetic Individuality', in Sally Mapstone (ed.), *William Dunbar, 'The Nobill Poyet'* (East Linton, 2001), 134–49; MacDonald, 'Parameters of Culture', 82–3, 85–6; Julia Boffey, 'The Maitland Folio Manuscript as a Verse Anthology', in Mapstone (ed.), *William Dunbar*, 40–50; Theo van Heijnsbergen, 'Modes of Self-Representation in Older Scots Texts', in Mapstone (ed.), *Older Scots Literature*, 340–1. Cf. also Julian Goodare, *State and Society in Early Modern Scotland* (Oxford, 1999), 76–8; Jane E.A. Dawson, *Scotland Re-formed, 1488–1587* (Edinburgh, 2007), 210.

5 Quotation from Robert Hudson, 'Ane vther epitaph of the said Sir Richard', MF, p. 448, line 6; '[a]pproximately half the poems [in the Quarto] are by Sir Richard, or written in honour of members of the family', Bawcutt, 'Manuscript Miscellanies', 196.

6 There is a significant literature concerned with the historical, cultural and literary constructions of 'youth' in the early modern period. See, for example, Konrad Eisenbichler (ed.), *The Premodern Teenager: Youth in Society 1150–1650* (Toronto, 2002); Ira Clark, *Comedy, Youth, Manhood in Early Modern England* (Newark, 2003); Jennifer Higginbotham, *The Girlhood of Shakespeare's Sisters: Gender, Transgression, Adolescence* (Edinburgh, 2013); Margaret L. King,

realm acts as a microcosm of the broader political and civic one. The poem by Richard Maitland to his son at court is a singular example of this association, and is here explored along with other literary patterns of filiation. Yet an additional, less frequently examined thematic thread is traced by this essay. This might be termed the 'maturation' or formation process of young women; in other words, the emergence of daughters into 'appropriately' fashioned wives and mothers. These lyrics show a rhetorical fascination for the female body, not just in terms of physical beauty but in the moral and social implications of reproductive power. As the bearers and nurturers of children, young women are portrayed as the moral guardians of a future generation. This lyric vein of fascination with the 'governance' of young women provides an imaginative 'meeting point' or coalescence between representations of female youth, children and marriage, and the moral regulation of femininity within the domestic realm.[7] This essay will suggest that 'young' femininity and masculinity evoke different imaginative and cultural associations.

Both manuscripts are also associated with 'daughterliness' in more tangible ways. Maitland's eldest daughter, Helen, is considered the owner of the Folio manuscript ('This buke pertenis to helyne m', claims one inscription).[8] Another daughter – 'Marie' or Mary – has been conjectured as a possible compiler or transcriber of the Quarto.[9] In 1959, Maurice Lee suggested that Marie 'sacrificed herself for many years to the requirements of' her blind father.[10] These suggestions

'Concepts of Childhood: What We Know and Where We Might Go', *Renaissance Quarterly* 60:2 (2007), 341–407. See also Adrienne E. Gavin (ed.), *The Child in British Literature: Literary Constructions of Childhood, Medieval to Contemporary* (Basingstoke, 2012); Phyllis Gaffney, *Constructions of Childhood and Youth in Old French Narrative* (Aldershot, 2011); cf. also Helen Berry and Elizabeth Foyster (eds), *The Family in Early Modern England* (Cambridge, 2011); Sandra Cavallo and Silvia Evangelisti (eds), *A Cultural History of Childhood and Family in the Early Modern Age* (Oxford, 2010). On the Scottish context, see Elizabeth Ewan and Janay Nugent (eds), *Finding the Family in Medieval and Early Modern Scotland* (Aldershot, 2008).

7 Pioneering work in social and women's history in late medieval and early modern Scotland is found in Ewan and Nugent (eds), *Finding the Family*; Elizabeth Ewan and Maureen M. Meikle (eds), *Women in Scotland, c. 1100–c. 1750* (East Linton, 1999). Cf. also Rosalind K. Marshall, *Virgins and Viragos: A History of Women in Scotland from 1080–1980* (London, 1983); Margaret H.B. Sanderson, *Mary Stewart's People: Life in Mary Stewart's Scotland* (Tuscaloosa, AL, 1987); and Margaret H.B. Sanderson, A *Kindly Place? Living in Sixteenth-Century Scotland* (East Linton, 2002). See also David Sellar, 'The Family', in E.J. Cowan and L. Henderson (eds), *A History of Everyday Life in Medieval Scotland 1000–1600* (Edinburgh, 2011), 89–108.

8 Bawcutt, 'Manuscript Miscellanies', 197.

9 Maitland had four surviving daughters: Helen, who married John Cockburn of Clerkington in 1560; Isabella (d. 1621), who married James Heriot of Trabroun (1560); Mary (d. 1596), who married Alexander Lauder in 1586; and Elizabeth, who married William Douglas of Whittinghame. Cf. James Balfour Paul (ed.), *The Scots Peerage*, 9 vols (Edinburgh, 1904), v. On Helen's ownership, see Priscilla Bawcutt, 'Manuscript Miscellanies', 197. In this essay, Mary will be referred to as 'Marie' in accordance with her own inscription in the Quarto manuscript.

10 Maurice Lee, *John Maitland of Thirlestane and the Foundation of Stewart Despotism in Scotland* (Princeton, 1959), 153–4; quoted in Bawcutt, 'Manuscript Miscellanies', 197, and

strengthen the notion that the Maitland manuscripts served as poetic family commonplace books. This raises the question of the degree to which Helen and Marie, in their respective roles as owner and possible compiler and transcriber, might have formally shaped and influenced their contents. In Marie's instance, this might be understood in creative terms. The Quarto may 'more certainly be a woman's book',[11] for it has been suggested that Marie herself may have been a writer, and that the manuscript is itself distinctively 'feminized' in its inclusion and choice of particular material.[12] Whilst this essay does not offer new evidence for this beguiling issue, it revisits the figure of Marie, 'the partner of her father's studies',[13] as an emblematic daughter, and suggests that her association with the Quarto provides an evocative context for its more imaginatively 'resistant' depictions of young wives and daughters.

Sons

Richard Maitland's own advice poem to his son (MF, XIV) is, in the context of early modern Scottish poetry, perhaps the most familiar example of what this essay calls imaginative filiation. In terms of genre, the poem has a long literary and cultural lineage that encompasses medieval 'advice' and exchange-poems between father and son, and also those poems that in broader generic terms portray an older man as adviser to a younger. Both modes depend on a relationship of superior wisdom or understanding compared to innocence, naivety, or folly. In Scottish writing, an earlier but neglected example is the poem entitled *Ratis Raving*, though the broader framework or dialogue of exchange between two male locutors or voices, experienced and innocent, is seen in other works such as the prose treatise *The Spektakle of Luf*.[14] Maitland's paternal advice poem distils

discussed in Sarah M. Dunnigan, 'Scottish Women Writers c. 1560–c. 1650', in Douglas Gifford and Dorothy McMillan (eds), *A History of Scottish Women's Writing* (Edinburgh, 1997), 29–31.

11 Bawcutt, 'Manuscript Miscellanies', 197.

12 Cf. Dunnigan, 'Women Writers c. 1560 – c. 1650', 29–31; Sarah Dunnigan, 'Feminising the Early Modern Erotic: Female-Voiced Love Lyrics and Mary Queen of Scots', in Mapstone (ed.), *Older Scots Literature*, 441–66; Evelyn S. Newlyn, 'A Methodology for Reading Against the Culture: Anonymous, Women Poets, and the Maitland Quarto Manuscript (c. 1586)', in Sarah M. Dunnigan, Evelyn S. Newlyn and C. Marie Harker (eds), *Woman and the Feminine in Medieval and Early Modern Scottish Writing* (Basingstoke, 2004), 89–102. On early modern women and manuscript culture see, for example, Victoria E. Burke, 'Manuscript Miscellanies', in Laura Lunger Knoppers (ed.), *The Cambridge Companion to Early Modern Women's Writing* (Cambridge, 2009), 54–67; Gillian Wright and Jill Seal Millman, *Early Modern Women's Manuscript Poetry* (Manchester, 2005); Victoria E. Burke, Jonathan Gibson and Elizabeth Clarke (eds), *Early Modern Women's Manuscript Writing* (Aldershot, 2004).

13 David Irving, *The History of Scottish Poetry* (Edinburgh, 1861), 407.

14 See Helen Cooney (ed.), *Writings on Love in the English Middle Ages* (Basingstoke, 2007), 189. On *Ratis Raving*, see Chapters 1 and 10 in this collection. On early modern conduct books and instructional literature, see Merridee L. Bailey, 'In Service and at Home: Didactic Texts for Children and Young People, c. 1400–1600', *Parergon* 24:2 (2007), 23–46.

through the medium of the father–son relationship concern and anxieties that are beaded through the Folio manuscript as a whole. The paternal injunction to '[b]e nocht blawine with windis of all airts / Constante in gude of wisdome is ane sing [sign] / Be wyse and tentie [careful] in thy gouerning' (lines 27–9) reflects a standard litany of anti-curial poetry – the court is a place of treachery and deceit that requires the fledgling courtier to be vigilant but honest. An anonymous lyric, for example, complains against court parsimony and injustice by means of a folktale-like moral parable:

> Thre brether war we
> all borne of ane cuntre
> The hardest fortoun fell me
> The grit god be my gyde (MF, LXXVI, lines 5–8).

The misfortune to befall the youngest brother is to end up at the court. Amongst Maitland's own poems in the Folio are those that record the moral laxness of court practices. Success and favours at court are bought by 'ane purse of fine gold fow [full of]'. Indeed:

> All courte men youris as ye wald
> gude gold and syluer with yow tak … [in order to manipulate courtiers, take fine gold and silver with you]
> kyndnes of courte is coft and sald [bought and sold]
> neirnes of kyn na thing thai rak [they do not rate] (MF, CXII, lines 44–5; 48–9).

Maitland's poem constructs a world that functions through a self-aggrandizing economy of exchange and barter – where the motivation is greed and profit as opposed to disinterested obligation – rather than a free exchange of 'kyndnes' or 'fidelitie'.[15]

Maitland's poem exemplifies another recurrent thematic thread of the collection and, as later discussed, of the Quarto too, which concerns the fallibility of youth (though the follies of old age are not exempt either). This can be expressed in two ways. The first is as a kind of moral 'degeneracy'[16] – 'young perverst creaturis / To palyardrie replaidis' [display lechery]. The second, as in the lyric inscribed 'williame stewart to ye king' (MF, p. 355, which is surely influenced by, or indebted to, Lyndsay's play *Ane Satyre*), is to personify a misguided and misdirected political and civic realm: 'young counsale that dois yow all desaiff' [deceive] (MF, cxxviii, line 43). Honesty and integrity is required not only in conduct but in the practice of language itself: 'Be nocht ane scorner nor feinyeit [feigned] flatterer / nor yit a rounder [gossip] of Inuentit talis' (MF, XIV, lines 9–10). This is of accord with the thematic concerns of Maitland's other poetry,

15 The loss of 'kyndness' is a key value in Maitland's poem, 'This warld so fals Is and vnstabill' (MF, CLXXV).

16 As in the lyric ascribed to Alexander Scott, 'Ye blindit luiffaris like' (MF, XCIII, lines 81–2).

where purity and transparency of language signifies an equivalence in moral and ethical intent.[17]

Still, the Folio attribution to 'richart maitland of ledingtoun knycht' (MF, p. 24) casts the poem's generic and conventional subject matter in a personal light – this is William of Lethington's rite of passage into court life, and an opportunity for Maitland to invest general counsel with topical resonance. (Though there are no allusions that are direct, the poem's particular association with William's 'court entry', as it were, sharpens the resonances of implied courtly corruption.) The commemorative and dedicatory poems to Maitland, found in the manuscript's closing section where his death is recorded, draw attention to the illustrious lineage of the family, and the moral exemplariness of Maitland and his heirs. Of course, such praise in the context of a 'family' manuscript is to be expected; but what the poem to his son suggests is that even inherited nobility and moral lineage is subject to the moral pressures exerted by life at court. The virtues of moderation and self-governance are key:

> Preis nocht to be exaltit abone vther' (MF, XIV, line 49)

> Be gentill lawlie and meik in thyn estait
> ffor and thow be vncourtess proude and hie
> Than all the warld sall the detest and hait (MF, XIV, lines 66–8).

The son incarnates the power of name and kinship.[18] This is Maitland's prescription to his son about how to assume a role at court whilst preserving public and private morality. Parental law assumes a place within a larger moral hierarchy – obedience to father entails loyalty to state, prince and God. Ultimately, the poem is less preoccupied with the specific frailties of young masculinity than with the possibilities of how they might be moulded to fit a harmoniously ordered social and political realm.

This is also the case in another father–son advice poem in the Folio: 'My sone gif yow to the court will ga' (MF, xlvii), anonymously attributed and inscribed, 'how the father teichit the sone'. It is, too, presented as an embodiment of parental or paternal 'law' – the 'bidding' to which the son must 'everie day tak tent [take care] thairto / Suppois that thow haue meikle ado' [much bother] (MF, XLVII, lines 3–4). The poem presents its counsel in more formal, discursive terms: 'Myn awin deir sone I the requeir / Thir documentis that thow wald leyr

[17] The notion of rhetorical purity or perspicacity is a key aspect of Scottish Protestant literary culture in this period. Verbal duplicity is also a chief satirical target of the Maitland manuscripts, cf. MQ, 173, 'Sum of the poetis and makeris that ar now', which condemns the practice of printing seditious broadsides and ballads.

[18] Here, the idea of 'kinship' suggests a filial and political nexus of power. 'A courtier had a real function in government: he stood at the head of a network of clients, and it was these clients who staffed the lower levels of the administration and outer circles of the royal court', (Goodare, *State and Society*, 81). 'Kinship could still operate in this new context. During 1587–92, the period of Maitland's ascendancy nine new members were appointed to the court of session: four were his relatives', citing Lee, *Maitland*, 153–4.

[that you would learn these documents] / And keip thame weill bayth less and mair' (MF, XLVII, lines 121–3). It is, in essence, a list of instructions: 'And that I forbid ye to do / bot gude sone do my bidding to ...' (lines 63–4). This serves as a reminder of the inherent persistence and power of the father–son bond. And this, in turn, is firmly anchored in the broader spiritual and moral values that underpin the poem, its strength and value emblematic of the virtues by which the son is urged to live a 'gud lyf' (line 33), 'Intentfullie' (line 15) undertaken in service to God. This father–son relationship is likewise related to what the poem terms 'In mesour ay' [always in moderation] (line 66) – that is, restraint or balance in moral and social conduct ('I forbid the be barganour [quarreller] / In cumpany or grit bostour' [great boaster], lines 69–70). In other words, masculinity is ultimately governable. In contrast to the portrayals of young femininity discussed below, the frailty and vulnerability of masculinity is shown as amenable to discipline or restraint, and capable of maturation into a social and civic ideal. In ways that the Quarto manuscript differently exemplifies, the familial and domestic realm is a mirror to the broader social, civic and political realm; discord within one signifies discord in the other. Maitland's poem implies that the security of the bond between father and son, partly envisaged here as a question of obedience, also determines the moral stature of an individual. Filial loyalty, as a desired virtue in young men, is one aspect of 'godly living'.

Wives and Daughters

The close association of the familial sphere and the larger, all-encompassing socio-political one is imaginatively evidenced in other poems in the Folio and Quarto concerned with young femininity, or female youth. These provide a 'feminized' counterpoint to the 'son at court', or advice to a young man, genre. Though there is no explicit analogue (i.e., advice poetry addressed specifically to a daughter), it might be suggested that a parallel can be located in those lyrics that draw associations between femaleness and youth. This is explicitly manifest in the manuscripts' depictions of, and allusions to, 'yong wyffis'.[19] Though the son at court is vulnerable to the contagion of the court environment, the figure of the young wife is even more troubling because she can 'spread' or communicate such 'contagion'. Almost consistently, these are negative depictions that condemn young wives for moral corruption (the striking exception is found in the Quarto, discussed below), reflecting deeply rooted literary and cultural associations between 'wives' and moral perfidy – as seen in the medieval genre of the *molestiae nuptiarum*, for example.[20] In this respect, the Bannatyne manuscript, compiled in the later 1560s, is an important precedent for the Maitland

[19] In terms of marriage, 'The age of consent was fourteen for men and twelve for women', Sellar, 'The Family', 96. On marriage age, see Chapter 10 in this collection.

[20] Literally, 'the pains of marriage'; this refers to a body of writing that disparages both marriage and women, and is defined by a common rhetorical discourse of dissuasion. Cf. Howard

manuscripts in terms of being a poetic miscellany that reflects concerns of the *querelle des femmes* debate, or 'the woman question', a late medieval European cultural, intellectual and literary controversy that still had fashionable currency in the mid-sixteenth century.[21] In the subsection of the Bannatyne in which the 'contra' feminine side of the debate is depicted, wifely transgressions (including mythological and literary exempla) serve to bolster the 'proof' of woman's immorality. The daughters of Eve in particular include habitually transgressive wives. The poetry of the Maitland manuscripts suggests that the 'pre-existing' moral vulnerability of young women is intensified further when the roles of wife and mother impose new duties and responsibilities.

In a poem ascribed to Maitland himself in both Folio and Quarto – 'Sum wyves of the borroustoun [burgh]'[22] – clothing serves as a signifier of acquisitive materialism. This use of female clothing as a visual emblem of corruption is echoed elsewhere. The anonymous poem, 'To my lordis of renoun', in both Folio and Quarto, contains a kind of sartorial blazon whereby the ways in which the fashionable arrangements of young female clothing draw attention to 'skin ... weist ... bellie ... buttokis' (MQ, LXX, lines 121, 123, 124, 125). Though Maitland's lyric opens with a general allusion to 'wyfis' who '[o]n vaneteis ... waistis geir' [waste possessions ... on vanities] (MF, XCIV, line 55),[23] it proceeds to narrow this 'designation' in terms of both class (these are specifically 'burges wyfis', line 53) and youth. The association between sumptuary excess and degrees of female moral and sexual corruption echoes an earlier poetic vein in late medieval Scottish poetry and its 'motif of a socio-econonomically self-promoting feminine sexuality'.[24] Typically, Maitland's lyric offers counsel:

> thairfore young wyfis specialie
> off all sic faltis hald you fre [of all such faults keep yourself free]
> and moderatlie to leif now leir [be taught how to live moderately]
> in meit and clayth accordinglie
> and not sa vanlie waist your geir (MF, XCIV, lines 66–70).[25]

R. Bloch, *Medieval Misogyny and the Invention of Western Romantic Love* (Chicago, 1992); Alcuin Blamires, *The Case for Women in Medieval Culture* (Oxford, 1998).

21 NLS, Adv.MS.1.1.6; cf. W. Tod Ritchie (ed.), *The Bannatyne Manuscript*, 4 vols (Edinburgh, 1928–32). See, for example, Gisela Bock and Margarete Zimmermann, 'The European *Querelle des femmes*', *Disputatio: An International Transdisciplinary Journal of the Late Middle Ages* 5 (2002), 127–56. It has been suggested that the *querelle* poetry of the Bannatyne manuscript may have had particular political resonance in its association with the reign of Mary Stewart: cf. David Parkinson, '"A Lamentable Storie": Mary Queen of Scots and the Inescapable *Querelle des Femmes*', in L.A.J.R. Houwen, A.A. MacDonald and Sally Mapstone (eds), *A Palace in the Wild: Essays on Vernacular Culture and Humanism in Late-Medieval and Renaissance Scotland* (Leuven, 2001), 141–60; Sarah Dunnigan, *Eros and Poetry at the Courts of Mary Queen of Scots and James VI* (Basingstoke, 2002), Ch 1.

22 In the Folio, the poem is extracted from lines 51–110.

23 MQ, II, lines 53–5.

24 C. Marie Harker, '*Chrystis Kirk on the Grene* and *Peblis to the Ploy:* The Economy of Gender', in Dunnigan, Harker and Newlyn (eds), *Woman and the Feminine*, 41.

25 MQ, II, lines 66–70.

The next two stanzas suggest that such virtuous moderation will come from eschewing 'dangeir' (a term that has echoes of its meaning as sexual temptation in courtly love poetry) and keeping 'honest cwmpanie'. Young women, Maitland's poem suggests, might be particularly vulnerable to the sin of 'leychorie' (MF, xciv, line 79); by implication this means prostitution since this 'leychorie' enables the acquisition of 'geir' (line 80). This is part of a 'false economy' in the selling and buying, or the trade and circulation, not only of young female bodies but social status and nobility. Maitland's poem evinces distaste for aspirant social mobility: the wives of burgesses dressed in their finery of 'velwet hude' and 'camreche courcheis' [cambric kerchief, i.e., a delicate cloth covering worn on the head] (lines 92, 93) have only the semblance of the innate 'honour' (line 97) possessed by 'lordis wyfis' (line 99).

Against such duplicity, Maitland's poem professes to speak 'plane' (line 106). The corruptive instability of young female desires is opposed to the purity and permanence of a reformist rhetoric. Moreover, the broader moral framework that encompasses this satirical exposure and denunciation of female materialism and fetishizing self-adornment points to the need for containment – for the re-establishment of social order. Maitland's poem implies that such order might have its beginning within the family. The appeal to a 'properly' regulated domestic realm is implicit in the narrator's exhortation:

> Leif burgess men or all be loist
> On your wyffis to mak sic cost [such expense]
> Quhilk may gar all your bairnis bleir [which may make all your children cry]
> Scho that may not wante wyne and roist [meat]
> Is abill for to waist sum geir … (MQ, lines 86–90).

Wives should be governed, this stanza implies, because their greed leads to the neglect of children. As in so many of Maitland's poems that address questions of contemporary morality and social practice, this greed is portrayed as a vice of the present generation of young women, for 'thair motheris' (line 63) would never have been so profligate or neglectful.

Interestingly, this concern for the welfare of children is echoed in another lyric by Maitland in the Quarto, which directly picks up the refrain of the previous poem ('bairnis bleir'). 'O hie Eternall god of micht' (MQ, IV) is an occasional 'new yeir' poem that uses the turn of the year as an opportune moment for moral reform. Maitland's poem has 'all staitis and degrie' (line 91) in its sight, but women will only be able to wear the symbolic garments of 'Wisdome meiknes and grauitie' (line 52) once they renounce material desire. Without women doing so, the narrator emphasizes, children will be made vulnerable – the inheritors of a material and spiritual burden of guilt and impoverished by maternal greed:

> Bot for to weir habulyement [habiliment, clothing]
> according to their stait and rent [status and landed property]
> and all thingis forbeir
> that may thair bairnis gar repent [make their children repent]
> now into this new year (lines 56–60)

For sum of thame wald be weill fed
and lyik the Quenis ladyis cled
Thocht all their bairnis sould bleir (lines 76–8)

The sphere of the domestic and familial is female, of course, but this foregrounding of the maternal–child relationship has a particular satirical point (fathers are never indicted). In the manuscripts' social and moral world, the figure of the 'bad mother' has the potential both to endanger and corrupt children. Generational welfare depends on responsible and 'regulated' mothers. The vulnerabilities of young women impinge on the children whom they nurture. This in turn binds issues of female reproduction to those of broader social and moral import; the need for the 'governance' of young women, as opposed to young men, has a different moral charge.

It might be suggested, however, that the particular context of the Quarto manuscript – its inclusion and arrangement of particular poems, its 'authorial' associations – casts this relationship between mothers and children in an interesting light, one that in part resists the negative associations more persistently drawn between feminine and moral realms in the Folio. The 'contra' feminine side of the *querelle* is by no means wholly excluded from the Quarto (in the anonymous and vitriolic 'To ane Vnthankfull freind' (MQ, LXXXIII), for example, in which a male narrator recriminates himself for attempting to 'satefie ane whore', line 41). Yet on the whole the prevalent attitude to women (especially young women) is more morally forgiving, or tolerant, as evidenced by the inclusion of poetry that focusses on the 'redemptive' qualities of woman. Such poetry praises and exonerates, rather than castigating women as the inheritors and perpetuators of sin, and allows the poetic articulation of female voices and specifically 'feminine' kinds of conflict. It is this aspect that suggests Marie Maitland was a possible shaping, and not just simply an inscribed, presence, ensuring that in comparison with the Folio, the sympathies of the Quarto rest with the 'pro-feminine' side of the *querelle des femmes* debate. Alexander Arbuthnot's *Ane contrapoysoun to the Ballat falslie intitulit the properties of gud Wemen* (MQ, XXXV) supports this idea. The poem systematically takes issue with and refutes some common assumptions in the rhetorical, philosophical and theological terms of the debate, as, for example, in this extract:

Quhen god maid all of nocht
he did yis weill declair
the last thing that he wrocht
it wes ane woman fair
In workes we sie ye last to be
Maist plesand & preclair [most pleasant and bright]
ane help to man god maid hir than
quhat will ze I say mair [whatever you will, I say more] (lines 81–8).

Arbuthnot's narrator locates him (or her?)self in a medieval pro-feminine tradition that not only draws on theological points for its reclamation but suggests imaginative literature as another source or 'proof':

Repeit the poetis auld
& reid thame gif thow can
thair thou sall find les thou be blind
the Vertewis of wemen (lines 99–102).

Arbuthnot's poem is a substantial and important text of the Quarto, and its engagement with the *querelle* tradition is more complex than can justly be summarized here. But I would suggest that the note of pro-feminine sympathy which it strikes is significant in terms of the manuscript's overall attitude to the representation of women and the feminine. This, in turn, provides a suggestive framework for considering poems that explore those themes of erotic desire and marriage that are particularly germane to the young women figured within the poetry (and arguably to a conjectural readership of young women surrounding the manuscript). The female beloved is frequently a moral 'luiking glas' (line 20) for all 'ladyis fair' (line 18):

remorss and tempaurance dois hir accompanie
and from hir staitlie presence dois all filthie vycis flie
no virtew sho dois want sho is both trew and kynd
(lines 23–5, 'In prais of ane Gentle woman').

This beloved is almost exonerated from being an object of desire in the first instance. This is symptomatic of the Quarto as a whole. Its love poetry to and about women[26] frequently differentiates between beauty and 'bontie'; between physical grace and a moral or emotional grace of superior value:

Gif Bewtie had me bound in thrall
and wer overcum with lustis sensuall
Then micht I thocht my wisdome faillit me
Bot sen her bontie supernaturall
To Bewtie couplit is collaterall
In heichest staige of excellent degrie … (MQ, XXXIX, lines 19–24).

Interestingly, this poem as a whole might be considered a more nuanced articulation of conventional courtly erotic desire, for in its final two stanzas it permits the rhetorical possibility for the beloved woman (who has been apostrophized throughout) to 'answer back'. Indeed, to a much greater degree than the Folio,[27] the Quarto contains female-voiced poems. These are typically spoken in the voice of a complaining female narrator – thus exemplifying a pervasive literary and mythic paradigm of the female voice – as the source of lamentation or grief, attested by the abandoned women of Ovidian lament who are reimagined and reinterpreted in medieval and early modern elegiac lyricism.[28] In the anony-

[26] The Quarto contains a substantial number of love lyrics in conventional courtly love lyric and Petrarchistic style. Several are presented as 'gifts' of love, and perhaps were intended for a Maitland daughter.

[27] For example, 'Still vndir the levis grene' (*The murning Maiden*), MF, CXXX.

[28] On conventions of elegy see, for example, Jennifer C. Vaught and Lynne Dickson Bruckner (eds), *Grief and Gender: 700–1700* (New York, 2003); Karen Weisman (ed.), *The*

mous Quarto lyric, 'With siching sad and surging sorrow soir' (MQ, LXV), the female plainant, described as if by an inverse blazon,[29] mourns the loss of 'ane freind with murning vaill [mourning veil] / amang the muses nurischit with their flouris' (lines 95–6). She declares herself an exemplary 'mirrour of mishap' (line 84) whose articulation of human frailty and philosophical quietude compels the 'frame' narrator to 'turne my face away / from hering of the wofull werye schout' [hearing the sad, despairing cry] (lines 154–5).

Yet the female elegiac mode offers more than plangency of expression and affective power; there is room for some sharp moral and social insights into the questions of female autonomy and agency that frequently lie at their heart. This is strikingly the case with the Quarto's poem entitled 'Ane Elagie translatit out of frenche in English meter', ascribed to 'G.H.' (MQ, LXVI). It is prefaced by the lyric 'With siching sad' (MQ, LXV), whose speaker also presents herself as an exemplary female plainant. Given the Folio and Quarto manuscripts' preoccupation with the vulnerability, however varyingly conceived, of 'yong wyffis' and children, this poem is imagined from the double perspective of both 'subject-positions'. It is a substantial monologue in which the persona is a young wife, unhappily married. She therefore belongs to the poetic tradition of the *mal mariée*. The poem also has a more explicit and particular debt in that it is based on an elegy by Clement Marot, though (as frequently with Scottish Renaissance translation practice) this is not just straightforward imitation but involves a degree of verbal and imaginative transposition.[30] The lyric portrays a failed marriage in manifold ways. A series of moral and spiritual ideals ('the husband to the deathe man [must] euer abyide / Gud or bad or quhat sort euer he be', lines 28–9) are shown to have been violated by the conduct of a husband who betrays the values and precepts of companionate marriage. This nuptial bond may be recognized spiritually and legally by Church and state, but the elegist implies that it lacks all other legitimacy. In the poem's close, she seeks an alternative form of self-realization and self-vindication in relation to God: 'thow creat me & formit hes of nocht [created out of nothing] / thow hes me als to that perfectioun brocht / quhairin I am' (lines 132–4).

As I have argued elsewhere, the lyric departs from the Marotic source in providing this new epilogue of spiritual transformation in which she renounces her

Oxford Handbook of the Elegy (Oxford, 2010). On female elegy, see Colette H. Winn, 'Early Modern Women and the Poetics of Lamentation: Mourning, Revenge, and Art', *Mediaevalia: An Interdisciplinary Journal of Medieval Studies Worldwide* 22 (1999), 127–55; Lisa Perfetti (ed.), *The Representation of Women's Emotions in Medieval and Early Modern Culture* (Gainesville, FL, 2005).

29 'Hir bodye small wes widderit and berent / as is the staik quhilk someris drouth opprest / hir visage pale declarit hir to be schent / In sichis and sobbis reposit wes her rest / hir febill handis togidder oft scho prest' (MQ, p. 202, lines 49–53).

30 This is the twentieth elegy in Marot's *La Suite de l'adolescence Clementine* (1533); cf. C.A. Mayer (ed.), *Oeuvres Lyriques* (London, 1964), 260–3. In the original edition, the poem was entitled 'L'infortunée en mariage'.

former status as an earthly bride in favour of superior marriage to Christ.[31] But this is not the poem's only reinvention of the end of Marot's elegy. The Maitland version also enables the plainant to renegotiate another spiritual identity – this time as a daughter of God – in the wake of voicing dissent against the parents who implicitly condemned her to pain. Where the French lyric leaves the speaker communicating her grief to her mother at the unhappy marriage, the Scots elegist issues a rebuke to the parents who failed her when their power and comfort was most needed.

> Quhair sall I then our out my bitter plaint [put forth my complaint]
> quhomto sall I my cruell paine lament
> to pleinyie to my parentis is bot Vaine
> that quhilk is done can not be brocht againe
> Quhen that ye mater wes not past remeid
> O god give then thay had taine better heid [taken better heed]
> Alace quhair then wes their experience
> I prayis their mynd bot curs thair negligence
> quhy wald thay not at leist seik my consent
> to freindis counsall quhy tuik thay nocht gud tent
> Sua their reme[m]berance dois augment my wo
> To mak my plaint then quhomto sould I go (lines 117–27).

Though Protestant marriage regulation as a whole stressed the importance of parental consent more than its Catholic counterpart, in early modern Scottish law parental consent 'was not required and parental disapproval was, strictly speaking, irrelevant'.[32] The elegy emphasizes the lack of consent on her part, and therefore suggests that the marriage contravenes the 'one absolutely necessary requirement for a valid marriage' in marriage canon law.[33] And at least within the poem's emotional and moral compass, parental governance is questioned; the child indicts the parents for a negligent lack of judgement and wisdom, for ignoring her own will and 'friendis counsall'. Submission to God in the poem's new epilogue, and the attendant renunciation of parental authority, is a vindicated act of daughterly disobedience. The poem becomes a kind of conduct book 'in reverse', shunning Juan Luis Vives's instruction to the Christian maiden that she 'regarde greatly their [her parents'] commaundements and

31 Dunnigan, 'Feminising the Early Modern Erotic', 444–5.

32 Merry E. Wiesner, *Women and Gender in Early Modern Europe* (Cambridge, 1993), 57–9; Sellar, 'The Family', 97. For more on parental involvement in their children's marriages, see Chapter 10 in this collection.

33 'This was expressed in the maxim *consensus non concubitus facit matrimonium* [consent and not intercourse makes a marriage]', pertaining to both pre- and post-Reformation (Sellar, 'The Family', 96). On the theological and legal stipulations of late medieval and early modern marriage in Scotland, see Sellar, 'The Family', 97ff; and A.D.M. Forte, 'Some Aspects of the Law of Marriage in Scotland: 1500–1700', in Elizabeth M. Craik (ed.), *Marriage and Property* (Aberdeen, 1984), 104–18. Interestingly, there are other intimations of, or allusions to, questions of consent to marriage in the Quarto. For example, in 'Ane Ballat to be singe' (MQ, XL), the lover warns 'o ladye schein / cast not your perle to suyne' (lines 110–11); this double-edged advocacy that she make a wise choice might well refer to the choice of a marriage partner.

mekely obey theim', considering them 'a verie image of almightie god, ye father of all thynges'.[34] Within the context of the Maitland manuscripts, then, this significant poem might be seen as a counterpoint to those poems previously discussed that condemn the figure of the deviant young woman, and that portray the relationship between parents (especially mothers) and children as a moral cornerstone of society. In depicting the failure, or at least the limitations of that religious and educational ideal, the Maitland elegy represents an interesting point of imaginative resistance and daughterly non-conformity.

Conclusion

This essay has suggested some of the ways in which young women and men, and children and parents, are represented in the Maitland manuscripts. The illustrative poems locate female and male youth at particular junctures of social, sexual and emotional formation (entrance into political court life; marriage and child-rearing). These become points of imaginative exploration that, in turn, evoke anxieties and concerns consonant with the underlying social, moral and spiritual fabric of both Folio and Quarto. Familial and domestic relationships are delicately layered and interconnected within their poetic world: a daughter's suffering is imputed to neglectful parents; the profligacy of young mothers is detrimental to the welfare of their children. Though a contrast in sympathy and perspective has been suggested in the portrayal of young married women, all these poems – and the manuscripts taken together as a whole – articulate a sense of moral and social crisis.

Yet both Folio and Quarto can be considered 'reformatory' or 'reformist', not only in doctrinal sympathy, but in articulating a series of possibilities or ways by which the social and moral realms might be reconfigured. Maitland's recurrent concern with the vulnerability of children is tersely summed up in a clear moral imperative: 'help ay the fatherles' (MQ, LIV, line 6). If erotic love morally and spiritually imperils vulnerable daughters and wives, then the Quarto opens up an alternative discourse or affective world of 'amitie' or friendship between women, which encompasses erotic love.[35] And though both manuscripts expose some moral inadequacies or failings in the nexus of familial relationships, they also point to the necessity of these relationships – not simply as a means of 'governance', but of shoring up instinctive bonds. As this miniature fable delicately sums

[34] *A Very Frutefull and Pleasant Booke called the Instruction of a christen woman, made firste in latyne, by the right famous clerke maystr Lewis Vives, and tourned out of latyne into Englishe by Rycharde Hyrde* (London, 1557), Book I, cap. xv, sig. P–Pv.

[35] See Dunnigan, 'Scottish Women Writers' and 'Feminising the Early Modern Erotic'; Newlyn, 'A Methodology'; Bawcutt, 'Manuscript Miscellanies', 198; and Sajed Chowdhury, '"Thair is Mair Constancie in O[u]r Sex / Then Euer Ama[n]g Men Hes Bein": The Metaphysics of Authorship in the Maitland Quarto Manuscript (ca. 1596)', *Textual Cultures: Texts, Contexts, Interpretation* 7:1 (2012), 50–76. See also Jane Farnsworth, 'Voicing Female Desire in "Poem XLIX"', *Studies in English Literature 1500–1900* 36:1 (1996), 57–72.

up: 'The lyon for hir tender whelpis dois roir / and quhy? Because in thame scho set hir stoir' (MQ, lxxix, lines 1–2).

Collectively, these representations of youth, women and children provide imaginative points of connection between these two diverse manuscript collections. There is perhaps one other imaginative bridge, however – one that binds a historical daughter to her father. Even though there is no incontrovertible proof of Marie's authorship, the strikingly pro-feminine nature of certain Quarto lyrics persuasively suggests a compiler's careful and motivated poetic selection – as if in symbolic reply to the Folio's more censorious depictions of, and culturally anxious attitudes to, young women. Because Marie's creative and intellectual identity haunts the allusions to Sappho and Olympia Morata (in a lyric addressed to 'Maistres Marie'),[36] so a poem such as 'Ane Elagie' might be considered the echo or imprint of a daughter's writerly dissent. And even 1586, the date of inscription that appears beside Marie's name in the Quarto manuscript, seems to bear its own imaginative, ironic echoes – the year of her father's death, and of her own marriage.

[36] *To your self* ('If sapho saige for saphic songe so sueit), MQ, LXXXV, line 9. On this dedicatory lyric and its allusions to a feminine literary and mythic lineage, see Dunnigan, 'Scottish Women Writers', 29–30; cf. Harriette Andreadis, *Sappho in Early Modern England: Female Same-Sex Literary Erotics 1550–1714* (Chicago, 2001). Olympia Morata (1526–55) was an Italian humanist and protestant convert, and an interesting intellectual and cultural model for identification with Marie.

Envoi

In Their Own Words: A Mother to Her Son

12

Elizabeth Melville, Lady Culross: Two Letters to Her Son James

Jamie Reid Baxter

Introduction

While eight of the poet Elizabeth Melville's nine letters to her young clerical protégé John Livingstone have been in print since 1845, the present note contains the first edition of her two holograph letters to her son James Colville.[1] These letters are almost our only direct source of information about Melville's relations with any of her offspring. We have no proof of the exact date of Melville's own birth c.1578, or that of her marriage to John Colville c.1596. Neither do we know the birth dates of any of her children. We do, however, know that her eldest son was Dr Alexander Colville (c.1595–1666), who graduated M.A. from Edinburgh on 22 July 1615.[2] We also know that the youngest son was Samuel (M.A. St Andrews, July 1634).[3] Melville's other sons were James (fl. 1625–41), Robert and John (both fl. 1629), and they had at least two sisters: one unnamed, who died before August 1625 but is mentioned in both letters to James, and Christian (fl. 1634–46).

Elizabeth Melville spent her own childhood at the long-vanished Halhill Tower, near Colessie in north Fife, with her sister Margaret and her brothers James and Robert. Their mother was Christian Boswell (d. 1609) of the family of Balmuto, an estate near Burntisland, and their father, Sir James Melville of Halhill (1535–617), was a busy courtier and diplomat. His famous *Memoirs*,

[1] They are found, with nine letters to John Livingstone and one of 20 September 1630 to the countess of Wigtoun, in Edinburgh University Library, MS Laing III.347. The eight holograph letters to Livingstone were printed in W.K. Tweedie (ed.), *Select Biographies*, 2 vols (Edinburgh, 1845–47), i, 351–69. The ninth letter to Livingstone, dated June 1629, was published in Rev. Mr James Kirkton, *The Secret and True History of the Church of Scotland*, ed. C.K. Sharpe (Edinburgh, 1817), 51.

[2] David Laing (ed.), *Catalogue of the Graduates of the Faculties of Arts, Divinity and Law, of the University of Edinburgh Since its Foundation* (Edinburgh, 1857), 29, where an ancient annotation records 'S.S.theologiae doctor' against Alexander's name.

[3] R.N. Smart, *Alphabetical Register of the Students, Graduates and Officials of the University of St Andrews, 1579–1747* (St Andrews, 2012). Smart's identification of Elizabeth's son Alexander with the Alexander Colville who matriculated in December 1613 and graduated in July 1617 is wrong; this is surely the future Dr Alexander Colville of Galgorm, Ballymena, a scion of the Colvilles of Cleish. See J. Reid Baxter, 'The "Real" Dr Alexander Colville of Galgorm', *Familia 2014 (No 30), Journal of the Ulster Historical Foundation*, 57–76.

written in old age, are exclusively concerned with public matters, 'to serve for an exempler of lyf and better behavour ... concerning the service of princes and medling in ther affaires'. However, his genuine care for his children's upbringing is clear from the opening words of the *Memoirs*' prefatory letter to his son:

> sen thou hes schauen thy self sa willing to satisfie my expectation of thee, in following and obseruing many of my formar preceptis during thy yong yeares, I grant now vnto thee thy requestis the mair glaidly, quhilk is to put in wret for thy better memorie sindrie thingis that thou had hard me rehers betymes, baith concernyng maneris, with some meit preceptis for thy barnely age; and also how to temper the rage of furious youth be the reull of godlynes and raisoun; quhilk twa tretises haue serued also vnto the rest of thy brether and sisters. [4]

The implication is that Sir James had earlier written 'twa tretises', now lost, full of 'preceptis' appropriate to childhood and adolescence respectively, for the use of all his children male and female. His daughter's letters to her son suggest that, in her own way, she followed her father's example in giving her children written advice. Sir James's reference to 'the reull of godlynes' is not merely conventional: arriving in France ten years before the Scottish Reformation, he spent his youth at the court of Henri II without being in the least tempted to renounce the Protestant convictions he had inherited from his father. So strong was Sir James's faith that in later life, he 'professed he had got assurance from the Lord that himself, wife and all his children should meet in heaven'.[5]

His elder son James, who succeeded to Halhill in 1617, participated in illegal, non-kneeling Presbyterian communion services in 1620, after James VI's bishops had imposed geniculation by virtue of the Articles of Perth in 1618.[6] The younger son, Robert, trained for the ministry, but his fervent Presbyterianism meant no bishop would allow him to have a parish of his own, until episcopacy was overthrown in 1637–38. For years before that turning-point, he had assisted his sister's brother-in-law, Mr Robert Colville (d. 1631), minister of Culross, himself stoutly committed to the Presbyterian cause.[7] In the first decade of the seventeenth century, Elizabeth, the most significant religious poet of Renaissance Scotland, addressed sonnets of spiritual encouragement to the persecuted and imprisoned Presbyterian spokesmen John Welsh and Andrew Melville.[8] Her

[4] James Melville of Halhill, *Memoirs of His Own Life* (Edinburgh, 1827), 1. 'Brether' suggests that James and Robert were not Sir James's only male offspring, but there is absolutely no trace in the records of any other sons.

[5] Tweedie, *Select Biographies*, i, 346.

[6] David Calderwood, *Historie of the Kirk of Scotland*, 8 vols (Edinburgh, 1842–9), vii, 416. In 1638 or 1639, this James Melville's daughter Elizabeth, Lady Culross's niece and namesake, became the second wife of the Presbyterian Sir John Scot of Scotstarvet, who signed the Covenant in 1638: Sir William Fraser, *The Melvilles, Earls of Melville, and the Leslies, Earls of Leven*, 3 vols (Edinburgh, 1890), i, 147. See the anonymous *Epithalamium* in NLS, Adv. Ms.17.1.9, fols 92–4.

[7] See e.g. Calderwood, *Historie*, vi, 376, 454, 457; vii, 256.

[8] J. Reid Baxter, *Elizabeth Melville, Lady Culross: Poems from Manuscript, with* Ane Godlie Dreame (Edinburgh, 2010), 10, 11, 68. See also J. Reid Baxter, 'Elizabeth Melville, Calvinism

involvement in the 'Presbyterian resistance' to the ecclesiastical policies of James VI and Charles I was extensive, and she fully deserves her place in James Anderson's *The Ladies of the Covenant*.[9]

Given the consistent stance of Sir James Melville's children and grandchildren with regard to Church polity, it seems likely that he had Presbyterian sympathies himself. However, his *Memoirs* stop in 1597, and say so little about the Kirk that even John Knox is never mentioned, let alone Andrew Melville or the other Presbyterians who fled the earl of Arran's persecution in 1584.[10] This exclusion of ecclesiastical affairs must be deliberate, for Sir James had the closest of personal links with the birthpangs of Scotland's Reformed Kirk. First, there was the Catholic government's execution in December 1548 of his Protestant father, Sir John Melville of Raith, ostensibly for treasonable communication with the English Protestant invaders. Second, there was Sir James's own adoption by a friend and protégé of Sir John of Raith, namely the childless lawyer Henrie Balnaves of Halhill (c.1512–70). In 1546, Balnaves had joined the murderers of Cardinal Beaton, who were holding St Andrews Castle. As a result he became a firm friend of John Knox, who during his imprisonment in France revised (and wrote a preface to) Balnaves's *Treatise on Justification*, itself composed in a French prison. Later, the lawyer would be the recipient of the young Sir James's kindness at the French court. In March 1567, he adopted Melville as his heir. Hence the title 'Melville of Halhill'.

Elizabeth Melville's parentage and ancestry did not merely endow her *a priori* with a rich protestant spiritual background and heritage. The Melvilles were no mean family in terms of status and connections. Her father and two of her uncles were impressively close not only to Queen Mary, whom they supported during the Civil War of 1569–72, but also to her son King James. Sir Robert Melville of Murdocairnie, Queen Mary's choice as Keeper of Linlithgow Palace, would become James VI's long-serving Treasurer Depute in 1582 and die as 1st Lord Melville of Monimail. His son Sir Robert of Burntisland, 2nd Lord Melville, was a Privy Councillor from 1600. Elizabeth's uncle Sir Andrew Melville of Garvock was Master of the Household to Queen Mary and then to James VI. Another uncle, William, commendator of Tungland, was a Lord of Session from 1587 to 1614. On Elizabeth Melville's mother's side, her uncle George Boswell was surgeon to the king, and her first cousin John Boswell, laird of Balmuto, enjoyed good personal relations with James VI. He was knighted with his son and heir at the baptism of Prince Henry Frederick in 1594, alongside several others including Elizabeth Melville's brother-in-law, Andrew Balfour of Montquhanie.[11]

and the Lyric Voice', in D.J. Parkinson (ed.), *James VI and I, Scotland and Literature: Tides of Change 1567–1625* (Leuven, 2013), 151–72.

[9] James Anderson, *The Ladies of the Covenant* (Glasgow, 1862), 32–48. See also Alexander Whyte, *Samuel Rutherford and Some of his Correspondents* (Edinburgh, 1894), 43–9.

[10] See Gordon Donaldson, 'Scottish Presbyterian Exiles in England 1584–85', in Gordon Donaldson, *Scottish Church History* (Edinburgh, 1985), 178–90.

[11] Contract of marriage with Margaret Melville dated 27 December 1589, NRS, RD1/34, fols 240 ff; not mentioned in Fraser, *The Melvilles*. For those knighted in 1594, see Calderwood, *Historie*, v, 344.

Despite her distinguished family background and the amount of information that we possess about several of her relatives both by blood and by marriage, we have surprisingly little concrete information about Elizabeth herself. Her writings show that she had received a thorough education. Her father's formative years at the French court had exposed him to a culture in which highly educated women, most notably the prolific Marguérite de Valois, queen of Navarre, not only wrote poetry but put it into print. Sir James himself liked poetry. Not only is a specially composed homiletic poem on the folly of kirk-burial the principal feature of the graveyard mausoleum he built for his wife in 1609, but he also quotes poets in his *Memoirs*, including Du Bellay.[12] His daughter began composing sacred verse at a young age. Alexander Hume announced as much to the world in 1599 when he published his *Hymnes and Sacred Songs*, in which the prefatory epistle dedicating the book to her also praises the quality of her poetry. Four years later, in 1603, Elizabeth took the unprecedented step of going into print – the first Scotswoman to do so – with her celebrated short epic *Ane Godlie Dreame*.[13]

Her marriage contract, unlike that of her sister Margaret, is not extant, but the presence of the signature of her husband, John Colville laird of West Comrie, on a document of February 1597 indicates that she was then already his spouse.[14] John Colville was the son and heir of Alexander (d. 1597), commendator of Culross, judge and Privy Councillor.[15] The little we know of John Colville indicates that he was a less impressive figure than his brothers Alexander of Blair, justice-depute (d. 1664),[16] or Robert, minister of Culross (d. 1631).[17] On the latter's death in March 1631, Elizabeth would write to John Livingstone that God

> hes tane away our deir pastour, who hes preached the Word of God among us almost fourty yeirs, plainly and powerfully a soir strok to this congregatioun, and

[12] *Poems of Elizabeth Melville*, 69; Melville, *Memoirs*, 268 (Scots, anon), 387 (Du Bellay), 389 (Pacuvius, tr. Guéroult).

[13] *Poems*, 71–91.

[14] NRS, RD1/59, fol. 96v: 5 February 1597, tack (*lease*) by Sir Andrew Balfour of Montquhanie 'with expres assent & consent of Margaret Melville my spous'. Signatories include Margaret and Sir James Melville of Halhill; the witnesses include James Melville and 'Johne Colville of Comrie', whose sole connection with Balfour and Margaret Melville was via Elizabeth.

[15] Alexander's older half-brother, Sir James Colville of East Wemyss, first Lord Colville of Culross, was a trusted ambassador with very strong links to Henri de Navarre and his son Louis XIII over many years. See Sir James Balfour Paul (ed.), *The Scots Peerage*, 9 vols (Edinburgh, 1904–14), ii, 553–6.

[16] Laing (ed.), *Catalogue of the Graduates ... University of Edinburgh*, 14, with marginal note *questor rerum capitalium*. For Alexander Colville's intense commitment to Presbyterianism, see A.A. Bonar (ed.), *Letters of Samuel Rutherford* (London, 1891), note preceding Letter XCVIII (p. 204).

[17] D. Beveridge, *Culross and Tulliallan*, 2 vols (Edinburgh, 1885), i, 145–7, 168, 171. Beveridge's 'facts' are not always accurate and should be checked against more recent scholarship, as should Anderson's *Ladies of the Covenant* and Bonar's *Letters of Samuel Rutherford* – the latter both claim, for example, that Elizabeth Melville's husband was called 'James Colville'.

> cheifly to me, to quhom he wes not only a pastour and a brother, bot, under God, a husband and a father to my children. Nixt his awin familie, I have the greattest los.

Elizabeth's words are a startlingly strong implied criticism of the inadequacy of John Colville both as a husband and as 'a father to my children'. He would seem to have fallen far short of her ideal, itself perhaps based on her own father's care for his children. Writing to John Livingstone nine months later, Lady Culross, speaking of her family, said:

> He quhom ye knaw is lyk to ovirturne all, and hes brokin all bands, Lord pitty him. Thair wes som begining of order, bot all is wrong again, for the death of his brother maks him to tak liberty, so I have doubill los.[18]

This may be a reference to her husband, but since in October 1632 John Colville is recorded as a Kirk elder, perhaps Elizabeth was speaking about two of her sons, and the troublemaker was the undergraduate Samuel.[19] Lady Culross herself was not proud of her record as a wife and mother. When she asked Euphan McCullen, 'a poor woman ... but rich in faith ... to pray for her in regard of the outward condition of her family', Euphan said that the Lord's answer had been 'he that provides not for his own house hath denyed the faith'; to which Lady Culross replied: 'Now you have killed me; for I goe to preachings and communions here and there, neglecting the care of my family.'[20] This self-condemnation is hardly borne out by her extant letters.

The Letters to James

James Colville was named for his maternal grandfather, and was probably therefore the second son. A very approximate date of birth would be c.1600. He first appears in a letter written on 9 April 1619 by his mother's first cousin Sir Robert Melville of Burntisland to the courtier Sir Robert Ker of Ancram, a first cousin of James's father John Colville, and a leading member of Prince Henry Frederick's household.[21] Burntisland wrote: 'I dout not bot Mr Alexander and James Coluille has acquaint yow' with the details of a request. His final comment that Lady Burntisland 'had not Mr Alexander Coluille to be her scrib'[22] strongly implies that by 'Mr Alexander' he means Elizabeth's son. Ker would later be James Colville's patron at court in London, as we shall see, but there is no further reference to any Colville in Ancram's surviving correspondence. If James was at court in 1618–19 with Alexander, then he is unlikely to be the James

18 Tweedie, *Select Biographies*, i, 358, 363.

19 Beveridge, *Culross*, i, 178–9.

20 Tweedie, *Select Biographies*, i, 339.

21 Ker's and John Colville's mothers were sisters, viz. Margaret and Nicolas Dundas of the family of Fingask. Ker would be made 1st earl of Ancram in 1633.

22 David Laing (ed.), *Correspondence of Sir Robert Kerr, First Earl of Ancram, and his son, William, Third Earl of Lothian*, 2 vols (Edinburgh, 1875), i, 6–7.

Colville who matriculated at St Leonard's College, St Andrews, in 1621, since matriculands were generally no older than fifteen.[23] Be that as it may, neither of Elizabeth's letters to her son addresses him as 'Mr' James. The edited texts of both are given below, followed by a discussion of what they, taken in conjunction with some other sources, can tell us about Elizabeth's relations with her children. Punctuation is largely (and paragraphing entirely) editorial; *u*, *v* and *w* have been standardized to modern usage; contractions such as *yt*, *qt*, *wt* have been silently expanded to *that*, *quhat*, *with*.

The first letter is dated 27 August 1625, and the mention of the lairds of Carlton and Earlston indicates that James was in the south-west of Scotland, a hotbed of resistance to episcopacy and the royal ordinances for the Kirk known as the Five Articles of Perth (1618).[24]

> God resists the proud and gives grace to
> the humbill etc.[25]
> Watche and praye[26]
>
> James ye wreit not to me and I knaw not quhat to wreit to you. God hes usit many meins to warne and wakin, to counsell and derect. If that do not the turn, quhat can I say or do to you? Reid this letter. I think ye knaw the handwreit.[27] Be ernist with god, crave his derectioun. Ye knaw quhat pains he hes tane upon you, and quhat danger he hes savit you from, and others also, blissed be his name. Also the death of your kynd and loving sister, who wes hevylie trublit in mynd and body. Pryde wes the cheif thing that trublit hir, and the greving of hir deir mother as she callit me then. Bot efter a soir battell, she gat a happie victorie, blissed be god. Nou she rests in the arms, all tears are wyppit away.[28]
>
> Ye knaw not hou soone god cals you to a tryall: remember bygans, and iff that be forget, luik for som other thing then ye have yet felt. I knaw ye pertein to him who will not los you. Bewar to do against your consciens, greve not that sprite.[29] Iff ye have alreddy, preas[30] to repent and to com haim from your wanderings, and he will be reddy to receve you.[31] Seik ernistly his derectioun, and the prayers and counsell of my deir and worthy freinds thair: James Traill,[32] also the laird of

23 Smart, *Alphabetical Register of the Students … St Andrews*, 123.

24 See Jenny Wormald, 'The Headaches of Monarchy: Kingship and the Kirk in the Early Seventeenth Century', in J. Goodare and A.A. MacDonald (eds), *Sixteenth-Century Scotland: Essays in Honour of Michael Lynch* (Leiden, 2008), 365–98.

25 James 4.6.

26 Matthew 26.41.

27 Presumably referring to a now-lost enclosure, containing spiritual advice from a source that Elizabeth regarded as more authoritative than herself. Note the reference to other letters in the postscript.

28 Revelations 21.4.

29 Ephesians 4.30; *Godlie Dreame*, line 15. Elizabeth has no doubt that James is one of the Elect.

30 Strive.

31 A reference to the parable of the Prodigal Son (Luke 15.11–32).

32 This may be the Cromwellian Lieutenant Colonel of that name (1597–1663), brother of Robert Traill (1603–76) minister of Greyfriars, Edinburgh; the family was from Blebo, near St

Cairltoun[33] and Alexr Gordoun of Erlstoun,[34] who hes bein kynd and comfortabill to me, cheifly in my grittest neid, and also to hir who is with god.[35] The lord recompence them, they will do you gude.

Crave ernistly som setled cours and forget not your buik, iff ye be wyse. Iff ye do, God will remember you. Stryve against your cheif sin, do nothing that may nourish it. Gues quhat it is; iff your sister wes so trublit, juge who hes most caus. Remember quhat calling ye was over ernist to imbrace, quhilk efter ye confessit wes neither meit for body nor mynd. I say it also, and I think god hes said it to your hart. Be ernist in prayer joined with humiliatioun, and follow his derectioun, who hes had a grit cair of you from your infancie to this hour. Remember quhat I have oft said, God wreit it in your hart. I feare ye get a wakening shortly, if not allreddy. God wakin you in mercy as I hope he will.

I will give you no counsell in perticular, [the] lord counsell you by his sprite and give you grace to follow it. His grace be with you. In haist, your loving mother the 27 of agust 1625
E Melvill

Iff the letters come first in your hand, delyver them to the rest shortly.[36]

[on outer face]
To hir belovit sone James Coluill
[in different, cursive quasi-secretary hand]
Lord help me for I know no
other refuge but in thee
O Lord in thee is all my trust
give eare unto my wofull cry[37]

Andrews. James Traill was a protégé of Andrew Melville's former student, the Ulster magnate Sir James Hamilton (1559–1644), and from 1633 Traill was tutor to Hamilton's heir. In March 1620, 'James Traill from the north of Fife' had been named as one of those, including Lady Culross's elder brother James of Halhill, attending the traditionalist non-kneeling communions celebrated by John Scrimgeour, minister of Kinghorn (Calderwood, *Historie*, vii, 415). On 9 September 1644, the will of Mr Robert Melville, Lady Culross's younger brother, recorded a James Traill as owing £666 13s (NRS, CC15/5/5, p. 182).

33 Almost certainly John Fullartoun of Carlton in Galloway, 'a grave and chearful Christian' according to John Livingstone: Tweedie, *Select Biographies*, i, 344. See Bonar, *Letters of Samuel Rutherford*, no. CLVII (p. 288).

34 John Livingston notes that Gordon (1587–1654), the wealthy laird of Earlston near Dalry, Kirkcudbrightshire, was 'a man of great spirit … he refused to be made a knight … for wisdom, courage and righteousness, he might have been a magistrate in any part of the earth': Tweedie, *Select Biographies*, i, 343. See also Bonar, *Letters of Samuel Rutherford*, no. LIX (p. 132).

35 That is, James's nameless sister.

36 A reference to a parcel of letters, presumably from Fife, addressed to other members of whatever circle James found himself in at the time.

37 The hand is conceivably James Colville's. The third and fourth lines are the beginning of John Marckant's hymn 'The Lamentation [of a sinner]', found in Scottish metrical psalters from 1566 onwards. It also appeared in the *Gude and Godlie Ballatis* from 1578 on. Lady Culross alludes to it in several poems. For example, 'Then thou shall hear those pleasant songs / That to thy lord and love belongs' (*Poems*, 9, lines 59–60), is derived from Marckant's lines

Three main things emerge from this brief letter. First, that James is proud, and rather touchy about being counselled by his mother; secondly, that she has an overwhelming concern for his spiritual well-being, and thirdly, that she abhors the sin of pride and sees it as James's principal problem. She singles it out in the first of her biblical superscriptions and tackles it head-on in the letter. James's touchiness, his spiritual health and the deadly danger of pride are closely linked, and the three issues reappear in Elizabeth's second letter to her son. This is dated 30 January 1629, when James was at court in London and under the patronage of Sir Robert Ker of Ancram, now a Gentleman of the Bedchamber, whom we have already met corresponding with Sir Robert Melville of Burntisland.

Awake and strenthin the things that remain quhilk ar reddy to de etc.[38]

James, I receivit your letter quhilk wes sent with Mr Jhone Scrimger.[39] I have moir caus to quarrell then ye: I wreit with Mr Robert Colvill[40] to you, bot receved no answer, ye wreit with your brother to your father,[41] bot not a word to me, quhilk maid me think ye wes als miscontent with my letter as ye seim to be at my silence.

As for that cours that ye have tane, I think it better then wors. My counsell is that ye hold you wher ye are untill ye have som warrand to change; ye knaw that manie hie heads ar laid low within this short whyll.[42] Ye have great caus to be thankfull to that lord[43] who hes holdin you back from sic coursis, thocht against your will, and his [has] saved you from disperrat dangers that many hes perrished into, not so guilty as ye, considering all things. I beseik you, remember quhat pains the lord hes tane upon you from your infancie untill this tyme, and quhat warnings and wakenings he hes sent, and quhat use ye have maid of them. Quhat ye find inlaiking, preas to mend.

Be ernist in prayer I charge you. Read and lern the word of god in ernist and with reverence, stryve against this idoll sins[44] that your natour is most inclynit unto. Remember how low ye have bein brocht in body and mynde, and how sweitly the lord delt with you and preservit you and us also, wonderfuly and contrair to deservings. Be thankful, I charge you, and remember the words of Christ to the man that

61–4: 'And I shal sing the songs / Confirmed with the iust / That vnto thee belonges / Which are mine only trust'.

38 Revelations 3.2.

39 Former minister at Kinghorn on the Fife coast, deposed 1620 (Calderwood, *Historie*, vii, 417–24). See Tweedie, *Select Biographies*, i, 139, 312.

40 Her brother-in-law, minister of Culross.

41 The brother is probably John, who, we are told later, 'hes sent Latine vers to his father'. John's letter presumably enclosed James's letter to his father.

42 The duke of Buckingham had been assassinated on 24 August 1628; the eldest son of the Prince Palatine and Elizabeth Stuart had been drowned at Amsterdam on 7 January 1629.

43 Presumably God; in 1629, Sir Robert Ker of Ancram was not yet a lord.

44 This term is used in 1637 by Melville's friend Samuel Rutherford: 'it is impossible that your idol-sins and ye can go to heaven together and that they who will not part with these can, indeed, love Christ at the bottom but only in word and show, which will not do the business'. See *Letters*, no. CCLXXX (to John Gordon), 542.

laye so long at the pooll.[45] Ye knaw the place, reid it and preas to practis it, least wors com nixt. I beseik you and chargis you, as a mother who hes borne you with great pain, and brocht you up with great trubill and manie sair hurt, to watche and praye that ye fall not in tentatioun,[46] that ye esschew evill companie so far as ye can, and evill occasiouns. Stryve against natur, cheifly against pryde and impatience, refrain from wyn and women, and esschew all occasiouns that may snair you that waye, so far as ye can. Feare your awin waiknes, and beg ernistly strent[h] and grace from him who hes aboundance to give,[47] and will nevir faill them[48] who despairs in themselfs, and seiks him in humilitie and som measur of faith.[49]

Be spairing and spend not superflewisly – God knaws quhat cace we ar in. Be humbill, I beseik you: there is moir then caus. Be faithfull and diligent in that calling ye ar in for the present. Greatly ar ye bound to that worthy man[50] who hes bein a gude instrument, under God, since your coming thair, to save you from many fearfull and disperrat dangers. Be thankfull to God, and dewtifull to him and that gud lady, untill it pleas God to derect you further quhat cours to tak. Keip the lerning quhilk ye had, I beseik you, and tyne[51] it not, for iff ye do, it will offend God and greve my harte. Your brother Jhon keips all he had, and hes sent Latine vers to his father; he is weill, blessed be God. Your brother Robert also is with Robert Leslie in Swadin.[52] I can heare na word from your eldest brother this long tyme.[53]

As for us heare, iff ye knew our cace, I hop it would humbill you. Our destres cam to a great hicht and wes lyk to com to greatter, bot it hes plesit the Lord to begin som outward change, blissed be his name. Your father hes sold kinnether for xii thousand merks to his brother Mr Robert, not willingly, bot driven by extremitie.[54] Also, he hes sold the Cumry to him for fyve thousand merks, upone a reversioun of vii yeirs in Alexanders person only. His father nor na other hes power to redeim it, bot only he. Wreit so soone as ye may, and advertis him, not to discurage bot to incurage him to do quhat lyis [in] him to releve it. Iff it had bein sold without redemption moir wold have bein gottin for it, bot I wold not consent to that, becaus I hope in God that he will mak him abill to redeim or [ere] then: they cair not how soone, neither do I. Therfor curage, and do quhat ye can to help your brother for the hous, and I hope the heuch[55] sall be worth that soum.

45 John 5.14 'Behold thou art made whole; sin no more, lest a worse thing come unto thee.'
46 Matthew 26.41.
47 *Poems*, 67, line 8: 'His strenth is yours, his prayer cannot faill'.
48 *Poems*, 7, line 13: 'I never failed thee in thy need'.
49 *Poems*, 96, lines 55–6: 'all that fall, that call and shall / Repent and seek to Him by Fayth'.
50 Sir Robert Ker of Ancram.
51 Lose.
52 Third son of Patrick, 1st Lord Lindores; from 1628, serving with Gustavus Adolphus for the second time. In 1632 he was reported as being at court in London. Extensive information about Robert Leslie is available in the Scotland, Scandinavia and Northern European Database http://www.st-andrews.ac.uk/history/ssne (accessed 12 July 2014), in which his identity no. is 2932.
53 Dr Alexander Colville, resident in France.
54 The sale is recorded under 24 July 1629, as item 1458 in *RMS*, viii, 491.
55 Coal pit

Our burdens wes so great that all freinds thocht it a great eas to us, for if it hade not com that way, warding and comprysing[56] wes verry neir. So I wes forced to yeild, and hops that all sall turne to the best. Thank god, and be ernist in prayer, that we all may be humblit under his hand. Then will he rais us up and comfort us according to the tyme that he hes afflicted us and according [to] the dayis that we have sein evill.[57] Your deir sister that is with God desyrit you all to feare god, to be humbill and to follow your mothers counsell, iff you desyrit God to blis you heir and for evir: I wishe ye hade sein and heard that quhilk I heard and saw. It mycht have bein a sensibill preaching to you all your dayis. Since it can not be, the lord speik to your harte and grant ye may be warned by sic a neir and deir exampill.

I may wreit na mair. Remember my humbill deuty and hartly affectioun to Sir Robert[58] and his lady, God blis them and theirs and recompence their kyndnes. I am moir bound to them then I can expres. Nou the sprite of god be with you and gyde and derect you.
In haist.

Valifeild[59] the penult of Januare 1629
your loving mother
E Melvill

[The following postscript is damaged, with loss of text]
For Christs saik, be ernist in prayer, and rem[ember] upon your self and us also and forget not the d[estres]sed kirk of god heir and in other parts – nevir sic neid.[60] I fear som hevy publicte calamities sall be the first thing that sall mak us forget our privat crossis. So many tokins of his wraith! Lord mak us sensibill and work that repentence quhilk he requyrs. Tyme now to draw neir to God [61] [...] all the greifs perplexities straits and extre[miteis I have bein in] and yet am in (for … uo all thir [...)] iff my bairns fear evill I will forget all greif, and rejois and thank God who upon that conditioun hes promised to be a father to you all and provyd all things. If not, ye will feill the smarte and it will help to bring my graye head with sorrow to the grave.[62]

56 Scottish legal terms: imprisonment for debt, and sale by creditors to recover debts (distraining).
57 Psalm 90.15.
58 Identified as 'Sir Robert Ker' in another letter (Tweedie, *Select Biographies*, i, 367). His 'lady' was his second wife, Lady Anne Stanley, daughter of the earl of Derby. They had married in 1621.
59 The home of Lady Culross's sister-in-law, Grizel Colville, wife of Sir John Preston, fourth of Valleyfield (*Scots Peerage*, ii, 550).
60 On 7 January 1629, according to John Row, *The Historie of the Kirk of Scotland 1558–1637* (Edinburgh, 1842), 347, the great and much-persecuted Edinburgh minister Mr Robert Bruce had been confined to his home at Kinnaird by a personal letter from Charles I. This was at exactly the time of the drowning of Prince Frederick Henry in Amsterdam.
61 James 4.8.
62 Genesis 42.38, where the speaker is Jacob talking of the possible loss of his beloved youngest son Benjamin.

Commentary

In these two letters, we see 'a mother who hes borne you with great pain, and brocht you up with great trubill and manie sair hurte' endeavouring to guide a beloved son who is trying to make his way in the world. She implores him to make his spiritual welfare his first concern. One is inevitably reminded of Elizabeth's father and his treatise designed 'to temper the rage of furious youth be the reull of godlynes and raisoun', mentioned above. In 1625, James was still in his native land, apparently surrounded by his mother's 'deir and worthy friends'. But in 1629, he was far away, and in circumstances unimaginably different from those of his Fifeshire home or his mother's close-knit Presbyterian circles. His 'loving mother' suggests and quotes scriptural passages for him to meditate on: James's upbringing has ensured that he knows his Bible. Both letters movingly testify to the depth of Elizabeth's love for a haughty and touchy young man who does not seem to know what he wants of his mother: 'ye wreit not to me and I knaw not quhat to wreit to you'; she thinks him 'als miscontent with my letter as ye seim to be at my silence'.

Yet James preserved these two letters, an indication of his filial piety and his ultimate respect for his mother and her counsels, a respect enjoined on him by his dead sister. In both these letters, despite her invaluable inclusion of family news, Elizabeth's overriding concerns are spiritual: 'iff my bairns fear evill I will forget all greif, and rejois'. But alongside her sternly loving, pious advice to James, she shows herself capable of pragmatic realism, too. She says (twice) with regard to temptation and the opportunities for keeping bad company – which must have abounded at court – to avoid these things 'so far as ye can'. Her warning not to spend 'superflewislie' is grounded in the reality of the family's circumstances, which give James no grounds whatever for haughtiness. In the 1625 letter, we saw her worries about James's pride, which apparently ran in the family: she says it afflicted her dead daughter, and no fewer than four times she addresses the need for James to be humble. He is to seek God 'with humilitie and som measur of faith'; he is to 'be humble'; a proper understanding of the family's circumstances 'would humbill' him; and finally, his dead sister wanted all her siblings 'to feare God, to be humbill'. In a sermon of 1590, the great Presbyterian minister Robert Bruce had said that 'quhosoevir hes trew faith, of necessitie he man be humble. And as faith and humilitie go togither, so pryde and incredulitie go evir togither.'[63] The adjective 'humble' appears fourteen times in Elizabeth's extant poetry, and the verb 'humble' twice.[64]

63 Edinburgh University, New College Library, *Sermons on Hebrews XI*, MS Bru 2, fol. 67. See J. Reid Baxter, 'Presbytery, Politics and Poetry: Maister Robert Bruce, John Burel and Elizabeth Melville, Lady Culross', *Records of the Scottish Church History Society* 34 (2004), 6–27.

64 See for example, *Poems*, 33, lines 103–4: 'the humble men / exalts thou then'; p. 87, lines 376–7: 'Thocht in this earth ye sall exaltit be / Feir salbe left to humbill yow withall'. And note especially Bruce Manuscript, fol. 180, 'Ye humbell hairtis that did defy / all worldlie vanitie' (Poem no. 15, lines 217–18).

As for James's outward existence, as opposed to his spiritual life, the 'calling ye was ouer ernist to imbrace quhilk efter ye confessit wes neither meit for body nor mynd' referred to in 1625 may have been a military career. Whatever the abandoned calling was, the 1629 letter shows us that James was trying his luck at court in London and that Sir Robert Ker was of real importance in James's life at this stage. Both cultured and sincerely religious, Ker was a correspondent of William Drummond of Hawthornden, to whom he addressed his sole surviving sonnet, on the solitary life. Eleven vernacular psalm paraphrases are extant from his pen, some of them being reworkings not of the Geneva Bible, but of Buchanan's Latin poetic versions.[65] Ker would still be James's patron in June 1632, when we find his mother writing to John Livingstone, who was about to travel to London:[66]

> I haue a sone at court wt Sir Robert Ker. Tak pains to delyver him [James] this letter,[67] and mak aquaintence with him. Give him your gude counsell becaus he is my sone. I hope, iff he culd be any waye steadeabill, thatt he sall be at your service.[68]

We have no certain reports of James after this, but on 13 November 1641, the Scottish Parliament recorded that a group of businessmen had sent 'James Colville, ane Gentleman of good woorth and knowledge' to follow a case at Hamburg, the origins whereof went back to 1628. This could be Elizabeth's son. At Hamburg, Colville experienced only 'strange usage and great delays and was forced to constitute Master Joseph Everie, agent for your majesty at Hamburg, procurator, to follow that process, who, having now pursued the same these four years bygone, has in no way advanced in the said process'.[69] James must have gone to Hamburg in 1637 or 1638. He was apparently named, with Alexander and Samuel, in 'a bond of provision' by his father dated 3 May 1643.[70] There are no further sightings of him.

The tone of the letter of 27 August 1625 implies that James's nameless 'kind and loving sister' had died not long before that date. She makes a powerful reappearance just before the close of the letter of January 1629. Here we learn that unlike his mother, James had not been present during her final illness. What Elizabeth writes of her dead daughter, 'hevylie trublit in mynd and body', hints at the depth of their relationship; for all her problems with pride, the girl was troubled by her 'greving of hir deir mother as she callit me then'. She tells James

[65] See Laing, *Correspondence of Sir Robert Kerr*, ii, 487–506.

[66] See Tweedie, *Select Biographies*, i, 146.

[67] A letter, now lost, enclosed with the letter to Livingstone.

[68] Tweedie, *Select Biographies*, i, 367.

[69] *APS*, v, 386. See also Steve Murdoch, *The Terror of the Seas? Scottish Maritime Warfare 1513–1713* (Leiden, 2004), 181–6, which does not mention James Colville, but notes that Scots in favour of reprisals against Hamburg 'were quick to exploit Charles I's political weakness during the Covenanting Revolution (1638–1641) to reopen the affair' (p. 186).

[70] J.P. Wood (ed.), *Douglas's Peerage of Scotland*, 2 vols (Edinburgh, 1813), i, 355. This bond, which implies that Robert and John are both dead, appears not to survive.

that 'Your deir sister ... desyrit you all ... to follow your mothers counsell.' Elizabeth's own respect for the young woman, whose deathbed struggles ended in 'happie victorie', is manifest when she writes to James that 'I wishe ye hade sein and heard that quhilk I heard and saw. It mycht have bein a sensibill preaching to you all your dayis.'[71] The fact that the pious south-western lairds named in 1625 had been 'kynd and comfortabill ... to hir that is with god' indicates the daughter had some strong link with the south-west and indeed may have died there. A letter of July 1637, from the great Presbyterian preacher Samuel Rutherford, informs us that Lady Culross had another daughter, who lived in Kirkcudbright. Christian Colville, named for her maternal grandmother, Christian Boswell of Balmuto, was married to William Glendinning (or Glendoning), son of Mr Robert Glendinning, the doughty Presbyterian minister of Kirkcudbright. When William Glendinning was imprisoned for refusing to silence his reverend father (suspended from his duties by Bishop Sydserff), Rutherford wrote to Lady Culross that 'your son-in-law W.G. is ... strong in his Lord ... and his wife is his encourager, which should make you rejoice'.[72] Christian Colville was clearly a worthy daughter of her mother.[73] All three of Rutherford's extant letters to William Glendinning end with special greetings to his spouse, and we should not read anything into Christian's absence from her mother's twelve extant letters: the letter of January 1629 also omits any reference to her youngest son, Samuel.

'Your brother John', whose studiousness and Latinity his mother clearly regards as exemplary, was probably younger than James, but is otherwise unknown.[74] He would seem to have been in Sweden, since Elizabeth adds that 'your brother Robert also is with Robert Leslie in Suadin'. The brothers were presumably two of the hundreds of Scottish mercenaries fighting for Gustavus Adolphus in his war (1626–29) against his Catholic cousin Sigismund III of Poland. Just as family connections underpin James Colville's link to Sir Robert Ker, kinship may well underlie his brothers' soldiering in the Swedish service with Colonel Robert Leslie. The latter's own mother, Jean Stewart Lady Lindores, widowed in 1608, had become the third and final wife of Robert Colville's aged great-uncle, Sir Robert Melville of Murdocairnie, first Lord Melville Monimail (1526–1621). Like the Leslies of Lindores and the Balfours of Montquhany, Lord Melville lived at no distance from Halhill.[75]

[71] It is hard to believe that Lady Culross did not record in (now-lost) verse what was clearly a major spiritual and emotional experience; the poet-pastor James Melville wrote moving short lyrics on the deaths in infancy of two of his children. See Robert Pitcairn (ed.), *Autobiography and Diary of Mr James Melvill* (Edinburgh, 1842), 270–1, 309.

[72] *Letters*, no. CCXXII. For his imprisonment, see *Letters*, prefatory note to no. CXXXVII, see also nos CCLXVII and CCLXXVI.

[73] See M.D. Young, *The Parliaments of Scotland: Burgh and Shire Commissioners*, 2 vols (1992), i, 278–9.

[74] Wrongly identified by Smart (*Alphabetical Register... St Andrews*) as the John Colville who graduated in 1635 and became minister of Kirknewton (Hew Scot, *Fasti Ecclesiae Scoticanae*, i, 150). See note 3 above.

[75] The Colville boys' great-aunt Margaret Dundas of Fingask's eldest son by her third marriage (*Scots Peerage*, v, 463) was Sir George Douglas of Mordington. In 1623 he had taken a

Elizabeth's eldest son, Alexander, was named for his paternal grandfather. He is allotted a key role in his mother's strategy for saving her beloved home at West Comrie, but interestingly, she appeals to James to write to Alexander about this; it rather sounds as if James enjoyed closer relations with his mother and his brother than the latter pair did with each other. Alexander took his Edinburgh M.A. in 1615.[76] On 30 June 1619 he left Scotland for France and 'immediately obtained appointment as master in Hebrew and physics at the protestant academy in Sedan', where he married the niece of a French colleague in 1631,[77] and was a friend of the aged Andrew Melville.[78] This edition cannot encompass his later career, fascinating though it is – not least for its interaction with that of his youngest brother, Samuel Colville. Of Samuel it must suffice to say here that he is mentioned in his mother's December 1631 letter to John Livingstone: 'I feare my prayers be turned into sin. I find and seis the clein contrair in me and myne, at least som of them. Samuell is going to the colledge in Sant Andrews, to a worthy maister thair, bot I feare him deadly.'[79] In 1637, Samuel Rutherford would write to Elizabeth of 'your son, who is your grief', almost certainly a reference to Samuel, who had graduated in July 1634.[80]

Coda

Elizabeth Melville's January 1629 letter to James, a layman, indicates that her clerical son Alexander seems to have kept his distance from her, and not only in a geographical sense. In 2002, David Mullan described Lady Culross as 'an imperious mother', on the basis of the letters to James.[81] We have seen that these two letters are in fact more solicitous than imperious, but the nine extant letters to the young cleric John Livingstone are indeed often imperious (as well as querulous and even self-deprecatingly humorous).[82] While referring to Livingstone as

Scottish company of foot to join Gustavus Adolphus in Germany: Margaret Dundas, *Dundas of Fingask* (Edinburgh, 1891), 30.

76 See note 2 above.

77 Marie Claude Tucker, 'Colville, Alexander, *de jure* third Lord Colville of Culross', *ODNB*. Her claim that in 1656 Colville was again teaching at Sedan seems improbable, in view of his appearances in Scottish sources.

78 In a letter of 9 May 1620 from Sedan, one John Hume informs Mr John Adamson, minister of Liberton, that 'Mr Melvine and Mr Colvine maike thaire commendations to yow most hartelye': David Laing (ed.), *Original Letters Relating to the Ecclesiastical Affairs of Scotland*, 2 vols (Edinburgh, 1841), ii, 622.

79 Tweedie, *Select Biographies*, i, 363.

80 Bonar, *Letters of Samuel Rutherford*, 81.

81 David G. Mullan, *Scottish Puritanism* (Oxford, 2000), 158.

82 The letters to Livingstone printed as I–VIII in W.K. Tweedie (ed.), *Select Biographies*, 2 vols (Edinburgh, 1845–47), i, 351–69, were actually written in the following order: Letter III (pp. 356–7) – 17 June [1629]; Letter VIII (p. 369) – 19 September [1629]; Letter I (pp. 352–4) – [?October] 1629; Letter II (pp. 355–6) – [?July 1630]; Letter IV (pp. 357–9) – 25 March 1631; Letter V (pp. 359–609) – 17 June 1631; Letter VI (pp. 361–5) – 10 December

'My werry worthy and deir brother' and herself as 'Your loving sister in Christ', and repeatedly asking for his prayers, Elizabeth really does write like a 'mother in God', lecturing Livingstone, counselling him, scolding him, and even suggesting subject matter for sermons. It may be that Elizabeth had earlier tried to play a similar role in her son Alexander's exercise of his vocation, and been firmly rebuffed. The young Livingstone, by contrast, records his gratitude to a number of upper-class Presbyterian ladies in his 'Life'.[83] In his 'Memorable Characteristics', he has more to say of Elizabeth Melville than of any of the other much grander *grandes dames* to whom he was beholden.[84]

Whether the young Alexander Colville rejected his mother's spiritual direction or not, his later moderate stance as a Resolutioner would have disappointed her, and his readiness to conform to prelacy at the Restoration in 1662 would have wounded her to the quick.[85] For Lady Culross, the cause of Christ could know no compromise. In *Ane Godlie Dreame*, she had preached to the persecuted faithful: 'Thocht waters greit do compas yow about, / Thocht tirranes freat, thocht Lyouns rage and roir / Defy them all'. She had gone on to write a sonnet of spiritual encouragement to the imprisoned minister John Welsh, facing the death penalty for *lèse-majesté* in 1605–6; a very few years later, in a sonnet to Andrew Melville imprisoned in the Tower of London, she wrote with reference to earthly life and worldly powers, 'defy this dung and drosse'.[86] And finally, in 1662, unlike her own eldest son, her spiritual child and friend John Livingstone would reject episcopal jurisdiction. He went into exile and died in Holland. Whatever Melville's own sons made of the maternal 'counsell' that her early-deceased daughter had wished them to follow, Livingstone had taken it to heart.

1631; Letter VII (pp. 366–8) – 19 June [1632]. Reasons of space preclude an explanation of the methodology and evidence used to reconstruct the chronological sequence.

83 See Tweedie, *Select Biographies*, i, 139–40, and especially 148.

84 Tweedie, *Select Biographies*, i, 346–8. See also 300, 316, 339.

85 Alexander sat on the Committee to review and visit Presbytery and Synodal Books in 1662: G.R. Kinloch (ed.), *Selections from the Minutes of The Synod of Fife* (Edinburgh, 1837), 181.

86 *Poems*, 88, 68, 11.

Guide to Further Reading

In *Finding the Family in Medieval and Early Modern Scotland* (Aldershot, 2008) we argued that medieval and early modern Scottish family history is possible, that it makes a rich contribution to our broader understanding of premodern Scottish history, and that Scotland can make an important contribution to the broader European picture. In that volume we identified additional areas of research to be explored. While some important works on the family have emerged since then, including Katie Barclay, *Love, Intimacy and Power: Marriage and Patriarchy in Scotland, 1650–1850* (Manchester, 2011); David Sellar, 'The Family', in Edward Cowan and Lizanne Henderson (eds), *A History of Everyday Life in Medieval Scotland* (Edinburgh, 2011), 89–108; and Deborah Symonds, 'Death, Birth and Marriage in Early Modern Scotland', in Elizabeth Foyster and Christopher Whatley (eds), *A History of Everyday Life in Scotland, 1600 to 1800* (Edinburgh, 2010), 83–107, there is still much work to be done on the history of children and youth.

Within the Scottish literature only a few short studies have explicitly addressed the topic of premodern childhood. These include Rosalind Marshall, 'Childhood in Early Modern Scotland', *Scottish Local History* 59 (2003), 30–4; Rosalind Marshall, *Childhood in Seventeenth Century Scotland* (exhibition catalogue) (Edinburgh, 1976); Craig Beveridge, 'Childhood and Society in Eighteenth-Century Scotland', in R.A. Mason et al. (eds), *New Perspectives on the Politics and Culture of Early Modern Scotland* (Edinburgh, 1982), 265–80; and Keith Brown's chapter, 'Children', in *Noble Society in Scotland* (Edinburgh, 2000).

The lives of youth have received more attention. Although age is not considered specifically for the contributions that it can make to understanding society, young people appear within discussions of service, illegitimacy and education. Service and apprenticeship are particularly fruitful areas of research as most of those involved were young people. Works include Winifred Coutts, 'Women, Children and Domestic Servants in the Seventeenth Century', *Transactions of the Dumfriesshire and Galloway Natural History and Antiquarian Society*, 3rd ser. 61 (1986), 73–83; Elizabeth Ewan, 'Mistresses of Themselves? Female Domestic Servants and By-Employments in Sixteenth-Century Scottish Towns', in A. Fauve-Chamoux (ed.), *Domestic Service and the Formation of European Identity* (Bern, 2004), 411–33; Diane Baptie, 'Apprentices in the North-East of Scotland', *Scottish Archives* 9 (2003), 37–44; and A.M. Allen, *The Locksmith Craft in Early Modern Edinburgh* (Edinburgh, 2007). Demographic work on mobility often incorporates discussions of servants. Rab Houston, 'Geographical Mobility in Scotland', *Journal of Historical Geography* 11:4 (1986), 379–94, and Ian Whyte and Kathleen Whyte, 'The Geographic Mobility of Women in Early Modern Scotland', in Leah Leneman (ed.), *Perspectives in Scottish Social History* (Aberdeen, 1988), 45–53, provide information on the economically independent young. Crises affect children as well as adults; the impact of one such crisis is examined in Karen Cullen, 'The Famine of the 1690s and its Aftermath: Survival and Recovery of the Family', in Ewan and Nugent (eds), *Finding the Family*, 151–62.

Studies of sexuality and illegitimacy, mainly informed by the Kirk Session records and criminal court records (important access points for social history), are rich resources on youth. Although young people are not the focus of studies on pregnancy, illegitimacy, wet-nursing and infanticide, young women are the main historical actors within them. Leah Leneman and Rosalind Mitchison opened up this area with their many publications on early modern illegitimacy. Their findings are detailed in the companion volumes *Girls in Trouble* (a new edition of their 1989 *Sexuality and Social Control*) and *Sin in the City* (Edinburgh, 1998). Essays on wet-nursing by Gordon DesBrisay in Elizabeth Ewan and Maureen Meikle (eds), *Women in Scotland c. 1100–c. 1750* (East Linton, 1999) and the *Journal of the Canadian Historical Association*, new ser. 8 (1997) include many young women, as do essays on women and crime by Gordon DesBrisay, Anne-Marie Kilday and Lynn Abrams in Yvonne Galloway Brown and Rona Ferguson (eds), *Twisted Sisters* (East Linton, 2002). Deborah Symonds, *Weep Not for Me* (University Park, PA, 1997), examines balladry as well as court records to reveal young women lamenting acts of infanticide, while Anne-Marie Kilday explores infanticide in her studies *Women and Violent Crime in Enlightenment Scotland* (Woodbridge, 2007) and *A History of Infanticide in Britain, c. 1600 to the Present* (Basingstoke, 2013).

Youth may not form the analytical core in studies of premodern education, yet young people are certainly present in Shona Vance, 'Schooling the People', in E.P. Dennison et al. (eds), *Aberdeen Before 1800* (Edinburgh, 2002), 309–26, and Steven Reid, *Humanism and Calvinism* (Aldershot, 2011). More material on elite children's education, especially that of girls, is discussed in Katherine Glover, *Elite Women and Polite Society in Eighteenth-Century Scotland* (Woodbridge, 2011). The tools of an eighteenth-century education are examined in Matthew Eddy, 'The Alphabets of Nature: Children, Books and Natural History in Scotland, circa 1750–1800', *Nuncius. Annali de storia della scienzia* 25 (2010), 1–22. For a glimpse into schoolboy mischief, see Eila Williamson, 'Schoolboy Scribbles in a Burgh Court Book', *Scottish Archives* 8 (2002), 96–112. University students, as well as their potential for disruptive activities, are studied by Colin McLaren, *Aberdeen Students 1600–1860* (Aberdeen, 2005). The leisure pursuits of the young are discussed in John Burnett, *Riot, Revelry and Rout: Sporting in Lowland Scotland before 1860* (East Linton, 2000); Margo Todd, 'Profane Pastimes and the Reformed Community', *Journal of British Studies* 39 (April 2000), 123–56; and J.T. McGavin, 'The Kirk, The Burgh and Fun', *Early Theatre* 1 (1998), 13–32. The forthcoming Robert Anderson et al. (eds), *Edinburgh History of Education in Scotland* (Edinburgh, 2015) will also provide new insight on the education of the young from the medieval to the modern period.

Parenting is another area of research that examines adult perspectives on the young. Essays by David Mullan, 'Parents and Children in Early Modern Scotland', 73–84, and Melissa Hollander, 'The Name of the Father: Baptism and the Social Construction of Fatherhood in Early Modern Edinburgh', 63–72, in Ewan and Nugent (eds), *Finding the Family*, are important studies on parenting, as is L. Diack, 'Motherhood and Poverty in Eighteenth-Century Aberdeen', in T. Brotherstone et al. (eds), *Gendering Scottish History* (Glasgow, 1999), 172–85. Formalized parenting practices are also examined in Peter Parkes, 'Celtic Fosterage', *Comparative Studies in Society and History* 48:2 (2006), 359–95, and Jane Dawson, '"There is nothing like a good gossip"', *ROSC* 15 (2002–3), 88–95. Relationships between seventeenth-century parents and children are examined in David G. Mullan (ed.), *Narratives of the Religious Life* (Aldershot, 2010).

For additional references to studies including youth and children see the online bibliography at WISH (Women in Scottish History) http://www.womeninscottishhistory.org; 'Guide to Further Reading', in Ewan and Nugent (eds), *Finding the Family*; Katie Barclay, Tanya Cheadle and Eleanor Gordon, 'The State of Scottish History: Gender', *SHR* 92 (2013), 83–107; and Elizabeth Ewan, 'The Early Modern Family', in T.M. Devine and Jenny Wormald (eds), *Oxford Handbook of Modern Scottish History* (Oxford, 2012), 268–84.

Beyond Scotland, the field of child and youth studies is a thriving topic within the historical discipline. Philippe Ariès, *Centuries of Childhood* (New York, 1962), sparked interest in the topic and more than forty years later social scientists are still engaging with his work. His concept that childhood is socially and historically constructed was a watershed and many have worked to build on these ideas. Early responses such as Lawrence Stone, *The Family, Sex and Marriage* (New York, 1977), and Lloyd deMause, *The History of Childhood* (New York, 1974) present a violent and brutalized premodern world where a separate childhood characterized by familial affection did not exist until the Enlightenment. Linda Pollock's *Forgotten Children* (Cambridge, 1983) was the first to challenge this theory and present a more nuanced understanding of the historically constructed childhood of the early modern era.

Building on Pollock's assertion that there was indeed a recognized stage of childhood prior to the Enlightenment, a number of general histories of childhood have been produced, many of them intended as undergraduate textbooks. Hugh Cunningham has sought to assess how Western conceptions of childhood have evolved over five centuries in his studies *Children and Childhood in Western Society Since 1500* (London, 1995) and *The Invention of Childhood* (London, 2006). Colin Heywood has produced a well-known survey of childhood from the medieval period to the present, *A History of Childhood* (Cambridge, 2011). Recent surveys that have taken account of the highly nuanced and complex portrayal of childhood that has emerged over the last two decades include Paula Fass (ed.), *The Routledge History of Childhood in the Western World* (London, 2013), and Elizabeth Foyster and James Marten (general eds), *A Cultural History of Childhood and Family*, 6 volumes (London, 2010).

National surveys include Colin Heywood, *Growing Up in France* (Cambridge, 2007), and Anthony Fletcher, *Growing Up in England* (New Haven, 2008). Surveys of medieval childhood include Nicholas Orme, *Medieval Children* (New Haven, 2001); Alexandre Bidon and Didier Lett, *Children in the Middle Ages, 5th–15th Centuries* (Notre Dame, 1999); and Shulamith Shahar, *Childhood in the Middle Ages* (New York, 1990). More geographically specific medieval surveys are Barbara Hanawalt, *Growing Up in Medieval London* (Oxford, 1993); Sally Crawford, *Childhood in Anglo-Saxon England* (Stroud, 1999); and Louis Haas, *The Renaissance Man and His Children: Childbirth and Early Childhood in Renaissance Florence, 1300–1600* (New York, 1998). An excellent review essay on these and other works is Margaret L. King, 'Concepts of Childhood: What We Know and Where We Might Go', *Renaissance Quarterly* 60 (2007).

Recognition that childhood was complex and that youth experienced a distinctly different world than their younger counterparts emerged in the 1990s, sparking the publication of a number of general studies including Michael Mitterauer, *A History of Youth* (Oxford, 1992); Paul Griffiths, *Youth and Authority* (Oxford, 1996); Ilana Krausman Ben-Amos, *Adolescence and Youth in Early Modern England* (New Haven, 1994); P.J.P. Goldberg and Felicity Riddy (eds), *Youth in the Middle Ages* (Woodbridge, 2002); and Konrad Eisenbichler (ed.), *The Premodern Teenager* (Toronto, 2002). The idea of a distinct youth culture goes back to earlier studies of popular culture such as Natalie Davis, 'The Reasons of Misrule: Youth Groups and Charivaris in Sixteenth-Century France', *Past and Present* 50 (1971), 41–75. Courtship practices have been a particularly fruitful area, and works include Diana O'Hara, *Courtship and Constraint* (Manchester, 2000); John Gillis, *For Better, For Worse: British Marriages, 1600 to the Present* (New York, 1985); and Eric Carlson, 'Courtship in Tudor England', *History Today* 42 (August 1993), 23–9.

Over the last twenty years general studies have provided the foundation for more detailed examinations of the experience of childhood and youth. Many are highly sophisticated, engaging in the major theoretical issues of gender studies, social history, and child and youth studies; they seek to move the study of the young from the oft-cited 'children's table' of history, to an integral and vibrant lens through which to enrich and move forward our understanding of the premodern world. The inaugural issue of *The Journal of the History of Childhood and Youth* (2008) provides an excellent overview of some of the most interesting and evocative questions currently being explored.

Studies of children, youth and poverty have added a depth and complexity to our understanding of the centralizing state in early modern Europe. In the last decade these include Joel Harrington, *The Unwanted Child: The Fate of Foundlings, Orphans, and Juvenile Criminals in Early Modern Germany* (Chicago, 2009); Patricia Crawford, *Parents of Poor Children in England, 1580–1800* (Oxford, 2010); Cheryl Nixon, *The Orphan in Eighteenth-Century Law and Literature* (Farnham, 2011); T.M. Safley, *Children of the Laboring Poor: Expectation and Experience among the Orphans of Early Modern Augsburg* (Leiden, 2005); and

Nicholas Terpstra, *Abandoned Children of the Italian Renaissance: Orphan Care in Florence and Bologna* (Baltimore, 2005).

Also important to our understanding of children and broader historical processes are A. Fletcher and S. Hussey (eds), *Childhood in Question: Children, Parents, and the State* (Manchester, 1999), and A. Baggerman and R. Dekker, *Child of the Enlightenment* (Leiden, 2009). The economic contributions of young people has also nuanced our understanding of pre-industrial economies; this is demonstrated in Ann Kussmaul, *Servants in Husbandry in Early Modern England* (Cambridge, 1981); Cordelia Beattie, *Medieval Single Women* (Oxford, 2007); and A. Curry and E. Matthew (eds), *Concepts and Patterns of Service in the Later Middle Ages* (Woodbridge, 2000).

The intersection of gender and age has yielded some excellent studies of children and youth. Among these are Naomi Miller and Naomi Yavneh (eds), *Gender and Early Modern Constructions of Childhood* (Farnham, 2011); Benjamin Roberts, *Sex and Drugs Before Rock 'n' Roll: Youth Culture and Masculinity during Holland's Golden Age* (Amsterdam, 2012); Kim Phillips, *Medieval Maidens: Young Women and Gender in England, 1270–1540* (Manchester, 2003); Amy Froide, *Never Married: Single Women in Early Modern England* (Oxford, 2005); Ruth Mazzo Karras, *From Boys to Men: Formations of Masculinity in Late Medieval Europe* (Philadelphia, 2003); and Amy Leonard and Karen Nelson (eds), *Masculinities, Childhood, Violence* (Newark, 2011). For Scotland, Rosalind Carr, *Gender and Enlightenment Culture in Eighteenth-Century Scotland* (Edinburgh, 2014) often has young men at the foreground of her discussion.

Children and their role in religious thought have deepened our understanding of premodern religion. See M.J. Bunge, *The Child in Christian Thought* (Grand Rapids, 2001); C. John Sommerville, *The Discovery of Childhood in Puritan England* (Athens, 1992); Diana Wood (ed.), *The Church and Childhood* (Oxford, 1994); Karen Spierling, *Infant Baptism in Reformation Geneva: The Shaping of a Community, 1536–1564* (Louisville, 2009); and Jeffrey Watt, 'Calvinism, Childhood and Education: The Evidence from the Genevan Consistory', *Sixteenth Century Journal* 33:2 (2002), 439–56.

The very high rates of childhood illness and mortality have inspired a number of studies, with much of the history of children and emotions emerging out of such works. Examples include Claudia Jarzebowski and Thomas Max Safley (eds), *Childhood and Emotion* (London, 2014); R. Woods, *Children Remembered: Responses to Untimely Death in the Past* (Liverpool, 2006); Katie Barclay, Ciara Rawnsley and Kimberely Reynolds (eds), *Small Graves: Death, Emotion and Childhood in the Early Modern Period* (forthcoming); and Gillian Avery et al. (eds), *Representations of Childhood Death* (Basingstoke, 2000). An excellent study of healing and illness is Hannah Newton, *The Sick Child in Early Modern England, 1580–1720* (Oxford, 2012).

Material culture has been a fruitful source for scholars of children and youth. Joanna Sofaer Derevenski (ed.), *Children and Material Culture* (London, 2000) theorizes about and explores children and material culture in prehistory and the Middle Ages. See also Stephanie Tarbin and Philippa Maddern (eds), *Material*

Worlds of Childhood in North-Western Europe c. 1350–1800 (Farnham, forthcoming); D.M. Hadley and K.A. Hemer (eds), *Medieval Childhood: Archaeological Approaches* (Oxford, 2014); G. Avery and J. Briggs, *Children and Their Books* (Oxford, 1989); and A. Immel and M. Witmore (eds), *Childhood and Children's Books in Early Modern Europe, 1550–1800* (New York, 2006).

Finally, historical and literary studies of parenting and parenting practices shed light on adult perceptions and treatment of children. Important studies include Steve Ozment, *When Fathers Ruled: Family Life in Reformation Europe* (Cambridge, 1983); Benjamin Roberts, *Through the Keyhole: Dutch Child-Rearing Practices in the 17th and 18th Century* (Hilversum, 1998); Valerie Fildes (ed.), *Women as Mothers in Pre-Industrial England* (London, 1990); Valerie Fildes, *Breasts, Bottles and Babies: A History of Infant Feeding* (Edinburgh, 1986); Lianne McTavish, *Childbirth and the Display of Authority in Early Modern France* (Aldershot, 2005); Douglas Brooks (ed.), *Printing and Parenting in Early Modern England* (Aldershot, 2005); Marilyn Francus, *Monstrous Motherhood: Eighteenth-Century Culture and the Ideology of Domesticity* (Baltimore, 2012); Jacqueline Musacchio, *The Art and Ritual of Childbirth in Renaissance Italy* (New Haven, 1999); Grace Coolidge (ed.), *The Formation of the Child in Early Modern Spain* (Farnham, 2014); Merridee L. Bailey, *Socialising the Child in Late Medieval England, 1400–1600* (Woodbridge, 2012); and Naomi Miller and Naomi Yavneh (eds), *Maternal Measures: Figuring Caregiving in the Early Modern Period* (Aldershot, 2000).

Index

All references in **bold** refer to illustrations and maps.

St Andrew Studies in Scottish History

Previously published

I
Elite Women and Polite Society in Eighteenth-Century Scotland
Katharine Glover

II
Regency in Sixteenth-Century Scotland
Amy Blakeway

III
Scotland, England and France after the Loss of Normandy, 1204–1296
'Auld Amitie'
M.A. Pollock